THE LABOR OF LITERATURE

A VOLUME IN THE SERIES

Studies in Print Culture and the History of the Book

Edited by

Greg Barnhisel

Robert A. Gross

Joan Shelley Rubin

Michael Winship

The Labor of Literature

DEMOCRACY AND LITERARY CULTURE IN MODERN CHILE

Jane D. Griffin

University of Massachusetts Press
Amherst & Boston

Printed in the United States of America

ISBN 978-1-62534-209-6 (paper); 208-9 (hardcover)

Designed by Jack Harrison
Set in Adobe Garamond Pro with ITC Kabel display
Printed and bound by The Maple-Vail Book Manufacturing Group

Cover design by Jack Harrison
Cover photograph by Jane D. Griffin. Reproduced by permission of Santiago en 100 Palabras.

Library of Congress Cataloging-in-Publication Data
A catalog record for this book is available from the Library of Congress

British Library Cataloguing-in-Publication Data
A catalog record for this book is available from the British Library.

For my parents

Wayne Garrett Griffin

and

Susan Gail Entrekin Griffin

With love and gratitude

Contents

Acknowledgments

Research for this book was funded in part by Bentley University, the Jeanne and Dan Valente Center for the Arts and Sciences at Bentley University, the American Association of University Women, and the University of California, Irvine. My fieldwork in Chile was dependent on the participation of numerous cultural producers, including Pía Barros, Jorge Montealegre, Luis Cruz, Mauricio Sanhueza, Tanya Núñez, Ximena Ramos, Fernanda Arrau, Ignacio Cuevas, Roberto Toledo, Mario Aravena, César Rey, Olga Sotomayor, Luís Díaz, Nélida Muñoz, Amanda Espejo, Karen Peñaloza, Jonathan Velásquez, Ignacio Arnold, Carmen García, Javier Pinto, Victor Pueyes, and Horacio Eloy. I am grateful to my colleagues and friends—at Bentley University, UC Irvine, and beyond—for their generous feedback, including Jenny Rogers, Adriana Johnson, Resha Cardone, Kristin Sorensen, Heidi Tinsman, Ivette Hernández-Torres, Marcy Schwartz, Bonnie Field, Gesa Kirsch, Randy Ontiveros, Margaux Cowden, I-Lien Tsay, Janet Neary, Jane Tchaïcha, Luis E. Cárcamo-Huechante, Alice Nelson, and Christian Rubio. Resha Cardone, Gabriela Aguilera, Alexandra Missirian, and Jonathan Velásquez all made important contributions to the two appendices, for which I am incredibly grateful. I owe a heartfelt thanks (and many meals) to the Pohl-Díaz family and the Barros-Montealegre family for welcoming me into their homes during my many research trips to Chile. And, most important, to my pack of wild animals, Osito, Chanchi, and Loba: thank you for making me a home.

THE LABOR OF LITERATURE

INTRODUCTION

Literary Production and Cultural Democracy

We have to take the reins back into our own hands, combine conviction, voluntarism, and a grain of willfulness with a tradition of praxis and of learning new forms of communicating, producing, and organizing.
—PAULO SLACHEVSKY

IN 2006, the Santiago-based feminist writing collective, Ergo Sum, self-published its twentieth annual volume of short stories, all written by predominantly unknown authors who participated in the group's 2006 writing workshops. The book—if we can call it that—has no traditional front, back, or spine, but is instead a pair of denim pants tailored to fit a child's toy doll (fig. 1). On the pants' back left pocket is a bright yellow and orange sticker meant to look like the jeans' brand label; it reads: "*Tenemos pantalones*® [We wear the pants], Ergo Sum Writing Workshops, Directed by Pía Barros, 2006."[1] Ergo Sum's signature logo, the head of an ink pen with the symbol of woman (♀) embedded into it, also appears on the sticker label.

Upon opening the Velcro snap that holds the pants shut at their waist, the reader reaches in to extract a stack of bifold pamphlets, each containing an original short story and illustration. The stack of pamphlets is held together by a paper band, on the front of which we see the same brand logo the jeans carry on their back pocket; on the reverse side of this strip (fig. 2) we find bibliographic information, which includes the names of illustrators who contributed to the individual drawings that accompany each story, the name of the printing company that printed the pamphlets, the individuals responsible for editing the literary texts and the design of the overall object, and, most important, the name of the woman, Ely Albornoz, who single-handedly made all five hundred copies of this "book" on her home sewing machine. This bibliographic paper strip also notes the place and date of publication: "Santiago, Chile, November 2006."[2] Gently sliding the stack of folded papers

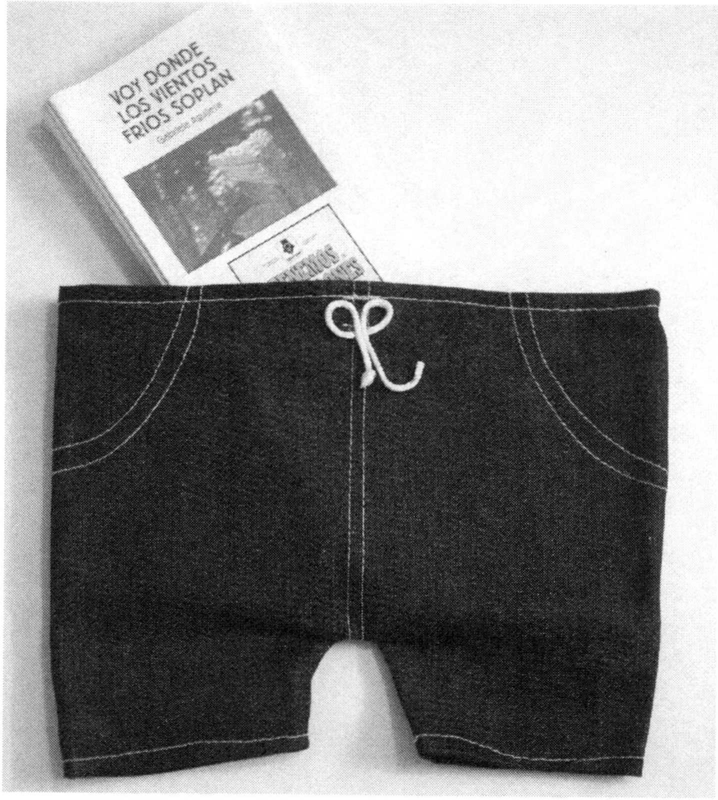

FIGURE 1. *Tenemos pantalones* (front side). Photograph by Nélida Pohl. Reproduced by permission of Pía Barros.

FIGURE 2. *Tenemos pantalones* (back side). Photograph by Nélida Pohl. Reproduced by permission of Pía Barros.

out of its binding, the reader is left to shuffle through the loose-leaf pamphlets and read the individual short stories they contain.

There are thirty short stories housed inside this miniature pair of pants, but the jeans themselves tell us a story of their own. In them we can read a history of the complex changes that Chilean literary culture has experienced over the past forty-three years—changes that are a direct result of the nation-state's dramatic political and economic transformations. These transformations began on September 11, 1973, when General Augusto Pinochet led a military coup that ousted the democratically elected socialist president Salvador Allende and began an authoritative dictatorship that lasted until 1990.[3] Once in power, General Pinochet enacted cultural and economic policies that had immediate and lasting effects on how literature in Chile has been produced, circulated, and consumed ever since.

Almost immediately after taking power, the Pinochet regime began to censor "all modes of communication, including all artistic and cultural expression."[4] Cultural censorship was so severe, especially during the early years of the dictatorship, that the National Truth and Reconciliation Committee, convened by President Patricio Aylwin following the removal of Pinochet as head of state in 1990, includes cultural censorship in its list of human rights violations committed by the regime. The only forms of cultural engagement sanctioned by the dictatorship were those that echoed its ideological commitments to militarism, Catholicism, patriarchy, and free-market capitalism.

To advance its capitalist agenda, the Pinochet regime began a neoliberal restructuring of the Chilean economy that privileged private institutions over public ones, the individual over the collective, and the accumulation of material wealth over the advancement of social justice and equality. As a result of this economic reform, multinational publishing firms came to dominate the local literary market, and their editorial policies privileged global market trends and profitability over national aesthetic sensibilities or social concerns. Thus the military state and the global market assumed the authority to decide what kinds of texts would circulate within the public sphere and how citizens would have access to them. These political and economic changes explain why the dictatorship has become infamously known for creating an *apagón cultural*, or cultural blackout.

The history contained in the miniature pair of jeans labeled *Tenemos pantalones*, however, disputes the widely held notion of a cultural blackout. This nontraditional publication represents a whole host of amateur and noncommercial forms of literary production that originated in direct response to authoritarian state politics in Chile during the 1970s and 1980s. Such alternative forms of literary production and circulation did not wither with the fall of dictatorship; they have instead gained momentum throughout the postdictatorship period. By manipulating the material form through which literary texts reach readers, Chileans have created a literary culture in defiance of state censorship and independent of capitalist definitions of value. Studying alternative literary publications gives us a new image of the dictatorship period as a time of editorial experimentation rather than of widespread cultural suppression; likewise, it helps us see how Chileans of the postdictatorship period have invented diverse forms of grassroots cultural activism that serve as a viable alternative to the hegemony of the neoliberal market.

In the late 1970s, and especially throughout the 1980s, defiant writers and artists all over Chile responded to the regime's cultural censorship and neoliberal restructuring by forming underground artistic collectives that specialized in what they termed *autoedición,* or self-publication. The *autoediciones* (self-publications) these groups produced were defined by their handmade quality and typically took the form of two- or three-folded paper pamphlets or makeshift journals. Underground literary collectives did not have the necessary state permission to meet as groups or make and disseminate printed materials, but they did so anyway as a means of democratic protest and artistic activism. By not only writing but, even more important, by publishing literary works autonomously and by hand, these literary producers emphasized the political and aesthetic power inherent in literature's material production. The material form of self-publications crafted during the dictatorship years made as much of a political and artistic statement as the language of the texts they contained.

The feminist literary collective Ergo Sum was only one of these many self-publishing literary *talleres,* or workshops, to originate in Chile under dictatorship. Like other self-publishing groups, Ergo Sum made literary pamphlets to publically distribute its writings; however, it cleverly packaged these pamphlets in what it called "book-objects": three-dimensional objects made out of everyday materials that took the shape of nonliterary object-commodities. *Tenemos pantalones* is a perfect example of this method in that it does not resemble a literary publication of any kind but rather an accessory for a child's toy doll. The material form of Ergo Sum book-objects exemplifies Judith Butler's theorization of a drag performance. Like human bodies appearing in drag, these objects donned mainstream identities in order to fulfill conventional expectations of what material culture and women's labor were supposed to look like under Pinochet's regime. For example, by taking the shape of everyday commodities, these objects acted out the fetishization of consumer goods within Chile's neoliberal political economy. And by crafting these books in the specific shape of objects characteristic of the female sex and domestic labor—such as miniature shopping bags, hope chests, sewing boxes, and homemade children's toys—Ergo Sum members dressed their publications according to the preferred gender ideologies of the military regime, which ascribed to women the roles of biological and ideological reproducers of the nation.

Yet it is important to understand these book-objects as more than a loyal performance of hegemonic social codes. At first glance, the objects could have passed as conventionally styled commodities, and that act of passing could have proven useful in the hostile cultural environment of Chile's dictatorship years. Yet the history of how these objects and the texts they housed inside them were made confirms another effect. Their seemingly uncritical performance of state ideologies was at the same time a sardonic interpretation of those very ideologies. In so far as Ergo Sum book-objects were literary publications that circulated without official permission, they directly defied the military's overt tactics of cultural suppression as well as the widespread tendency toward self-censorship that those tactics precipitated.

Similarly, through the very acts of meeting together, writing, editing, crafting, and circulating literary publications—all without the required permission of the state—the women who wrote the stories contained inside these traditionally feminine-looking objects were in fact rebelling against conventional notions of femininity espoused by the military regime. And, finally, the Ergo Sum collective mocked Chile's neoliberal political economy by denying their publications the ability to generate surplus value since the group's members distributed these objects through noncapitalist circuits of exchange. This history of feigned conformity and conscious defiance is embodied in the material form of *Tenemos pantalones.*

The political and economic context of the dictatorship years is essential to understanding the critical power of Ergo Sum's literary aesthetic and material process. It is therefore somewhat surprising that *Tenemos pantalones* was published in 2006, sixteen years after the authoritarian regime was civically removed from power. *Tenemos pantalones* is one of sixteen book-objects that Ergo Sum has published since the fall of Chile's dictatorship and one of thirty that it has published since the group's inception in the mid-1980s. All of its publications take the shape of three-dimensional objects that challenge our conventional expectations of the book form. They are also all made and assembled collectively by participants in the group's annual writing workshops, which Barros has directed out of her home for three decades. And they all contain original short stories written by workshop participants who are, for the most part, amateur and unknown women writers. These writers are also responsible for distributing the collectively produced book-objects, which they typically circulate through personal social networks and almost always for free or at a minimal fee to cover production costs. None of the writers, including Barros herself, are paid for the intellectual or manual labor of writing and making book-objects. These processes of artistic and material production have remained the same ever since Ergo Sum began its operation under military authoritarianism.

The question that book-objects such as *Tenemos pantalones* requires us to ask, then, is why this group has continued such a laborious and historically unrecognized form of literary production throughout the postdictatorship period. Another way to articulate this same inquiry is: if Ergo Sum used its editorial practice as a form of pro-democratic protest and artistic activism during the 1980s, then what purpose does that practice serve once democracy has been reinstated?

I have been thinking about this question ever since I first encountered Ergo Sum book-objects while studying abroad in Santiago as an undergraduate in 1999. When I returned to Santiago throughout the early 2000s to continue studying Ergo Sum as a graduate student, it became impossible for me to ignore the diverse array of other more recently published literary texts whose unconventional physical forms shared much in common with Ergo Sum book-objects. I thus had to ask not only why Ergo Sum had refused to abandon its alternative editorial method with the end of the dictatorship, but also, and perhaps more important, why so many other individuals and organizations had *started* literary projects in the postdictatorship period that employed unconventional editorial techniques reminiscent of those that originated during the dictatorship.

Of these many alternative projects, three share material practices and artistic philosophies uniquely similar to those of the Ergo Sum group. These are: (1) Cartonera cardboard book publishers, (2) Libros de Mentira (Fake Books), an online press and social media website, and (3) Santiago en 100 Palabras (Santiago in 100 Words), a massively popular annual writing contest. There are striking differences, namely in scale and institutional affiliation, among these alternative literary producers, but what they all share is an overt attempt to democratize Chilean literary culture. Moreover, they all define the democratization of literary culture as the process by which modes of literary production and consumption are made equally accessible to as many Chileans as possible. And, finally, all three of these literary producers, along with Ergo Sum, work to realize this process by creatively changing the material forms through which literary texts reach readers.

Like Ergo Sum, Cartonera cardboard book publishers craft their literary products by hand and from everyday materials, but unlike Ergo Sum, they do so within the traditional book format. Cartonera presses make their books out of recycled cardboard trash, often hand-sewing pages into their cardboard bindings and hand-painting unique covers onto each individual book. This method originated in Argentina in 2003, but it has since spread to twenty-three countries on five different continents, where it has empowered individuals with little-to-no prior literary or editorial experience to become published authors and publicly recognized editors, bookmakers, and book distributors.

Chile stands out within this global network of Cartonera publishers because it has more Cartonera presses per capita than any other country, and because Chilean Cartonera editors have assumed a leading role within the global network by organizing and hosting three important international meetings of Cartonera presses in Santiago.[5] Because Chilean Cartonera publishers consistently refer to their handmade editorial practice as "artisanal," it is important to understand the democratic potential of this practice within the historical context of Latin American *artesanía* and its relationship to capitalist culture industries—both national and global. Chilean Cartoneras also exhibit what is at best an ambiguous concern and at worst a blatant disregard for copyright protection and intellectual property laws. As such their editorial practice stands in direct contrast to Chile's newly democratic state and its national publishing industry, which have worked together to make copyright protection a key aspect of the state's new cultural policies during the postdictatorship era. The disobedient behavior of Chilean Cartoneras echoes that of self-publishing groups of the dictatorship years and reveals the ways in which the neoliberal democratic state, like its authoritarian predecessor, attempts to discipline literary culture according to its own political and economic agendas.

Libros de Mentira, on the other hand, alters the book's material form by "dematerializing" it, which it does through the production of what it calls "digital books." Founded in 2008 by three university students looking for an alternative to the neoliberal publishing market, the press provides its users with software tools and an online platform with which to design and publish their own digital books for free; these books often include embedded video clips, musical accompaniments, and audio components—sometimes recorded by the authors themselves. The site invites its online members to participate in all levels of book production and consumption, from writing and publishing original texts, to editing digital versions of works previously published in print form, to critiquing digital books in the comment boxes attached to each online publication. By encouraging its members to participate in all these activities at once, Libros de Mentira weakens the boundaries that exist within the capitalist field of literary production and that define readers, writers, editors, critics, and book manufacturers as separate individuals responsible for different kinds of intellectual, artistic, and manual labor. In contrast, through the design of its website, Libros de Mentira attempts to empower amateur writers and readers as publically recognized literary agents capable of wielding the kind of cultural capital that the commercial literary market traditionally reserves for consecrated professionals.

Finally, Santiago en 100 Palabras is an annual writing contest that began in 2001 and is based in Santiago's ever expanding subway system. The contest re-imagines the material form of literature by publishing winning short stories of one hundred words or less in a myriad of nontraditional ways, such as on billboards stationed on subway platforms and in train cars; as magnets, desk calendars, and other nonliterary everyday objects; in anthologized form as tiny pocket-sized books; and in digital form on the contest's website and through its smartphone app.

Because it distributes all of these publications in mass quantities to the Santiago public for free, the contest is an opportunity to rethink the relationship between literature, mass culture, and the public within cultural studies broadly and Latin American literary culture specifically. In neoliberal Chile, the mass production of literary texts is almost always associated with multinational publishing houses that commercialize and, as many argue, depoliticize literary works. Santiago en 100 Palabras, on the other hand, has not only found a way to mass-produce and distribute literature independent of the global publishing industry, but it has also done so in a way that empowers average Chilean citizens as the producers of that literature rather than as its mere consumers. It has done this by creatively and strategically acquiring the philanthropic sponsorship of national and multinational corporations that are themselves not members of the culture industries.

Chilean Cartonera book publishers, Libros de Mentira, and Santiago en 100 Palabras were all founded in Chile's postdictatorship period, yet they all share striking similarities with the Ergo Sum project, whose origins are deeply rooted in the dictatorship years. All four of these alternative literary producers have altered material modes of literary production in ways that make them more accessible to individuals who find themselves marginalized by institutional powers: the state with regard to the period of military authoritarianism and global capitalism with regard to the period of neoliberal democracy. They also increase access to literary consumption by distributing publications either for free or at a minimal cost. The inclusive nature of these projects constitutes their democratizing goals.

These four alternative literary producers are not alone in their struggle to democratize Chilean literary culture by experimenting with literature's material form. For example, Ergo Sum's emphasis on the gendered nature of artistic performance—which includes literary production—is also a quality found in avant-garde art and literature of the dictatorship period as well as in more traditionally published feminist and queer literary texts of the dictatorship and postdictatorship periods. Avant-garde artists of the 1970s and 1980s belonging to the *escena avanzada* (advanced scene) and the group CADA (Colectivo de Acciones de Arte / Collective Art Actions) experimented with a variety of artistic forms in ways that challenged established conventions of what art was supposed to look like and how it should reach viewers and/or readers. CADA, for example, was known to use things such as milk cartons, newspaper postings, and even small aircraft to disseminate politically impassioned pieces of poetry throughout Santiago.[6] Similarly, feminist and queer writers of the dictatorship period commonly put the gendered body on display through dramatic public performances of their writings, as is best evidenced by the work of Diamela Eltit and the queer art duo Las Yeguas del Apocalispsis (Mares of the Apocalypse). These performances constructed the gendered body as an artistic medium and material embodiment of the literary text.[7]

Even in narratives published in the traditional book form, many writers made the materiality of the human body central to their struggle for narrative power in postdictatorship Chile.[8] For example, as Raquel Olea has argued, women writers of the dictatorship and the early postdictatorship periods rejected conventional uses of language, which they saw as complicit with the military regime's authoritative power, and instead attempted to rewrite the female body through alternative grammars and voices—conflating the materiality of the female body with that of the literary text.[9]

All these examples show us how Ergo Sum's project echoes larger aesthetic tendencies of the dictatorship period—tendencies that strategically used gender, public performance, and nontraditional materializations of the art object as tools in the advancement of an anti-authoritarian political aesthetic. This kind of experimental artistic and literary production is *not,* as Olea tells us, a "literature of the masses."[10] Nelly Richard agrees with this claim in her book *Margins and Institutions,* where she argues that the avant-garde work of the avanzada scene was rejected and marginalized by mainstream institutions such as traditional leftist political organizations and the commercial art market.[11] This marginalization happened because intellectual artists sought to break with artistic convention, whereas the global publishing industry sought, and still seeks, to profit from it. It has done so by mass-producing sensational or "light" literature, understood by scholars as depoliticized, overly nostalgic, and historically reductive.[12]

Chilean literary scholar Luis E. Cárcamo-Huechante argues that bestselling novelists of the dictatorship and early postdictatorship periods employ a pragmatic use of language and repeat played-out literary tropes that by definition make their works nonexperimental.[13] He also argues that the ability of such authors to become market sensations vis-à-vis the bestseller phenomenon has amplified the process of "professionalization" that began, according to Ángel Rama, with the Latin American literary "boom" of the 1960s.[14] The professionalization of authors by corporate publishers perpetuates a notion of the literary text as a means of economic gain rather than as a tool for social or political critique.

The global publishing industry has also sought to capitalize on literary representations of national difference. For example, Kathrin Bergenthal and Ksenija Bilbija have both shown that the ways in which multinational publishing houses compile and market "national" literary catalogs are not representative of a particular nation's literary or cultural difference at all.[15] The Nueva Narrativa Chileana (New Chilean Narrative) of the 1990s is a perfect example of this phenomenon; Bergenthal's research shows that this canon did not comprehensively represent what was happening in Chilean literary culture at this important time in the nation's history, but was rather the invention of Spanish publishers—namely Editorial Planeta—that chose to publish works whose authors and themes reflected the conservative ideologies of their target audience: middle- and upper-class professional Chileans.[16]

Cárcamo-Huechante understands this kind of commodification of literary texts through the concept of the "market niche," which he argues compartmentalizes texts into limited categories that compete with each other—often to the death—for market share.[17] Francine Masiello sees the capitalist marketing of difference from a slightly more optimistic perspective. She argues that the neoliberal market seeks out representations of gender and sexual difference to market as tokens of trade, but she also contends that authors ironically indulge the market's desire for the spectacle of difference in ways that resist homogenization and advance progressive gender politics.[18]

The global publishing industry has also affected Chilean literary culture through its emphasis on the role of the cultural consumer. The market determines the value of mass-produced literature not by the quality of the work per se but rather by how many copies of a work are sold; bestseller lists and market rankings are the only markers of literary "value" relevant to corporate publishing houses, and those rankings are dependent on cultural consumers. In the words of Chilean sociologist Jorge Larraín, "the culture industry converts individuals into consumers" because it needs consumers in order to profit.[19] Larraín goes so far as to claim that since the military coup of 1973, material consumption has replaced social movements as the defining means through which Chilean social identity is formed and recognized.[20] According to Cárcamo-Huechante, even bestselling authors assume the role of literary consumers, or what he calls "writer-consumers," in their recycling of hackneyed literary forms.[21] If we agree with scholars such as

Sergio Villalobos-Ruminott who argue that the dictatorship was a process of "modernizing" Chile by bringing the nation in step with the global capitalist economy, then we can also agree that the modern Chilean citizen is by definition, to use Néstor García Canclini's term, a consumer-citizen; citizenship in modern Chile, as in the rest of the neoliberal world, is defined through acts of material consumption.[22]

Ergo Sum, Cartonera publishers, Libros de Mentira, and Santiago en 100 Palabras all aim to do something fundamentally different from either of these two models of literary production—vanguard experimentation and mass-produced commodification—although they do share degrees of similarity with each category. For instance, all four of these projects manipulate literature's material form in ways that are reminiscent of avant-garde experiments of the 1970s and 1980s, perhaps explaining why a handful of avant-garde writers have participated in one or more of these alternative literature projects. And like mass literature, these projects solicit participation from a mass audience that determines the legitimacy or value of literary publications.

Despite these similarities, alternative literary producers perform a unique function: they incorporate average citizens as literary producers, rather than mere consumers, and they do so without the requirement or expectation of either intellectual prowess or commercial success. In so doing, Ergo Sum, Cartonera publishers, Libros de Mentira, and Santiago en 100 Palabras all, to varying degrees, allow individuals to fluidly occupy the social positions of writers, editors, book manufacturers, critics, and readers and thereby blur the boundaries that have historically defined those roles according to limited and capitalist definitions of intellectual, artistic, and manual labor. Consequently, all four of these literary producers help erode the uneven power dynamics that have historically existed between those subjective social categories.

While the democratic impetus of the Ergo Sum project seems self-evident given the group's origins under dictatorship, the similar goals of Cartonera presses, Libros de Mentira, and Santiago en 100 Palabras may seem less urgent or necessary given that these projects originated under full democracy. However, there is widespread debate about the success of Chile's democratic transition since 1990—a process that has been riddled with institutional contradictions.[23] One contradiction that pertains directly to literary culture concerns the state's attempt to promote literary publications as commercial goods while simultaneously trying to make them equally accessible to all Chileans. All the presidential administrations that have governed Chile throughout the postdictatorship period have made serious attempts to strengthen national culture, and they have done so through diverse policies and programs related to public and school libraries, cultural production grants, and economic policies that strengthen national culture industries.

While many of these policies and programs have attempted to make literary consumption and publication easier for as many Chileans as possible, the state has simultaneously countered that effort by continuously increasing laws that protect copyright and intellectual property and by making the penalties for infringing those laws ever more severe. Through such policies, the state defines cultural goods as private property and polices who can make use of those goods and how. The increased economic value of literary publications strengthens Chile's national print industry, making it a more viable competitor against multinational corporations, but it also has the contradictory effect of limiting how average citizens can access and use print materials.

For these reasons and many others, we can rightfully critique the institutional failures of Chile's transition to democracy. Yet despite these failures, we must recognize that Chile has succeeded in re-establishing what Philip J. Costopoulos and Zaki Laidi refer to as "procedural democracy"—a term that refers to the political processes through which citizens choose their own leaders through free and fair elections.[24] The larger question is whether or not Chile has successfully realized an organic sense of what Costopoulos and Laidi call "cultural democracy"—a term they use to refer to the equitable functioning of social institutions such that "respect for interests and rights is guaranteed in ways that go beyond the safeguarding of fair electoral procedures."[25]

Costopoulus and Laidi find that on a global scale cultural democracy develops much more slowly than procedural democracy, and this is certainly the case in Chile. However, if we only look to hegemonic state and market institutions to measure Chile's democratic progress in degrees of successes and failures, we do not get a composite picture of the heterogeneous struggles for political, cultural, and economic equality that have been taking shape in Chile since the military coup of 1973. Institutional contradictions and limitations have not stopped Chilean citizens from believing in the struggle for cultural democracy; in fact, alternative literary producers demonstrate that institutional shortcomings have motivated citizens to work together toward the advancement of cultural democracy in ways that are not wholly determined by state or market institutions. Literary culture offers us diverse examples of grassroots artistic projects, all of which advance a democratic agenda.

Alternative literary producers are evidence that average Chilean citizens—by which I mean individuals who are neither public intellectuals nor professionals within the literary industry—engage in the struggle for cultural democracy through modes of literary production. Or, to put it another way, Chilean citizens claim political agency by defining themselves as literary producers rather than mere consumers. Studying the literary production of such individuals adds to our understanding of what Doris Sommer has termed "cultural agency." In her influential book *Cultural Agency in the Americas,* Sommer argues that creative practices and reflection constitute political agency in the sense that both activities allow a "political voice to speak through aesthetic effects [that] can renew love for the world while [enhancing] the worth of artist-agents."[26]

We typically think of reading and writing as the primary if not the only ways in which individuals generate cultural agency through literature. In addition to encouraging reading and writing, Ergo Sum, Cartonera publishers, Libros de Mentira, and Santiago en 100 Palabras turn the process of making and publishing literary objects into acts of creative reflection, and their techniques allow the material quality of literary publications to generate aesthetic effects just as the texts they contain do as well. By increasing the possible ways in which individuals can make literary texts, these projects increase the ways in which the literary text can produce individuals as empowered cultural agents.

Not only do alternative practices of literary production increase the ability of average citizens to exercise cultural agency, but they also attempt to solve one of the most widely agreed-upon problems with postdictatorship Chilean literature, which is its commodification into a mass-produced and mass-sold economic good. There is a general consensus within postdictatorship Chilean literary culture that the process of mass-producing and commodifying literary publications depletes them of their artistic aura. Recently some cultural studies scholars have examined ways in which cultural consumers recuperate a sense of aura in material culture through interpretive practices and acts of repurposing object-commodities in unforeseen creative ways.[27]

Ergo Sum, Libros de Mentira, Santiago en 100 Palabras, and especially Cartonera publishers all attempt to recover the artistic spirit of literary publications through modes of material production rather than through interpretive acts of consumption alone. They demonstrate that a large number of Chileans are unsatisfied with the kind of agency offered to them via modes of capitalist consumption and subversive reading practices. By exercising cultural agency through modes of material production, Chileans redefine their position within local and global cultural economies. While some of their strategies echo a current global uptick in non-industrial and noncommercial methods of cultural production and exchange, their presence in Chile holds particular meaning because of that country's recent political, cultural, and economic history.

In his 2005 book *Globalización, desarrollo y democracia: Chile en el contexto mundial* (Globalization, development and democracy: Chile in a global context), Manuel Castells speaks to the creative potential of new information technologies in postdictatorship Chile, but what he says applies equally to literary production:

> [*Literary production*] *is directly related to society's cultural and creative development.* This is not necessarily in order to develop new [ideas], but rather to invent new ways of producing, of communicating, and of living. Because in the end, [literary production] is the social and personal ability to transform creativity into a productive force that will, in its turn, allow for the development of that creativity in a virtuous cycle between the art of living and the efficiency of production.[28]

What we read in the pages that follow are stories of how Chileans have invented new ways of producing, of communicating, and of living. Their efforts, like those of the state, have not been perfect or without contradictions and limitations. The creative efforts of underground literary groups such as Ergo Sum did not topple the military regime of Augusto Pinochet. Nor have the alternative editorial strategies of postdictatorship literary agents unhinged Chile's neoliberal political economy. But Chileans have used their labor in producing literature as a means of negotiating the kinds of social positions they have occupied within both of these repressive structures. By fighting, even on a small scale, to regain some portion of control over material modes of literary production, the cultural agents we will read about in the following pages echo Ergo Sum's sentiment when it states: "We wear the pants."

1

Chilean Literary Culture since 1970

A Panorama

How do we make it so that culture, that cultural expression, happens all the time in this country and that it includes all citizens, all of them?

—Gregory Cohen

To understand how certain cultural practices qualify as "alternative," it is necessary to understand the traditional practices to which they serve as an alternative. Another way of phrasing this is to ask, if the four literary producers studied in this book are alternative, what then constitutes mainstream literary culture during Chile's military dictatorship and postdictatorship periods? The most reductive answer to this question is that mainstream publication is produced by the state and the commercial literary industry. However, both the state and the market are complex social institutions through which multiple actors produce literature in a myriad of ways. In this respect, it is enlightening to examine the identities of diverse literary actors and the particular methods of literary production they have practiced, beginning with the brief period of socialist democracy that directly preceded Pinochet's military coup.

Literary Culture and Socialist Democracy

While Salvador Allende was not the first Chilean president to make literary culture a central component of his political agenda, he was the first to implement cultural policies that allowed the state to intervene directly in the production and distribution of literary goods.[1] During his stunted three-year presidency (1970–73), Allende established the Chilean state as the primary agent responsible for the production and distribution of literary materials, principally books. In 1971, the government nationalized what was then one of the biggest publishing houses operating in Chile, Zig Zag press. The state renamed the press Editorial Quimantú and increased its production to historic levels. Quimantú quickly became the dominant force within Chilean literary culture under Allende's presidency. As a result, smaller and privately owned presses were pushed to the margins of the literary industry and found it difficult to compete with the state-owned publishing giant.[2]

The indigenous Mapuche name of the state-owned press as well as its business model and editorial agenda all reflected the government's mission to use literature and books as a primary means of promoting its specific brand of Chilean nationalism, which was based on historically marginalized social sectors, namely Native peoples and the working class. The press became famous for its Nosotros los Chilenos (We the Chileans) line of books, which centered on the histories and struggles of Native and working-class peoples of Chile. It made this line of books, as well as consecrated and canonical works of global literature, easily available to the Chilean masses by selling them in large numbers at newspaper stands for extremely low prices.[3]

According to Chilean book historian Bernardo Subercaseaux, the primary goal of Editorial Quimantú was to "secure the public's access to artistic goods."[4] It was not, somewhat surprisingly, to promote literature written by working-class and indigenous Chileans themselves. The state's vision was to create a society of readers in which great works of literature would be known to all social sectors rather than just the upper classes. It did this by importing global literature into Chilean literary culture rather than by promoting Chilean writings abroad. Within this cultural agenda, the Chilean people were highly encouraged to become active readers but far less incentivized to become producers of a national literary culture. The state's strategy for increasing the public's literary activity was to decrease the book's economic value, thus making reading a cultural activity that was equally accessible to all social sectors. The purpose of literature was to generate knowledge, national pride, and artistic sensibilities; it was not to make money for the state, the literary industry, or individual authors.

Literary Culture and Military Authoritarianism

In many ways, the cultural agendas of Allende's Unidad Popular (Popular Unity, UP) administration could not have been more opposed to those of General Augusto Pinochet's military junta; however, there were some fundamental similarities in the development and functioning of Chilean literary culture under these two conflicting administrations. A first similarity was that Chile's commercial publishing industry under Pinochet subsisted, as it had under Allende, in a position of marginality, this time albeit in relation to the global publishing market rather than to the state itself. Second, just as the socialist state had used Editorial Quimantú to select and promote the kinds of literary and other texts that it wanted the public to read, so too did the military state exercise its authority to determine what was appropriate and inappropriate reading material for Chilean citizens, the difference of course being that the former exercised this authority from a progressive position of, in Subercaseaux's words, "cultural agent," whereas the military junta did so from a repressive position of cultural censor.[5] Third, as Subercaseaux argues, the UP's choice to mass-produce books, as opposed to other cultural objects, privileged the book as "a media superior to other medias."[6] The military dictatorship also viewed the book in this same light, as evidenced by its decision to severely censor and "punish" the book more severely than other forms of material culture.[7]

A final similarity was that neither administration conceived of the Chilean public as producers of print culture. The UP, however, proscribed to the public the role of reader, while the military dictatorship attempted to interpellate citizens primarily as cultural consumers. While we can understand reading as the act of consuming a text, within the context of dictatorship Chile the act of reading is rendered irrelevant in comparison to the act of consumption, which is strictly defined as the economic activity of purchasing a cultural commodity—in this case books and other print materials.

There are numerous ways in which the dictatorship acted as censor and depressor of Chilean literary culture rather than as an agent of its development and growth. Within months of taking control of the government, General Pinochet's junta also took control over Editorial Quimantú, renaming it Editoral Nacional Gabriela Mistral (Gabriela Mistral National Press) after Chile's famous Nobel Laureate, Gabriela Mistral—the first Latin American ever to win the Nobel Prize in literature. The junta placed the newly named publisher under the direct control of military officials and severely downsized its production levels and staff. The new national press retained Quimantú's Nosotros los Chilenos line of books but changed its focus from publishing texts about minority social sectors to publishing Chilean military histories. By 1976 the press was sold into private ownership.[8]

More devastating for the general public than the takeover and eventual sale of Quimantú was the strict surveillance and censorship of literary culture that the military imposed on the nation. The surveillance and repression of print culture began almost immediately after the coup of September 11, 1973. Only a few weeks later, on September 23, the military conducted a fourteen-hour raid on the San Borja tower buildings in downtown Santiago, during which time they detained dozens of people and burned scores of books and other printed materials they considered seditious. Such raids continued throughout the entire military dictatorship period, even after some print and publishing entities were granted permission by the government to function.[9] The year 1977, however, marks the beginning of the military state's legal assault against Chileans' freedom of cultural expression.

Between 1977 and 1983, various military bands and decrees granted state officials full control over the regulation of literary production, publication, and circulation. After 1983 the state expected citizens to self-censor their own cultural activity according to the threats and mandates of previous decrees. This expectation was supported by the 1980 constitution, which gave General Pinochet legal privilege, until 1989, to restrict the release of information, including "the creation, publication, and circulation of new publications."[10] What books were allowed to circulate did so with difficulty. In 1977 the state imposed what has become the infamous VAT tax (Value Added Tax), a 20-percent tax placed on all book sales, which still exists today and is widely seen as a major inhibitor of book sales in contemporary Chile. The state further restricted the distribution of approved print materials by requiring domestic bookstores to self-censure their inventory and report to the military regime all books that were deemed "unsellable." It also took full control over the importation of foreign titles.[11]

For years, the prevailing belief has been that the state's repressive cultural policies created what has been infamously coined an *apagón cultural,* or cultural blackout.[12] A cultural blackout involves a decline in cultural production as well as in consumption. During the dictatorship, Chilean citizens censored themselves by not attempting to produce cultural goods and by lessening their consumption of cultural goods already in circulation. Moreover, intense state surveillance of the public sphere and nightly curfews caused an epidemic of self-censorship that affected what people said, how they interacted with one another, how they did business, and what they did in their free time. As Pamela Constable and Arturo Valenzuela report, "Bookstalls closed, nightlight vanished, and radio stations replaced Andean protest ballads with Mexican *mariachis* and American pop songs. Santiago became a tense, subdued city where commuters rode buses in silence and restaurant conversations were held in murmurs."[13] The term "cultural blackout," within the Chilean context, refers to a decrease in the production of material culture, including and perhaps especially print culture, as well as a depressed social and public life.

The cultural blackout affected print culture in special ways. Chilean writer Horacio Eloy reports that in 1975, only two years into the military dictatorship, the national production of books had already dropped by 41 percent from what it had been ten years earlier, and Subercaseaux informs us that by 1978, it had dropped by another 53 percent from what it had been in 1975.[14] Subercaseaux also points to the decrease in books imported to Chile from abroad (due to censorship and the VAT tax on books) and the dramatic disappearance of bookstores throughout the country during the decade of the 1970s.[15] Many editors and writers were reluctant to continue their work in print culture since they knew the probability of attaining permission to publish was nil; others shut down their operations completely because of their former affiliation with the UP.[16] A large number of presses refused to operate because submitting their work for state approval, as required by law, would signify an acceptance of the military's right to power.[17] Still others decided to move their productions abroad, creating the first-ever Chilean publishing houses to open and operate outside of Chile.[18]

In addition, state officials publicly burned books in mass graves while individual citizens frequently did the same to their own personal libraries for fear that, if discovered by military officials (who often raided personal homes), their possession of certain books would be grounds for political imprisonment or even exile. Citizens who could not bring themselves to destroy books were known to resort to other measures, such as burying books in their backyards to avoid political persecution.[19] Subercaseaux quotes one individual who, in reference to his own home library, stated, "We had to bury it, and it's still there in Concepción; more than once I've thought that just like people in World War II buried jewelry or money, we in Chile had to hide or burn books."[20] Similarly, Chilean writer Diego Muñoz talks about living in Santiago under dictatorship and finding public trash cans full of books and computer discs that had been abandoned and thrown out. He couldn't help but pick them up and take them home, and he says that he still has them as "symbols of a history that [he] hopes remains definitively entombed in the past."[21]

The military state also negatively affected Chilean literary culture through its neoliberal restructuring of the entire national economy, which included the print and publishing industries. The logic of Chile's new free-market economy privileged an editorial business model that sought to profit from book sales rather than use literary culture as a tool for social advancement or for the representation and reproduction of local culture. This business model preferred the publication of books that sold in high volume, which included the genres of self-help, family sagas, biographical and nostalgic historical novels, travel novels, and cookbooks. The book's insertion into consumer culture during this period has caused writer Pía Barros to equate Chile's neoliberal editorial market with "mall culture" in the sense that "symbolic goods are valued but not valorized."[22] Within this editorial environment, the value of a work of literature is determined by how many copies it sells, establishing the market as a cultural mediator and gatekeeper—a role not unlike the state's own function as cultural censor. These forms of economic and political censorship directly threatened literature's symbolic purpose as the nation's storehouse of spiritual beliefs, identities, and memory.

In addition to changing the book's function and purpose in society, Chile's new neoliberal economic environment changed the way in which citizens participated in literary culture. With the state acting as censor and the market as media gatekeeper, Chileans found it difficult to access modes of literary production; their role within material culture became principally that of consumer rather than producer. Yet the kinds of books and other printed materials available for consumption were limited. The market offered only those titles deemed acceptable by the military and profitable to the global publishing industry, and noncommercial venues of literary consumption—namely public schools and libraries—suffered severe cuts in government funding.

Because of the emphasis that the military regime placed on capitalist consumption, the television quickly became the cultural product par excellence of the dictatorship period due to its ability to breed a culture of material consumption far superior to that of any other artistic media—especially books. Horacio Eloy has noted the corollary relationship between the fall of book publications and sales and the rise of the television under dictatorship.[23] Likewise the present-day Consejo Nacional de la Cultura y las Artes (National Council on Culture and the Arts, CNCA) reports that reading lost the privileged position it held in Chilean culture prior to the military coup and that it diminished considerably with the rise of the television industry during the dictatorship years.[24] And, finally, Constable and Valenzuela argue that TV "was the ideal medium for a modern authoritarian government [because] it kept people home, created a direct link between the individual and the state, filtered reality through an appealing prism, and encouraged consumption instead of thought."[25] We might say that the dictatorship did as much to promote the television and consumerist culture (albeit through the private industry rather than a nationalized one) as the UP did to promote the book through Editorial Quimantú.

Literary Culture and Neoliberal Democracy

After the end of the dictatorship in 1990, Chileans' right to freedom of cultural expression was restored from a legal standpoint. Publishing houses and print media outlets no longer functioned under the threat of government harassment or direct raids, and individuals no longer felt the need to empty or hide their home libraries. Many Chileans who had been forced into exile returned, and literary culture, like the rest of the nation-state, began a slow but steady journey of recovery.[26] Despite improvements, many of the factors that so negatively influenced literary culture during the dictatorship did not change with the return of democracy. There are complex reasons for this, including the damaging changes the dictatorship had made to Chile's education system (changes so damaging that education has become one of the most contested areas of public reform during the newly democratic era). However, there is a general sentiment among literary producers that the greatest obstacle facing the democratization of Chilean literary culture in the postdictatorship period is the neoliberal market, which has remained firmly in place since Pinochet left power in 1990.[27]

The effects that Pinochet's regime had in diminishing Chileans' reading habits have been difficult to reverse. Even though in recent years Chile has experienced a rapid growth in information technologies, educational and public library programs, and state-financed cultural programs, there remain high levels of functional illiteracy and a decreased general interest in acquiring better reading habits.[28] According to the CNCA's 2011 publication *Plan Nacional de Fomento de la Lectura: Lee Chile Lee* (National Plan to Promote Reading: Read Chile Read), 52 percent of Chilean adults—across all socioeconomic sectors—do not consider themselves readers. The same report shows that Chile's reading population falls below the average in Latin America and that those Chileans who do read usually do not understand what they are reading.[29] Furthermore, in a 2008 survey, 49 percent of Chileans admitted that they never read books, citing (in order of importance) a lack of interest, lack of time, and lack of possibilities.[30] And, as of 2008, 40 percent of households have possessed less than ten books, meaning that only 10 percent of those individuals surveyed fell into the category of what the study classified as a "frequent reader."[31] Finally, according to a 2011 survey conducted by the University of Chile Economics Department, *Estudio de Comportamiento Lector* (Study of Reader Behavior), 85 percent of Chileans surveyed said they had not gone to a public library for over a year and 62 percent claimed never to have gone to a bookstore.[32]

These problems are in large part the result of the hegemony that consumerist culture established in Chile during the dictatorship years. Chile's commercial publishing industry has made a valiant comeback from its suppression by both socialist and authoritarian governments, but it still struggles greatly to compete within the global market. As independent publisher Jaime Pinos has stated, "Democracy is supposedly based on the free circulation of ideas and words—a notion that becomes very complicated when the existence of an independent press is truncated halfway between economic ruin and control by the big consortiums."[33] Within this globalized editorial landscape, Chilean democratization and national identity are commodified into marketing schemes used to make money rather than create social or political change. Paulo Slachevsky, editor of LOM Ediciones, writes: "Freedom of expression seems to be more a slogan than a reality due to the total concentration of modes of communication and the virtual censorship imposed by advisory publicity firms."[34] What both editors suggest is that global capitalism has replaced the dictator as censor and mediator of literary culture within Chile's current cultural economy.

Editors such as Pinos and Slachevsky are frustrated by the current monopoly held by multinational publishers within Chile's local literary culture.[35] This monopolization of publishing has arisen because free-market economics favor the mass production and commodification of books; transnational publishing firms have the kinds of resources required to produce literature in this way, and they are experienced in doing so, placing them at a greater competitive advantage over local independent presses that are not only less capable of such mass production but are also not interested in it for artistic, intellectual, and political reasons. Consequently, multinational corporations have acquired many locally owned publishing houses outright, and they have purchased the catalogs of other independently owned presses in piecemeal fashion. According to Chilean print culture scholar Belén Bascuñán, some very important works of the dictatorship years that were originally published by small and locally owned presses were later bought by foreign-owned corporate publishing firms.[36]

The most common and forceful counter-response to the monopolization of Chile's national editorial industry has come in the form of the *editorial independiente,* or independent publisher. Independent publishing is by no means a Chilean invention but rather a global editorial movement that attempts to offer a viable alternative to corporate publishing via locally owned and operated presses. Spanish writer and critic Constantino Bértolo defines independent publishing as "being independent of market logic, being a medium-to-small sized press, and having editorial politics that are different from those of the multinationals."[37]

Slachevsky offers a more political definition of the independent publisher as a political militant and purveyor of democracy. He writes, "To distribute books is to enact democracy, it is to allow for the other to assume the role of citizen and not consumer, it is to invite the other to think, to be alert. In this sense, I believe that working with books, from a cultural perspective, is to a certain degree political activism. I believe that independent publishers assume the role of political militants within the cultural sphere."[38] Slachevsky is not only arguing that independent publishers actively renounce the profit-seeking logic of multinational conglomerates; he goes so far as to connect that logic with consumerist culture at large. While he does not make direct reference to Chile's military regime, it is fair to assume that Slachevsky understands the efforts of independent publishers to counter capitalist consumer culture as political and democratic activities precisely because of the historical connection between Chilean consumer culture and the military regime.

Furthermore, the general ideology of independent publishing in contemporary Chile assumes that locally owned and operated presses are uniquely capable of producing literary works that project political concerns and cultural identities authentic to the Chilean experience, whereas multinational publishing conglomerates are only interested in publishing local authors whose literary aesthetics will earn high profits. There is convincing research showing that when multinational presses publish national literary canons, the criteria on which they construct those canons are based almost solely on expectations of market sales and not on a desire to publish a holistic and diverse representation of national writers and literary styles.[39] Research also suggests that local Chilean writers still have to resort to self-publication because their work is not attractive to multinational presses that currently dominate the local industry.[40]

The concern that the global publishing industry silences local cultural expression is not unique to postdictatorship Chile. In fact the symbolic struggle between the local and the global in Latin America began with the colonization of Native peoples by Europeans who systematically suppressed local cultural traditions as a means of political subjugation. The struggle took on new importance in the 1960s with the emergence of the Latin American literary "Boom" as an international editorial phenomenon orchestrated and profited by Spanish publishing houses.[41] Chilean literary icon José Donoso has stated that the "Boom" evidences a moment in Latin American literary history in which the novel "began to speak an international language" instead of representing "regional taste and aesthetic values."[42] Rather than seeing the "Boom" as a moment when the world became attracted to Latin America's unique cultural aesthetic, Donoso sees this as a moment in which the Latin American novel lost its local distinction and became more like what the rest of the world is—which, we might presume, is why it became so commercially successful worldwide. Chilean independent publishers of the postdictatorship period have attempted to reverse this trend so that Chile's cultural idiosyncrasies can reach global audiences rather than being silenced by a homogenized global culture, or what Donoso calls an international language.

In an attempt to counter these problems, independent publishing has grown in size and strength in Chile throughout the postdictatorship period, becoming a heterogeneous, organized, and outspoken voice of the private sector. Independent industry professionals, both writers and editors, have formed multiple associations throughout the 1990s and 2000s to collectively advance their common interests, which they do in the form of political lobbying and the organization of book fairs, workshops, and other literary events that promote opportunities for Chilean writers and editors to make and distribute their works. Some of these groups and associations include: Letras de Chile (Chilean Letters), Asociación de Editores de Chile (Association of Chilean Publishers), Asociación Gremial de Editores Independientes, Universitarios y Autónomos (Associated Guild of Independent, University, and Autonomous Publishers), and La Furia del Libro (The Book Fury).[43]

Even though these collectives share the same political objective to strengthen and democratize Chilean literary culture and the book industry, they differ in their methods of how to do so. For example, Editores de Chile works directly with the government in drafting and implementing public policies of cultural reform, whereas the Furia del Libro takes a much more rebellious and anti-institutional approach, preferring to function independently, without ties to the current political and cultural establishment.

Despite their diversity—or perhaps because of it—individual presses and writers often belong to many of these groups at the same time. This is because they all share a common commitment to the economic strengthening of Chile's publishing and literary industry so that it can more seriously compete within the global market. While they openly reject corporate culture, most of the individual members of these organizations are commercial enterprises. This does not mean that they are thriving businesses. They are professional entities that employ staff, yet many independent presses do not make enough profit to constitute the sole or even primary financial income of their editors and employees.[44]

The economic instability of individual publishing houses is precisely why associations of independent presses fight to increase the economic health of Chile's local publishing industry. Cultural studies scholar Raymond Williams explains that even though associations of artistic producers are almost always not-for-profit entities, they have traditionally served the same purposes as trade unions, "especially . . . under the pressure of economic conditions in an increasingly corporate market."[45] This is certainly the case in postdictatorship Chilean literary culture, whose independent publishers value the book equally as a social and economic good; in other words, they want socially valuable works to find market profitability. Another way to state this is that they believe the market to be the best way to increase the production and distribution of socially valuable texts.

In general, the relationship between these associations and the newly democratic state has been strongly cooperative. Cultural activity at large, and literary culture in particular, has proven to be a principal concern to all the presidential administrations that have governed Chile throughout the postdictatorship period. In fact, it is in large part because of the outspoken efforts of the independent publishing industry that the newly democratic state created and formalized a cultural state infrastructure that President Ricardo Lagos labeled as Chile's "new cultural institutionalization."[46]

In 1993 the state recognized the need for a public cultural agency dedicated solely to literary activity and consequently passed legislation creating the Consejo Nacional del Libro y la Lectura (National Book and Reading Council), which become responsible for regulating cultural policy specific to reading and writing, as well as to book production and circulation. This agency inspired the creation of similar entities pertaining to other cultural areas and eventually to the 2003 formation of a state ministry to oversee all cultural activity: el Consejo Nacional de la Cultura y las Artes (the National Council on Culture and the Arts, CNCA). While the CNCA now includes state councils pertaining to twelve areas of cultural production, only one of which is literary culture, it is important to recognize the historic role that literary culture played in the formation of the CNCA at large.[47]

To be sure, had it not been for the outspoken voices of independent publishers from the private sector, the state might not have formalized a new cultural infrastructure such as it did. Throughout the late 1990s and early 2000s leaders of Chile's independent publishing industry consistently voiced their concerns that the newly democratic state was not doing enough to support literary culture, arguing that more formal state policies regulating cultural activity were needed. In 2005 leaders of Chile's book industry came together to write *Una política de Estado para el libro y la lectura: Estrategias para el fomento de la lectura y el desarrollo de la industria editorial en Chile* (A State policy for the book and reading: Strategies to promote reading and the development of the publishing industry in Chile) that both criticized the state for not implementing a more forceful cultural agenda and also suggested how it might do so.[48]

This document attributes the economic weakness of Chile's publishing industry and the low levels of national literacy to the absence of any viable state policy on books and reading. The state responded almost immediately with its 2006 publication of *Política Nacional del Libro y la Lectura* (National Book and Reading Policy), which laid out strategies for fortifying national book production and reading habits over the following four years.[49] Many of the authors of *Una política del Estado para el libro y la lectura* served on the state council that authored this document, which is why Agustín Squella, cultural advisor to President Lagos throughout the creation of the CNCA, credits civil society for the implementation of Chile's new cultural institutionalization and the CNCA it created. More recently, in 2011, the CNCA openly stated that the 2006 policy would not have been written had it not been for the efforts and guidance of civil society, specifically Editores de Chile.[50]

Given the strong influence that the private sector has had on the formation and implementation of an official state cultural policy, it is no surprise that such policies have aimed to secure the economic health of Chile's national culture industries. Chile's first ever minister of culture and director of the CNCA, José Weinstein, presented the following statement to the 2004 international symposium "Industrias Culturales: Un aporte al desarrollo" (Culture Industries: Supporting development): "We have created the National Council of Culture and the Council of Books, the Council of Music, and now the Audiovisual Council. These Councils are the public instruments through which we must channel state policies intended to strengthen our culture industries."[51] The newly democratic state has foregrounded national culture industries as essential agents in developing cultural democracy in postdictatorship Chile.

This partnership between the state and the local industry is mutually beneficial: it is good for the state because culture industries, more so than other industries, can improve democracy in society since they produce symbolic products that (re)produce feelings of national belonging and cohesiveness. The state also sees culture industries as an area of economic growth for the nation and potentially powerful contributors to the national economy at large. Likewise, this partnership is good for citizens because, through their participation in a system of cultural democracy, they have more power in determining how to regulate cultural production and circulation.

Such a partnership would seem to be inherently more democratic than a divisive relationship because governing powers are shared between the state and citizens. Indeed, this is a strikingly different model than the one implemented by the dictatorship in which the majority of local literary producers were at best highly skeptical of and at worst outright opposed to the state's authority to regulate cultural production and circulation. In the postdictatorship era we see just the opposite: independent literary producers have called on the state to take a more authoritative role in shaping the kind of cultural economy that they want and that they believe is most conducive to building and maintaining cultural democracy. This is not to say that the state and the private sector always see eye-to-eye on how to direct public funds to the cultural sphere, but the two sides do interact in a way that is far more cooperative than their openly antagonistic relationship of the 1970s and 1980s.

Despite the diverse presidential administrations under which the CNCA has functioned since its inception in 2003, fundamental tenets of its purpose and policy have remained the same. Two of the most important of these are that the state attempts to empower citizens as readers as well as authors of written works, and that it attempts to place equal importance on the social and economic value of print culture. The state assumes responsibility for financing artistic production by Chileans principally through its FONDART grants but also through legislation that strengthens national culture industries. The state furthermore attempts to secure the rights of citizens from all social sectors to have equal access to cultural products by strengthening libraries, schools, and bookstores.

Through all these means, the state hopes to condition Chilean citizens as both producers and consumers of cultural goods while at the same time defining those goods as containing equal social and economic worth. In its 2011 *National Plan for the Promotion of the Book: Read Chile Read,* the CNCA writes: "In these times in which fast profits are sought after at all costs, it is worth remembering that reading serves the purpose of sharing, of recognizing oneself in the joy and the suffering of others, of experiencing profound emotions, of questioning oneself, of acquiring critical capacities and of not allowing oneself to be fooled, in order to know this world and other worlds in a more complex and diverse way."[52] This statement makes it clear that the postdictatorship state, like Allende's Popular Unity, sees literature and print culture as central ingredients for a healthy and democratic society.

Yet this does not mean that the CNCA privileges the social value of cultural commodities over their economic worth. For instance, the same cultural minister who presided over the publication of the 2011 *National Plan for the Promotion of Reading,* Luciano Cruz-Coke, has also been responsible for scaling back public resources that the state awards to fund artistic production, namely FONDART grants. In defending this course of action, Cruz-Coke has stated that "the Fondart has become a kind of stipend that the state awards to artists who otherwise would not be able to make a living on their own. This should not be. . . . Who can legitimize the artist if not the work of art?"[53] Cruz-Coke seems to be suggesting that if an artist's work is truly good, that is legitimate, it will naturally do well on the commercial market and the artist will not need funding from the state. In other words, in his view, the market is the ultimate judge of artistic value and legitimacy.

Each of these two statements, Cruz-Coke's and the CNCA's, are just two of many examples that reflect how the newly democratic state defines cultural objects as both social and economic goods. Although both statements emerged from the CNCA while it was under the administration of Sebastián Piñera's right-wing presidency, they are equally representative of the CNCA's cultural policies and agendas throughout the entire postdictatorship period.

In all three state administrations—socialist democracy, military authoritarianism, and neoliberal democracy—the book as cultural artifact has played an indispensable role in advancing the state's political agenda. For the socialist administration it was important in creating a public of active readers and therefore of intelligent citizens capable of participating in a democratic society; for the military regime it became a weapon of social discipline and neoliberal profiteering; and for the neoliberal state it has been a means of creating cultural democracy while also serving as a source of economic development.

What most distinguishes the cultural policies of the newly democratic state from those of the previous two administrations is that they put primary responsibility and power of cultural production, distribution, and consumption into the hands of Chile's local publishing industry and the public—or in other words, civil society. Both the socialist state and the authoritarian state worked to strictly control the process of book production and the accessibility of books to the public. While the socialist democratic state defined the value of the book almost exclusively based on its symbolic capabilities, the military state defined it almost exclusively based on its existence as an economic good. In contrast to these two models, the postdictatorship Chilean state has attempted to put equal importance on the symbolic worth of books as a storehouse of language, traditions, identities, and national culture and on the book's economic value as a material object that can generate economic capital for individuals, the national book industry, and the state.

Alternative literary producers share some similarities with the cultural agents we have discussed here—namely the belief that literature and the book (in the diverse material forms that they both take) make a unique and necessary contribution to Chilean nationalism and democracy. Due to these similarities, some alternative literary producers cooperate directly with such institutions as the CNCA, Editores de Chile, and La Furia del Libro. Ultimately, however, what distinguishes alternative literary producers is that they all minimize the economic value of literature and books, and it is not their primary (or even secondary) goal to professionalize Chilean literary culture. They all also work independently of Chilean culture industries and industrial literary production and, in so doing, produce literature in unconventional material forms.

2

Ergo Sum

Self-Publication and the Book-Object under Dictatorship

But what if these "commodities" refused to go to "market"? What if they maintained "another" kind of commerce, among themselves? . . . Use and exchange would be indistinguishable. The greatest value would be at the same time the least kept in reserve.

—Luce Irigaray, *The Sex That Is Not One*

In the late 1970s, the young up-and-coming writer Pía Barros began organizing writing classes to help predominantly working-class women compose letters to national and international institutions; their goal was to seek help in finding information about family members who had been disappeared by Chile's military regime. Barros soon realized that for many of these women, this was their first experience with the act of writing. She also noticed that her students restricted the focus of their writing to the drama surrounding their missing loved ones, even when they themselves had significant personal stories to share. As a result of this experience, Barros began a series of creative writing workshops designed specifically for women with no prior writing or publishing experience.

These workshops soon evolved into a literary collective made up mostly of women who, under the name Ergo Sum, engaged in a whole host of cultural activities that included public performances, political protests, community organizing, the collective writing and editing of literary works, and the handmade production of self-published literary objects. Resha Cardone, one of the few scholars to study this group, has declared Ergo Sum to be "Chile's first feminist political and literary collective."[1]

Throughout its thirty-year existence (as of 2016), Ergo Sum has produced a diverse range of cultural and political projects, including the handmade creation and unauthorized publication of what Barros labels *el libro-objeto,* or the book-object. Barros began the tradition of publishing book-objects in the mid-1980s during the height of the military dictatorship's campaign to suppress print culture. By choosing to form a literary collective, self-publish literary works, and do so in the form of three-dimensional handmade objects, Ergo Sum engaged in strategic acts of political protest against the military state. It is somewhat surprising, then, that this collective did not disband with the end of dictatorship and the country's return to procedural democracy in 1990. To the contrary, the group continues to meet weekly in Barros's Santiago home, and it publishes at least one book-object a year containing original short stories written by members of the group.

While some Ergo Sum members have participated in the group consistently for years (and even decades), the majority of its participants are transitory, most are inexperienced and unpublished writers (at least when they begin attending writing workshops with Barros), and the great majority of them are women. Barros's own works of fiction have made an undeniably important contribution to Chile's postdictatorship literary canon, and her work as an editor and pedagogue for the last forty years deserves much further scholarly attention. Yet the significance of Ergo Sum's production of book-objects transcends the achievements of its founder or other individual participants. Their activities are part of a diverse and nationwide editorial phenomenon: the self-publishing of literary works, known as *autoediciones.* Throughout the 1970s and especially in the 1980s Chileans used self-publication as a political response to the cultural censorship and free-market economic policies of the military regime.

Self-publishing became a vital and pervasive form of communication during the dictatorship period. Human rights organizations, cultural collectives, student groups, trade unions, and political organizations all self-published materials at a time when the state attempted almost absolute control over all forms of public communication.[2] Literary culture seized upon the autoedición editorial trend with vigor. Self-published literary materials, ranging from journals to two- and three-folded bulletins and newsletters, began appearing in the late 1970s and continued circulating throughout the 1980s, with the most active period spanning roughly between 1983 and 1987.

Horacio Eloy, a central figure in the autoedición movement and one of the only Chilean scholars to write about this editorial trend, describes it as a wide-reaching phenomenon: "[This] authentic counter-discourse and alternative cultural experience unfolds as much in Santiago as in Temuco, Valparaíso, Concepción, Valdivia, Iquique, Antofagasta, Chiloé, Punta Arenas, and other locations."[3] Thus these publications appeared across the length of the country, validating the importance of this cultural occurrence on a national scale.

Moreover, almost all literary self-publications emerged from a *taller,* or writing workshop, often associated with a literary collective.[4] While the literary journal was the most common form that these unauthorized self-publications took, Eloy more broadly characterizes these publications as "triptychs, sheets of poetry, journals and magazines that circulated with great difficulty and challenges through sales at poetry readings, on university campuses, in clubs, bars, political manifestations, union meetings, theaters, at artisan markets and, of course, hand-to-hand."[5]

Self-publications make us question the legitimacy of the term *apagón cultural* (cultural blackout) that is so often used to describe the dictatorship period. While cultural suppression certainly did exist, self-publications teach us that the term *apagón cultural* refers more appropriately to authorized forms of cultural activity during the 1970s and 1980s. Homemade literary materials prove conversely that there was a flurry of illegal and unauthorized cultural activity taking place during the years of military authoritarianism that is not properly represented by the term "blackout."

Many important literary voices and graphic artists of Chile's postdictatorship period began their careers in clandestine writing collectives, and the self-publications they produced in those collectives are some of the only evidence we have of what aspiring young artists created during the years of military authoritarianism. As Chilean writer Ramón Díaz Eterovic, himself a former self-publishing author, explains, "In a way, since there weren't many options available either through the [popular] press or publishing houses, these journals were to a certain degree the means by which that generation of writers let the world know what they were doing."[6]

Self-published literary texts are some of the only places to find the early writings of now famous Chilean authors and intellectuals such as Roberto Bolaño, Jorge Teillier, Diamela Eltit, Pedro Lemebel, Ana María del Río, Pía Barros, Carmen Berenguer, Jorge Montealegre, Diego Muñoz Valenzuela, and Ramón Díaz Eterovic, to name a few.[7] They also offer us a look into the early works of some of contemporary Chile's most important illustrators and graphic artists, such as Eduardo de la Barra, El Gato, Guillo, Hervi, José Palomo and Rufino, who also began their careers publishing in these underground journals.[8] Some of these writers and illustrators—including Pedro Lemebel, Ana María del Río, Pía Barros, Carmen Berenguer, Jorge Montealegre, Eduardo de la Barra, Hervi, and Rufino—published in Ergo Sum book-objects throughout the 1980s. Autoediciones are proof that Chilean writers, editors, and graphic artists rejected state restrictions and retaliated against them by meeting together in groups to write and publish works of literature.

The Ergo Sum project shared political and artistic ideologies as well as material practices with other cultural producers and political activists of the dictatorship period—namely the autoedición phenomenon at large but also other forms of feminist and avant-garde literary activism that took shape in Chile during the 1980s. Yet Ergo Sum ultimately developed what literary scholar Andrea Bell has called a "singularly innovative approach" to literary production that marks the group's difference from its contemporaries.[9] This difference is one of sexual difference since the book-objects the group produced can be considered books in drag.

By taking the form of commercialized object-commodities associated with patriarchal definitions of feminine sexuality—such as shopping bags, hope chests, and children's toys—Ergo Sum book-objects feigned conformity with the gender and economic politics of Pinochet's Chile. The shape of these nontraditional literary objects helped them to circulate in a political environment hostile to print culture in general and to books in particular. But as books in drag these objects failed to pass completely, and this failure produced a sardonic disavowal of the military's preferred definitions of feminine sexuality and artistic value. These objects were of course not only commercialized commodities associated with patriarchal definitions of feminine sexuality; they were literary works written and published by women and circulated without state permission. Ergo Sum book-objects challenged traditional Chilean expectations of what books should look like, of how they should circulate throughout the public sphere, and, most important, of what role women were to play in literary culture and public life.

It is most crucial to note, however, that the material practices differentiating the Ergo Sum collective from its contemporaries during the dictatorship period are also what connect this project to alternative literary formations of the postdictatorship era. These practices include the targeting of novice and amateur writers, the rejection of editorial norms associated with the literary industry and literature as an institution, and a belief that processes of literary production—rather than consumption practices alone—empower individuals as cultural agents and advance cultural democracy in postdictatorship Chile.

Underground under Dictatorship: Self-Publishing Literary Collectives

Despite the fact that the term *apagón cultural* has become almost synonymous with the entire period of Chilean dictatorship, it most accurately describes the 1970s only. According to Eloy, the idea of an apagón cultural "was put forth by some researchers as a metaphor that designates the most difficult and violent period of the dictatorship (1973–81) in which there was an evident lack of leadership for creators in this depressive stage in the development of Art and Culture."[10] While it serves as an accurate description of 1973–81, the idea of an apagón cultural is a less fitting way to capture the cultural climate of the 1980s. Print culture scholar Belén Bascuñán refers to this decade as an *auge editorial* (publishing boom) through which citizens used print culture as "a weapon in the battle for democracy."[11] There were multiple factors that gave rise to this publishing boom, including eased state restrictions on print censorship and the increased political protest and civil unrest of citizens across the country that sought to end the dictatorship and return to electoral politics.[12]

The publishing boom to which Bascuñán refers does not include underground literary self-publications, but rather printed books, journals, and other periodicals. Bascuñán's research shows that the two were often interconnected, and she calls the former *revistas de oposición* (opposition periodicals), also known as the alternative or leftist press that functioned most actively between 1983 and 1986.[13] Examples of well-known opposition periodicals include *Apsi, Análisis, Hoy, Cauce, Punto Final, La Época,* and *Fortín Mapocho.* The primary emphasis of these periodicals was investigative journalism; they reported on the government's excessive spending of public funds for private use by military officials, the disappearance and imprisonment of citizens, political repression, unemployment, and economic crisis. Carol Díaz Allendes and Hugo Neira Gasc report that at least some of these periodicals, namely *Hoy,* "played a crucial role in the circulation of human rights discourses."[14] *La Bicicleta* and *Pluma y Pincel* were complimentary cultural magazines that, according to Eloy, "re-vindicated a discourse of veiled opposition."[15]

While these publications did not circulate with nearly the same level of ease or scale as mainstream and pro-regime media sources, they did attempt to circulate on a massive level and to serve as legitimate and professional alternatives to state-controlled media outlets. For instance, opposition periodicals produced and circulated approximately one hundred thousand copies of each edition; likewise, cultural magazines such as *La Bicicleta* and *Pluma y pincel* experienced mass distribution, primarily through newsstands and kiosks stationed all over Santiago.[16] These periodicals evidence a kind of print culture that existed in opposition to the state but was not underground. The political strategy of these publications relied on wide-scale visibility and public recognition.

Publishing houses also formed an important part of the alternative press during the dictatorship, and many functioned in partnership with opposition periodicals, printing book-length works written by anti-regime journalists. For instance, the publishing house Las Ediciones del Ornitorrinco was associated with the magazine *Apsi,* Editorial Emisión with *Análisis,* Libros de Hoy with the magazine *Hoy*, and Pensamiento Ediciones with *Cauce*.[17] Pehuen Editores, CESOC (Centro de Estudios Sociales / Center for Social Studies), and Editorial Cuarto Propio were other key oppositional publishing houses functioning under dictatorship.[18] Chilean literary historian Bernardo Subercaseaux uses the terms "contesting" and "dissident" to describe these types of publishing houses and includes in this category Editorial Aconcagua (associated with the magazine *Política y Espíritu*) and many nongovernmental organizations that published various materials during the 1980s.[19]

Oppositional and dissident publishing houses also produced important book-length works of literature and journalism during the early and mid-1980s, such as Raul Zurita's *Purgatorio* (Editorial Universitaria, 1979) and *Anteparaíso* (Editores Asociados, 1982), Diamela Eltit's experimental novel *Lumpérica* (Ediciones del Ornitorrinco, 1983), Patricia Politzer's *Miedo en Chile* (CESOC, 1985), Patricia Verdugo's *Los zarpazos del puma* (CESOC, 1985), Carlos Prats González's *Memorias. Testimonio de un soldado* (Pehuén Editores, 1985), and *Chile la memoria prohibida* (Ahumada et. al., Pehuén Editores, 1989).[20]

Due to their public visibility, these magazines and publishing houses were some of the hardest-hit victims of state censorship in the 1980s. They often asked for and had to wait years to receive state approval to print materials for circulation; editors and journalists received direct threats from the government; state officials frequently raided their places of business, often banning, confiscating, or even destroying published materials; and some editors and journalists were detained, imprisoned, and even murdered.[21] Many dissident presses responded to these oppressive tactics by fighting the state in court, engaging in lengthy proceedings that they sometimes won and sometimes lost but that ultimately neither stopped them from functioning nor impeded the military from constantly bullying them.[22]

Díaz Allendes and Neira Gasc maintain that the legal fight sustained by anti-state publishers was as politically important to the struggle for democracy in Chile as was the content of the materials they printed. Similarly, Belén Bascuñán argues that for all the negative outcomes that resulted from the state's persecution of oppositional journalists and publishing houses (affecting both the industry and the individuals working in it), it produced at the same time unexpectedly positive outcomes: namely, it brought the problem of Chilean state censorship to the attention of the international community, it caused widespread appreciation of the role and importance of journalism in Chilean society, and it paradoxically sparked the publication of many books written by journalists, some of which are still inherently relevant and widely read today.[23]

Underground literary self-publications existed in solidarity with these cultural formations, but they were much less known to the general public because of their grassroots, amateur, and non-industrial nature. Barros explains that "even though newspapers (under surveillance by the military regime), would talk about a 'cultural blackout,' the country experienced a massive counter-cultural movement that was not registered by the mass media, though it was known on a small scale because of the inundation of mini-modes of communication such as journals, triptychs, diptychs, and an endless amount of precarious publications."[24]

The mini-modes of communication to which Barros refers circulated information about cultural and political happenings as a way of organizing particular communities in opposition to the military regime. Specifically, self-published literary journals announced which writing workshops were taking place at the time, which other literary publications were circulating and where to find them, the winners of literary awards, which publishing houses were functioning despite the hostile editorial climate, the availability of individual services related to print culture (editing, graphic design, etc.), and information about where to find literary meetings and readings.[25] Some self-publications also advertised businesses in the communities in which they were produced and circulated. Others offered subscription-based circulation.

While literary autoediciones reside in the same political and cultural camp as oppositional print media, there are important differences between them that need to be fleshed out in order to fully appreciate the diversity of editorial practices that Chileans employed in their fight against military authoritarianism.[26] The most significant difference is that opposition print media were industrially and professionally produced whereas underground self-publications were made using artisanal modes of material production and were, for the most part, noncommercial. Whereas anti-regime periodicals printed up to 100,000 copies per edition, books published by opposition publishing houses circulated in much smaller numbers, rarely exceeding 1,500 copies per print run.[27] Yet even though the figures of book production were significantly small, they far exceeded the circulation of self-published works, which typically ran between 50 and 100 copies per title and only on rare occasions reached as high as 300 copies per edition.

The small scale of production and circulation for self-published works was a direct result of the artisanal methods used to make them, or of what autoedición producers such as Horacio Eloy, Jorge Montealegre, Pía Barros, and Juan Carlos Vega all describe as their "precarious" nature.[28] These publications were precarious in part because they were made without the use of industrial technologies and therefore lacked the physical durability and professional quality of commercial publications. They were printed using mimeographs, photocopiers, and inexpensive paper, and they were hand-folded, stapled, glued, or tied together with string.

Another cause of the fragility of these texts was the dominant use of hand-drawn illustrations both on the covers and throughout the interiors, which contrasted to the industrially printed periodicals of the same era. Magazines such as *Apsi* and *Hoy* exhibited high production value with colorful photographs and professional-looking design layouts. According to the grassroots political activists Juan Carlos Vega (who self-produced flyers for the non-governmental organization CODEPU), the mimeograph is "a very artisanal form of printing."[29] Once printed on a mimeograph and/or reproduced on a photocopy machine, pages of self-published works were assembled into three different forms: the journal (which was typically hand-bound using staples, glue, or string), the triptych (a three-folded paper pamphlet), and the diptych (a piece of paper folded in two). Some handmade publications were simply large pieces of paper folded multiple times or various folded pieces of paper placed inside one another.

Triptychs and diptychs were especially popular forms of autoediciones because they were incredibly cheap to make and easy to assemble: all that was needed was a mimeograph and paper, the latter of which was folded by hand into halves or thirds. Speaking to the popularity of this publication form, Vega describes the dictatorship as "the period in which the most triptychs and diptychs were published in this country: a sheet of paper folded in two parts that reported activities and voiced complaints."[30] Likewise, the self-published diptych *Botella al mar* writes in its first edition (printed in 1985) about the pervasive presence of these kinds of publications in Chilean society: "It's not strange to find them in the most unexpected places, that little piece of paper carefully folded into three parts and that almost everyone calls a 'Triptych.' "[31] Precisely because they did not require industrial modes of editorial production, hand-folded flyers or bulletins became a common means through which all kinds of social collectives, from literary workshops to human rights organizations, would disseminate information as a means of political protest.

The paper used to make triptychs, diptychs, and handcrafted literary journals became a defining characteristic of this editorial form, and its usage speaks to both the historical conditions under which these publications were made and also to the political meanings they were meant to embody. Kraft and butcher paper were the most common kinds of paper used in these publications because they were cheap and easily available to the public, meaning that anyone could buy them without raising suspicions.[32] The choice to print on kraft or butcher paper was thus a choice to evade state censorship, which in turn proved the government's inability to fully control the cultural sphere; the message these publications sent was that no matter what censorship laws were in place or how many presses the government shut down, people could still publish literature out of anything, even the most common household goods or store-bought supplies.

Symbolically, however, cheap paper represented the poor and lowly state of Chilean society under military dictatorship. Underground self-publishing artists and activists wanted to change those conditions and, in the words of Jorge Montealegre, "convert misery into dignity."[33] They did so by intentionally retaining the simplicity and impoverished quality of kraft paper even while transforming it into an aesthetic object. Almost all autoediciones included hand-drawn illustrations rendered in black ink that accompanied poems, short stories, editorial pieces, and essays of cultural criticism.[34] As the producers of the diptych *Botella al mar* explain, "Just as the poster takes on a quality far superior to commercial manipulation when in the hands of authentic illustrators, so too do triptychs prove to be more than just a test run of primary and modest literary concerns. And this is for a simple reason: they must blend together the skill of good graphic design with the quality of the written message."[35] Oppositional journals are not the kind of "commercial" publications that the authors of this statement rank as inferior to the graphic designs of handmade triptychs, but they did boast bright print designs and color photography that stood in stark contrast to the hand-drawn graphic illustrations characteristic of autoediciones such as *Botella al mar.* Through an artisanal material practice, counter-cultural literary groups showed that even in the most dire of conditions, creating beauty and change out of misery was possible. In the words of Montealegre, "everything mattered."[36]

Not all self-publications of the dictatorship period were handmade in literary workshops. It was also common during this time for books to be printed by industrial presses but to be financed solely by the author, thus qualifying them as self-publications.[37] Because of the strained economic and political conditions under which local presses functioned during the dictatorship period, authors often had to pay publishing houses to print and market their works.[38] Because of this, some authors opened presses with the sole intention of publishing and circulating their own works. Subercaseaux describes these kinds of presses as "private publishing houses that almost exclusively publish the works of their owners."[39] Whereas the examples that Subercaseaux cites functioned in accord with the "market criteria" that dominated Chile's editorial industry at the time, this style of self-publication was not exclusively commercial; Editores Asociados, for example, is believed to have opened for the primary purpose of publishing, in 1982, Raúl Zurita's avant-garde work *Anteparaíso,* and not necessarily of functioning as a commercial enterprise.[40]

These examples of self-publication were not artisanal in nature but rather pertained to the literary industry; they were books that were industrially produced via the printing press, they circulated with permission from the state (which, as we have seen, does not mean that they circulated with ease, but just that they had permission to exist) and they were bought and sold through sanctioned modes of capitalist exchange (some self-publishing presses even engaged in commercial marketing strategies). These types of presses therefore stand in stark distinction to the artisanal method of self-publication practiced by grassroots literary collectives.

In industrial book production, the writer is responsible for the symbolic production of the text but not the physical construction of the book as material vessel of the text; conversely, in most underground literary collectives, writers and graphic illustrators were the same individuals working cooperatively to print, fold, cut, and assemble makeshift publications. As Barros explains of her own self-publishing workshop, "All authors, both men and women, participated in the entire process of textual production: from the workshop where they learned to create the text, to the process of visualizing the text in private dialogue with a graphic artist . . . , to printing, folding, assembling and inserting it into the object at hand, to the process of direct sales. Nothing was foreign to them, not even people's refusal to buy them."[41]

This editorial practice weakens the boundaries that capitalist print culture has historically used to differentiate intellectual labor (producing the text as a symbolic good) from manual labor (producing the text as a material good) and to define the former as more valuable than the latter. Likewise, artisanal editorial production defines the raw materials from which the publication is made—kraft or butcher paper, hand-painted ink, string, glue, and the like—as contributing to the object's aesthetic value in the same way that the words of the text do. Individuals who handmade their own publications thus exercised cultural agency from multiple social positions simultaneously—as writers, editors, bookmakers, and book distributors—as well as through multiple artistic mediums—language, paper, ink, string, and other materials. They appreciated intellectual labor and manual labor equally, and they understood literature's aesthetic quality as deriving as much from the work's textual composition as from its material manifestation as a physical object.

Through artisanal literary production, underground literary collectives created social relations different from those produced through industrial print culture. Commercial publishing establishes a social relation between author and editor, editor and bookmaker, author and bookmaker, author and book distributor, and so forth. Such relations are determined by the market and exist primarily for economic purposes.[42] In contrast, underground self-publications are the product of groups of individuals who have come together in the formation of a collective identity based on shared artistic sensibilities and political ideologies. Specifically, participants in the autoedición underground shared an outsider identity, as subjects politically and culturally oppressed by the state. Barros states that micro-practices of literary production "re-vindicated above all else that those who stayed behind and suffered, those who acquired a collective consciousness in opposition to dictatorship and repression had the right to express themselves.' "[43] Individuals who expressed themselves through opposition periodicals shared strong political and cultural ideologies with those participating in underground literary collectives, to be sure, but because of the professional nature of opposition periodicals and the fact that there were only a small number of such periodicals authorized by the government, the number of people whose works were published by them was relatively small. Underground literary collectives on the other hand functioned on a grassroots level and had a much lower barrier for entry, offering a greater number of citizens the opportunity to build a pro-democratic political identity through the collective and unauthorized process of literary production.[44]

The marginal political identity of these groups was reflected not only in their non-industrial literary production but also in the precarious legal status of their publications. Jorge Montealegre, editor of the self-published journal *La Castaña* (fig. 3), acknowledges that he and fellow underground literary producers would have preferred legitimacy over their marginalized legal status: "We tried to be legal, we asked for authorization to circulate, but we didn't get it. (After all, my friends, there was a dictatorship). The [marginal] explication was valid because for us marginality wasn't an option or an inclination. We were just in the margin."[45] The fact that many counter-cultural groups would have preferred legitimacy to marginality is also evident in the qualifiers "Restricted Circulation," "published for internal circulation" and "permission in process" that were printed on many handmade literary publications. It is unclear if these publications were actually accorded a "restricted circulation" status by the state or if these declarations were simply attempts to show compliance with the state and ease political persecution in the event that these publications were discovered by officials.[46]

There were, however, a large number of self-publications that made absolutely no attempt to obtain authorization from the state and deliberately circulated, as Horacio Eloy claims, "without anyone's permission."[47] The illegitimate status of these publications is evidenced in a number of ways, including the overall lack of International Standard Book Numbers (ISBNs), copyright, and intellectual property rights protections.[48] In *not* asking permission, underground literary producers purposefully engaged in illegal activity since, in the words of *Análisis* editor Felipe Pozo, "What you could not do was found modes of communication without authorization."[49] Not only was it illegal to open up new publications without permission, but it was also illegal to form a social collective without authorization.

FIGURE 3. Two editions of the self-published literary and graphic arts journal *La Castaña* (no. 5, 1986, on the left; no. 7, 1987, on the right). Photograph by Jane D. Griffin. Reproduced by permission of Jorge Montealegre.

Resha Cardone's research tells us that during the 1970s, when the majority of these grassroots artistic collectives formed, the military regime only authorized the legal existence of two writing workshops, meaning that the substantial number of cultural groups working across the length of Chile were doing so illegally.[50] Ramón Díaz Eterovic, director of various self-publications, including the journal *La gota pura,* argues that within the culture of fear that was emblematic of the dictatorship years, the very acts of writing poetry and collectively producing texts were in themselves subversive because they went against the "sign of the times."[51] Producers of *Botella al mar* agree, writing that "the times in which we live are not only urgent and unsure, but they are also painful and even inhuman. It is from this that every means of communication, every piece of information or petition that the force of young writers can take on, acquire in themselves a testimonial value."[52] According to Chilean cultural critic and scholar Nelly Richard, the conscious participation in cultural activity was, for these writers and artists, itself an overt political act, especially considering the pervasiveness of self-censorship in Chile at this time.[53] Their actions not only questioned the very legitimacy of Pinochet's laws themselves but also seemed to argue that the government's actions were more criminal than their own.

Thus, although relegated to the margins by the state, counter-cultural literary producers strategically appropriated the marginal subject position and resignified it into a politically charged social and cultural identity. Self-published journals such as *Al margen* (At the margin) and *Textos por Latinoamerica: Serie Cuadernos Marginales* (Texts for Latin America: A series of marginal compositions) went as far as to don a label of marginalization in their very titles, wearing it publically as if with pride. The poetry journal *Presión 27* carried the subtitle *La Cultura Sin Censura* (Culture without Censorship), openly announcing its rebellious opposition to the military state's policies of cultural repression. The choice to inhabit the margin as a position of political critique is also evidenced by the very decision to produce and circulate literary publications underground. Clandestine publishing was a political strategy and one that carried with it both advantages and limitations.

The social, and therefore political, power wielded by these literary collectives did not derive from their public visibility or social influence since both were relatively small due to the artisanal nature of their literary production. Underground literary collectives chose to generate political power by giving individuals tools to create their own subversive editorial practices; they did not place emphasis on how many readers their self-published texts reached.[54] This practice stands in contrast to the leftist news media, which believed that "the return to democracy was possible by creating consciousness in readers" and that this consciousness needed to happen on a large scale, thus explaining the massive print runs of oppositional periodicals. While the oppositional media did not share the military regime's neoliberal privileging of materialist consumption, it did, somewhat ironically, focus its political strategy on the number of readers able to consume its publications. The autoedición movement, on the other hand, viewed literary *production*, and not consumption, as determining literature's social purpose.

Ergo Sum: Sexual Difference and the Book-Object

Ergo Sum is an exceptional contributor to the autoedición counterculture. The group's origins correspond to the beginnings of this underground publishing trend. In the late 1970s, Barros began teaching various writing workshops, and by the early 1980s, she had spearheaded the formation of a self-published women's literary magazine titled *Nos=Otras.* That publication fits the description of other autoediciones described above: the text consists of three large single sheets of paper printed on a mimeograph and then folded in half and inserted one into the next, creating a magazine-like effect and a total of twelve pages of text. In addition to publishing in this style, Barros experimented in a wide range of other editorial methods, both alternative and traditional. Her "Soffia" writing workshop released two anthologies of short stories, *Somos trece: Soffia* (We are Thirteen: Soffia; 1981) and *Cuentos: taller Soffia* (Stories: Soffia Workshop; 1984), both in traditional book form.[55] In addition, Barros and her students sometimes detached their texts from any physical vessel other than the human body by reciting works in public that they had not published in written form.[56]

Despite Barros's firm entrenchment in the underground autoedición phenomenon, in 1985 she initiated a noted divergence from the editorial norms established within this trend. During that same year Barros's individual writing workshops (Soffia, Kafka, and Ergo Sum) came together to self-publish an anthology of their collective writings under the shared name of Ergo Sum, marking the emergence of Ergo Sum as a literary activist group that is still functioning today (as of 2016), thirty years after its founding. The year 1985 also marked the beginning of what would become Ergo Sum's signature editorial form: the three-dimensional book-object. Over the years Ergo Sum book-objects would take many shapes, but what they all have in common is that they are containers filled with loose-leaf triptychs, each presenting a short story written by an Ergo Sum workshop participant and an original illustration drawn by an artist associated with the group. The choice to publish its writings in three-dimensional containers and not in the preferred autoedición form of a literary magazine or journal, or even just as individual triptychs and diptychs, is what most differentiates this group from its counter-cultural contemporaries.

Understanding why Ergo Sum strayed from the editorial norms of Chile's underground self-publishing phenomenon requires an understanding of the group's feminist politics. Chilean feminist discourse and praxis of the late twentieth century were grounded in the belief that national and regional institutions were inherently patriarchal and that feminist organizations and movements needed to remain militantly independent of them. Some Chilean feminists expressed this belief through literature as an explicit means of pro-democratic protest. Women writers galvanized at least two major events under dictatorship that directly challenged the state's efforts to silence artists, intellectuals, women, and homosexuals; both gatherings were staunchly anti-institutional. The first was the 1984 conference "Mujer, Cultura, y Contracultura: Congreso Internacional de Literatura Femenina" (Women, Culture, and Counterculture: International Congress on Feminine Literature), and the second was an international conference hosted in Chile in 1987 titled "Escribir en los bordes: Congreso Internacional de Literatura Femenina Latinoamericana" (Writing in the margins: International Congress on Latin American Women's Writing).

Both of these literary events—organized by, for, and about women writers—emphasized their autonomy from any institutional support. When the organizers of the 1987 conference edited a book documenting the event, they explained that their work "began in a completely autonomous way, without any institutional support, which therefore highlights the achievement of its formation, its creative independence."[57] In expressing their institutional autonomy, pro-democratic women writers under dictatorship were publically announcing their independence from an illegitimate, patriarchal, and terrorist state government.

They were also, however, differentiating themselves from other women who were mobilizing at the same time but with full institutional support from the state. General Pinochet made women a focal point of his political agenda, and one of the best examples of this is the Centro de Madres de Chile (Chilean Mother Centers), or CEMA-Chile, led by Pinochet's own wife, Lucía Hiriart. The political purpose of these centers was to incentivize women to assume the roles of wives, mothers, and homemakers. These centers trained women to use those traditional feminine roles to biologically reproduce more citizens for the nation and instill within those citizens love and loyalty to a patriarchal brand of Chilean nationalism. In announcing their institutional autonomy, feminist literary activists were not only expressing their disapproval of the military state but also their rejection of the state's prescription of traditional female gender roles.[58]

Autonomy from institutions was also a defining characteristic of the avant-garde artistic production that emerged in tandem with the autoedición trend. In her now classic book *Margins and Institutions: Art in Chile Since 1973*, Nelly Richard explores the avanzada art scene of the late 1970s and 1980s, whose participants included, in her depiction, visual artists, performance artists, poets, philosophers, and cultural critics.[59] Richard defines avanzada art as inhabiting a marginal position in relation to institutions, specifically leftist political parties and trade unions, whose aesthetic politics of transparent representation stood in direct contradiction to the disguised and hyper-codified aesthetics of the avanzada scene.

More important, however, Richard understands the marginal position of this art in relation to artistic and literary institutions whose material conventions the avanzada scene sought to destabilize. "The 'advanced' scene's move to disobey conventionally formulated assignations that fix artistic and literary tradition (the framed picture for painting; the book for poetry or narrative), figuratively denounced the abuse of authority with which the military regime oversaw the borders of Order."[60] In striving for institutional autonomy, avanzada artists attempted to break literature's own conventional norms on both the discursive level of how language functions as a semiotic system and also on the material level of how art takes the form of particular physical objects. Richard argues that in breaking the authoritative mandates of conventional art and literature, avanzada artists rebelled against the authoritarian dictates of the military regime.

Pía Barros and Ergo Sum shared these feminist and avant-garde politics of institutional autonomy and material experimentation, which explains why the group refashioned editorial practices that differed from the trends established within Chile's underground self-publishing scene. Despite the autoedición's marginalization from authorized, mainstream, and industrial forms of print culture, underground self-publications did exhibit material traces of literature and print culture's institutional power. The strongest evidence of this is the very form of the literary journal itself, which during the dictatorship was a more publically accepted and recognizable form of publication than the book. Even though the ban on publishing books without the state's prior permission—the infamous *censura previa*—was lifted in 1983, the state's open affront against the book as a threat to national security did not desist. The 20-percent VAT tax placed on all book sales remained in place, and government authorities continued to raid private residences and publishing businesses and publically destroyed the books they found there throughout the 1980s. In addition, book production is difficult to accomplish without the use of industrial print technology; small-sized magazines and journals were much easier to produce with household technologies and everyday office supplies.

Autoedición journals further embodied traces of institutional affiliation through their indication of edition volume and number. We can read the editorial choice to have included such markers as an attempt to establish symbolic legitimacy for a literary object that was, at least in a legal sense, wholly illegitimate. French cultural theorist Pierre Bourdieu talks about the way in which all cultural fields are sites of competition for "symbolic capital," by which he means the accumulation of recognition, consecration, and prestige that come in the form of authors' reputations, the critical reception of publications, and the fame of a publishing house.[61] The generally young and unknown authors publishing autoediciones under dictatorship lacked a public reputation, did not have reputable publishing houses willing to print and distribute their works, and had minimal opportunities for receiving acknowledgement from the literary establishment or the state. This meant that they had to seek other forms of generating symbolic capital and public credibility. One way in which they did this was by imprinting markers of institutional legitimacy—that is, of industrial print culture—onto their artisanal literary publications. Thus while the very existence of self-published literary works was a disavowal of the political authority of Chile's military state, it was not a disavowal of the institutional norms practiced by industrial print culture and literature at large.

By choosing to make book-objects rather than makeshift literary magazines, bulletins, or journals, Ergo Sum does not join the majority of underground self-publishers in their quest to establish some form of institutional legitimacy or what Bourdieu calls consecration. Instead, the group consciously rejects institutional consecration by producing texts that do not immediately register as *literary* or as even belonging to print culture at all. Ergo Sum book-objects have no identifiable front, back, or spine as do the majority of self-published journals, and they are almost all three-dimensional objects, rather than folded sheets of paper (although the objects contain diptychs and triptychs inside them); neither do they have edition numbers, volume numbers, or even page numbers. In fact, the individual pages of texts included within Ergo Sum book-objects are not confined to any determined order, meaning that there is no hierarchical structuring of the stories included in these anthologies; readers can remove the stack of triptychs found in a given Ergo Sum book-object and rearrange them however they please, altering the physical constitution of the text every time they take the stories in and out of the object.

This kind of material production is in complete accord with feminist and avanzada objectives of rejecting and, when possible, deconstructing conventional institutional hierarchies. Without the physical markers that would immediately identify these objects as literary publications, Ergo Sum book-objects intentionally complicate their inclusion into literary criticism and historicism—institutions that rely on page numbers and on edition volume, number, year, and place of publication, in order to talk about literary works and fix them within an accredited record of meaning. As such, these works, unlike other autoediciones of the time, make little to no attempt to accrue symbolic capital; they are not meant to gain prestige, consecration, or critical recognition. Rather they are meant to expose the exclusionary and discriminatory practices through which symbolic capital is defined and acquired. In Cardone's words, the Ergo Sum workshop sought to "show that the [military] regime, the art establishment, the publishing industry, and even language itself were all authoritarian institutions."[62] The group was committed to remaining as autonomous as possible from such institutions as an expression of their feminist and pro-democratic political views.

While the group's feminist politics separated it from its autoedición contemporaries, its method of artisanal book production and self-publication distinguished it from other feminist and avant-garde literary activists of the 1980s. For example, several other women besides Barros directed their own literary workshops under dictatorship, and there were at least two self-published literary magazines dedicated specifically to the question of women's literature: *Safo: revista literaria femenina* (Safo: female literary magazine) and *Palabra de mujer* (Women's word).[63] Both of these magazines originated at the end of the dictatorship and lasted into the 1990s. Unlike Ergo Sum book-objects, these self-publications used methods characteristic of the autoedición movement at large. *Palabra de mujer*, for example, was printed on brown kraft paper and bound together with a decorative ribbon that matched the uniquely colored ink used to print each issue. Both *Safo* and *Palabra de mujer* publications took the more recognizable form of the magazine or journal, capitalizing on the institutional legitimacy of literature and industrial print culture even while working through non-industrial means.

Outside the autoedición phenomenon, women and feminist literary activists working during the dictatorship focused on manipulating the materiality of literature as a form of political and artistic protest against the regime, but they did so by defining literature's materiality as primarily, if not strictly, linguistic. Feminist women writers manipulated the language of the literary text as a means of drawing attention to the historical reality out of which the text was made. For instance, in her book *Composición de lugar: escritos sobre cultura* (Composition of place: Writings on culture), Chilean literary scholar Adriana Valdés argues that women writers removed, dislocated, and disappeared the speaking "I" of the narrative text and that this affect alluded to the bodies disappeared by the military regime. The result, she argues, is a text that exhibits a consciousness of itself as text; the condition of the text's production is visibly "written on it."[64] This strategy makes the reader cognizant of the fact that the work is a fiction written by an author and determined by its historical moment—extracting the reader from the realm of imagination and returning her to the reality of Pinochet's Chile.

Ergo Sum's literary production accomplishes the same goal through different means, namely through modes of editorial production rather than through discursive acts of writing. The shape of Ergo Sum book-objects directly references the historical moments of their production. Prime examples are the book-objects *21 son los relatos* (21 are the stories; 1986) and *Ensacados: 26 cuentos ilustrados* (Bagged: 26 stories, 1990). The former takes the shape of a miniature paper suitcase (fig. 4), representing the massive number of Chileans forced to leave their country and live in exile during the military regime. The latter takes the shape of a small burlap bag that, according to Cardone, meant to cite the "known military practice of putting the bodies of the disappeared into burlap bags before discarding them into the Mapocho river."[65] In the same way that Valdés sees the language of women's literature as carrying traces of the text's historical moment of production, so too does the physical shape of Ergo Sum book-objects remind the reader of the political context out of which these texts emerge. Ergo Sum has maintained this tradition even after the fall of dictatorship, as we saw earlier with the example of *Tenemos pantalones* (2006).[66]

While both of these strategies affect similar results, there are larger

FIGURE 4. Ergo Sum's book-object anthology *21 son los relatos* (1986). The book-object is made of kraft paper and takes the shape of a miniature suitcase that has openings on both sides where pamphlets of short stories printed on them slide in and out. Photograph by Nélida Pohl. Reproduced by permission of Pía Barros.

implications for choosing to put forth a political message through the discursive matter of the text alone as opposed to constructing it through the materiality of the published object as well. For example, Valdés's research shows that feminist Chilean writers critiqued the authoritarian regime through their narrative language, yet the texts she uses as evidence of this were published through traditional forms that upheld the same patriarchal and authoritarian institutions that feminist literature was protesting against, including, notably, the global capitalist publishing industry. A poignant example of this is Diamela Eltit's 1988 novel *El cuarto mundo* (The fourth world). The novel is centered on a set of boy-girl fraternal twins who take turns narrating the same story from their relative perspectives. It ends in an act of incest between the siblings and with the female twin giving birth to their *sudaca* (South American trash) daughter, who then "go[es] up for sale."[67] The final lines read: "Far away, in a house abandoned to brotherhood, between April 7 and 8, diamela eltit, assisted by her twin brother, gives birth to a baby girl. The sudaca baby will go up for sale."[68] Eltit reveals herself as the narrative's protagonist, the female twin, who gives birth to the book / incestuous daughter that then goes to market. Her feminine literary product (*la niña sudaca*) represents literature and the female body at once, both of which are submitted to the force of the market from the moment of their birth.

We can read this novel's conclusion as an example of Valdés's thesis that postdictatorship women's literature carries within it material traces of the historical moment of its production. In this case, at the time Eltit wrote and published her text, Chile's national literary market was suffering severe marginalization by foreign publishing conglomerates that had increased their monopolization of Chile's editorial industry as a result of the military dictatorship's neoliberal economic policies. Eltit critiques this situation by announcing the marginalized subject-position of her literary work as both feminine (*la niña*) and South American trash (*sudaca*).

Outside the narrative structure of the text, the way in which this book literally "goes to market" is emblematic of the changes that Pinochet's neoliberal economic policies brought to bear on Chile's editorial industry. *El cuarto mundo* was first published in 1988 by Editorial Planeta, a Chilean subsidiary of the Spanish-owned transnational corporation Grupo Planeta, and was released again that same year in paperback form by another powerful Spanish publishing house, Seix Barral. These two firms exemplify how the global publishing industry in general and Spanish corporations in particular came to dominate the Latin American publishing industry throughout the twentieth century. While the history of this monopolization predates Chile's military coup of 1973, the cultural and economic policies that the dictatorship implemented only increased that trend.[69] Because independent and dissident publishing houses functioned at a disadvantage to larger corporate and foreign-owned presses working in Chile in the 1980s, their small budgets could not (and today still struggle to) compete with the deep financial resources of corporate and foreign-owned firms.[70]

Diamela Eltit's publishing trajectory during the 1980s is representative of this shift in the national editorial landscape: she released her first novel *Lumpérica* with the independent press Ediciones del Ornitorrinco in 1983 and then switched to Planeta and Seix Barral by 1988 (Ornitorrinco would eventually shut down and *Lumpérica* then went to Seix Barral). While Eltit's entire literary and artistic oeuvre is highly critical of neoliberalism and how it has changed Chilean society since the dictatorship years, she herself has participated in this system by signing her books with companies like Planeta and Seix Barral. Her critique of the market is weakened, if not wholly contradicted, by the privileged position that Planeta and Seix Barral—as dominant foreign publishing houses—occupy within Chile's postdictatorship editorial industry. In publishing her books with these presses, Eltit has forged an institutional alliance with the literary industry and global capitalism, thus acquiring significant symbolic capital for herself and her work.

This strategy of working to change institutions (in this case the literary market) from the inside out is, according to Nelly Richard, characteristic of the avant-garde avanzada art scene to which Eltit belonged. Richard argues that the entire avanzada scene "opposed the rules, but from the inside," and quotes avanzada artist Lotty Rosenfeld as writing in the oppositional magazine *Hoy* in 1981, "If you want to modify institutions, you have to work on the inside, even if this produces a conflict of interest."[71] Beyond the conflicts that this model produces, it also offers obvious benefits: the most important of which is the opportunity to gain public visibility and recognition as a requisite step in the political fight of all minority groups, including, in this case, Chilean feminist writers under Pinochet.

Certainly using the capitalist publishing market and transnational presses is an excellent way to get minority voices heard on a massive scale. We see other examples beyond Eltit of women literary activists adopting this strategy. Editorial Cuarto Propio, which bravely opened in 1984, is perhaps the best example of this tactic.[72] While remaining independent from the state as a political institution, this model of women's literary activism does not seek autonomy from the market as an economic institution, but rather attempts to change that system from the inside out by becoming part of it while constantly challenging its norms. Both Diamela Eltit and Editorial Cuarto Propio have accomplished a great deal in making the Chilean literary market more inclusive of women and other minorities as authors and readers. Furthermore, we can understand Eltit's choice to publish with foreign presses as an effort to avoid the complicated reality of Chile's own editorial industry during the 1980s.

Ergo Sum's material praxis differs from Eltit's (and that of other women writers like her) in that it applies Chilean feminism's desire for institutional autonomy to its publication of literary texts. It does this, as we have already seen, by publishing its book-objects independently of industrial print culture and by remaining as independent as possible from market capitalism.[73] In addition to these editorial decisions, Andrea Bell also cites Ergo Sum's choice to publish in the short story genre as proof of the group's rebellion against the market. Bell argues that the business model of commercial literary publishing in the postdictatorship period marginalized the short story in favor of the novel. Kathrin Bergenthal's research on the "Mini-Boom" of the Nueva Narrativa Chilena (New Chilean Narrative) confirms this claim, showing how short story writers such as Pía Barros, Ramón Díaz Eterovic, and Diego Muñoz (all active participants in the autoedición subculture) struggled to gain public access for their works in a literary market far more interested in promoting and selling novels such as those pertaining to the so-called Nueva Narrativa Chilena.[74]

French feminist theorist Luce Irigaray is helpful in explaining the relationship between patriarchy and capitalism and, consequently, the political and aesthetic protest that Ergo Sum book-objects launch against these two codependent social structures. In her book *The Sex Which Is Not One,* Irigaray uses a Marxist analysis of commodity fetishism to explain how patriarchy creates women as objects of sexual difference to be exchanged among men and how this exchange establishes the possibility for capitalism to exist. As parallel semiotic structures, capitalism and patriarchy both abstract meaning from material objects by defining their symbolic value in relation to an external and arbitrary signifier—either capital or the phallus. This is similar to Subercaseaux's claim that the Chilean book, under postdictatorship neoliberalism, loses its soul to the materiality of its body, whose value becomes abstracted by the global commercial market.

As commodities, both books and women are reduced to their material existence at the same time that their materiality is erased, abstracted, turned into nothing more than "pure phenomenality of value."[75] Applying Irigaray's feminist theory to the editorial climate of dictatorship Chile helps explain Ergo Sum's choice to create books in the disguised form of object-commodities broadly speaking (such as the miniature suitcase and pair of pants) as well as in the form of object-commodities unique to the female sex in particular (hope chests, sewing boxes, shopping bags, children's toys). Because these texts have been dressed as feminized object-commodities, we can think of them as individual drag performances: book-objects donning a traditional feminine gender subjectivity as a means of critiquing a political, cultural, economic, and social environment that is hostile to both books (in their normal form) and to gender identities that challenge patriarchal hegemony.

One benefit of this drag performance is that it allowed Ergo Sum to meet, write, and publish without inciting attention from the state. The group's use of drag to avoid state persecution functioned in two ways: first, the physical objects in which the group chose to house its literary writings did not immediately register as literary, thus lessening the likelihood that these texts would fall victim to state censorship; second, the very techniques the group employed to handcraft its literary publications resembled conventional domestic tasks that the state expected its female citizens to perform. According to Cardone, Ergo Sum's methods of handmade book production mimicked "women's everyday domestic activity" as wives, mothers, and homemakers.[76] Cardone reports that in a typical workshop meeting, participants would find themselves writing, cutting (both editing text and also cutting paper), folding, organizing, piecing, and sewing book-objects together with needle and thread.[77]

Without a doubt, Ergo Sum's editorial production was a theatrical parody of Pinochet's gender proscription for women. The chores that individuals performed in the workshop were precisely the same acts that Pinochet's wife, Lucía Hiriart, and her followers were teaching women in the Centros de Madres de Chile discussed above. In the same way that autoedición bookmakers used kraft paper because it was the easiest material to acquire without raising suspicions, so too were women's traditional methods of labor an inconspicuous way for women writers to rebel against state mandates while at the same time seeming to conform to them.

The physical objects that Ergo Sum participants handcrafted also performed a feminine subjectivity consistent with patriarchal norms. For instance, a large number of Ergo Sum book-objects come in the form of miniature shopping bags, referencing women's assigned role within capitalism and patriarchy as cultural consumers, whether it be in their function as homemakers (purchasing food and clothes items for the family) or as sexual objects of men's desire (buying feminine adornments to dress themselves as sexual fetish for men). Shopping is also a reference to Western women's historical role as passive consumers and not as active producers of art and culture. Other book-objects that take the shape of feminized object-commodities include letters in envelopes, pantyhose boxes, and hope chests (fig. 5).[78] But perhaps the best example of the book-object's drag performance as a feminized object-commodity is Ergo Sum's first published anthology of short stories, the 1985 publication *Ergo Sum.*

The object is a thin box containing a stack of folded pamphlets, each containing an original short story and illustration, all of which are tied together by a black band. In an essay titled "Mujeres, creatividad y contracultura" (Women, creativity and counterculture), Barros describes the object as a box of "women's things" and asks: "What do we expect from a box of 'women's things'? Certainly buttons, a needle and thread; earrings, hairpins; knick-knacks. Anything, in short, belonging to 'labors appropriate to her sex' but not cerebral labor; a lipstick pencil but never any other kind."[79] By using the material form of a box of "women's things"—commodities unique to the female sex—Ergo Sum drew attention to the way in which patriarchal culture only recognizes "women's work" as either sexual or domestic labor. Earrings, hairpins, and lipstick pencils are all technologies used by patriarchy and capitalism to produce the female body as commodity fetish to be exchanged among men for the primary purposes of men's sexual pleasure and the biological reproduction of the species. Through such an "inoffensive precious container" as a box of "women's things," Ergo sum writers and Pía Barros were not only able to publish and distribute literature without state permission, but they were also able to make the direct claim that it is the woman's sex that prevents her from successfully performing intellectual labor—we expect women to have lipstick pencils but never any other kind.[80]

By performing women's assigned gender position within Pinochet's patriarchal and neoliberal political economy, Ergo Sum's literary publications reiterate the law of the state at the same time that they ironically contradict it in order to prove the limits of its power. In her widely respected theoretical analysis of drag performances, Judith Butler explains that "what is 'forced' by the symbolic, then, is a citation of its law that reiterates and consolidates the ruse of its own force. . . . The paradox of subjectivation is precisely that the subject who would resist such norms is itself enabled, if not produced, by such norms. Although this constitutive constraint does not foreclose the possibility of agency, it does locate agency as a reiterative or rearticulatory practice, immanent to power, and not a relation of external opposition to power."[81] Ergo Sum exercises power through the very kinds of citational practices Butler here describes—by citing the state's legal mandates on cultural censorship as well as its gendered discourse on the role of men and women in society. The group conforms to the state's repressive cultural policies in the sense that, at least at first glance, these objects are *not* books, but rather burlap bags, shopping bags, children's toys, and miniature suitcases and hope chests.

Likewise, the seemingly conservative gender identity of Ergo Sum's editorial practice and literary products grant these objects a degree of innocuousness that helped them exist within the hyper-conservative cultural milieu of dictatorial Chile. In other words, these texts and their makers openly perform their own voluntary subjection to the law in order to expose the inequalities that the law produces. Ergo Sum successfully produces literature without

FIGURE 5. Ergo Sum's book-object *Secretos y pecados* (1993). This book-object takes the shape of a miniature hope chest that holds a stack of loose-leaf pamphlets inside. Each pamphlet contains an original short story. Photograph by Nélida Pohl. Reproduced by permission of Pía Barros.

producing literature and, in so doing, mocks the state by adhering to its laws and violating them at the same time.

Yet in order to be subversive, drag performances must fail to pass completely; they must produce some level of material ambivalence toward the law that they feign to appropriate. For instance, even though Ergo Sum's techniques of book production were designed to mimic patriarchal forms of femininized labor, they were performed with the goal of redefining women's gendered identity rather than conforming to patriarchal notions of women's work and worth. Barros focused on everyday feminine chores in the hopes that these tasks would allow previously inexperienced and untrained women to think of themselves as artists and, in so doing, experience a political and feminist awakening. She argues that by "ironically adhering to traditional gender roles," Ergo Sum participants were able to progressively recast women's role in Chilean culture and society as active artistic producers and political agents rather than simply custodians of the patriarchal family and gender status quo.[82] It is difficult to determine whether or not the women who participated in the Ergo Sum writing and publishing workshops experienced the kind of feminist consciousness-raising Barros had in mind when she founded the group; however, Cardone does maintain that since its founding in the late 1970s, Ergo Sum has succeeded in "publishing a virtual torrent of writers of all skill levels, most of whom would never publish outside an Ergo Sum anthology."[83]

Just like the domestic chores performed by Ergo Sum workshop participants, the unauthorized literary publications they made ironically resignify rather than loyally reproduce the traditional gender norms they performed. Upon opening the box of "women's things" labeled *Ergo Sum,* we do not find that which we expect to find: hairpins, earrings, and lipstick pencils. Instead, we find a stack of triptychs on which are printed original short stories written (predominantly) by novice female writers. These textual bodies have *not* materialized according to the hegemonic gender norms that Pinochet's patriarchal discourse demanded. By ironically subjecting itself to the powers of capitalism and phallogocentrism, the *Ergo Sum* book-object exposes the failure of these systems to produce it fully, to convert it into equivalents that, outside of its relation to capital and the phallus, hold no meaning in and of itself. In their failure to pass as loyal iterations of the social, cultural and economic discourses dominating dictatorial Chile, Ergo Sum book-objects offer an answer to Butler's question: "What would it mean to 'cite' the law to produce it differently, to 'cite' the law in order to reiterate and coopt its power?"[84] Certainly these books cite the state's law of cultural censorship and gender conservatisms in a way that the law itself could never have intended or anticipated and that it could not control.

Ergo Sum's use of drag and parody is, at least to a certain extent, consistent with other dissident and feminist forms of literary activism that emerged in response to Chile's military dictatorship. For instance, oppositional magazines commonly used parody in their public critique of Pinochet and his authoritarian regime.[85] Yet because of their heightened public visibility, professionally printed parodies of the regime often resulted in direct retaliation by the state against the oppositional magazines responsible for their publication.[86] In contrast, Ergo Sum's use of drag is a much more subtle form of parody that successfully critiques the government without subjecting itself to the threat of state violence. In addition, we could read drag as sharing certain similarities with the model of feminist literary activism employed by Diamela Eltit and Editorial Cuarto Propio. In the same way that Eltit and Cuarto Propio engage with capitalism in the hopes of changing the system from the inside out, so too does drag work within and according to the logic of dominant discourse rather than externally from it. What differentiates Ergo Sum's practice and political critique, however, is its belief that literature's form of publication—its material body—is as capable of performing a sardonic political critique as the linguistic composition of the text itself.

We can read Ergo Sum's production of books-in-drag as a response to the problematic way in which both women's bodies and also books are dematerialized through their mutual existence as commodity fetish. For Irigaray, if "woman" is to mean anything other than object-commodity to be fetishized by and exchanged among men as well as exploited by capitalism, it is her *body* that must be liberated from its subjection to the law that determines its value in relation to what it is not (in Lacanian syntax, her "lack"). Irigaray thus asks the enigmatic question, "*But what if these 'commodities' refused to go to 'market'?* What if they maintained 'another' kind of commerce, among themselves?" then "value might well lie, as Marx says, in the relation among [things] rather than in the relation to a standard that remains external to them—whether gold or phallus."[87]

Ergo Sum book-objects refuse to be consecrated as legitimate works of art according to the traditional standards of the art world. The work of Pierre Bourdieu enhances our understanding of how Ergo Sum does this. For Bourdieu, symbolic value—the "consecration" of objects as works of art—is established when cultural actors (publishers, book distributors, critics, readers, and so forth) recognize and accept an object as a work of art. The process of recognition creates the object as a work of art, which is to say, as a fetish.[88] Ergo Sum book-objects "refuse to go to market" by rejecting the established rules of consecration. This fact is best illustrated in an anecdote that Barros tells of trying to sell Ergo Sum book-objects in bookstores. In personal interviews, Barros has recounted how the physical form of these literary objects actually prevented them from selling in bookstores, since customers did not *recognize* them as books but instead thought they were decorative objects in window displays. The failure to be recognized, and therefore consecrated, as literary works of art is precisely the purpose of the book-objects' drag performance. It is also a means of refusing to have the value of these objects determined by, in Irigaray's words, either "gold or phalluses."

If the value of these objects is not determined by external agents (that is, the market and literary establishment), then what does set their value? Is it even possible in any contemporary political economy to create value that is *not* determined by gold or phalluses? For Ergo Sum, the answer is that the workshop participants themselves establish the value of these objects as works of art through their own recognition of them as such; they do not rely on external measures or agents to consecrate their works as possessing symbolic value; the authors/bookmakers alone do that.

Ergo Sum's contemporaries—feminist literary activists, dissident presses, and oppositional periodicals—do not employ this system of value production. They succeed in granting marginalized subjects greater agency within the cultural field, but they still leave intact the general rules and hierarchies that structure that field. In contrast, the symbolic economy created by Pía Barros and Ergo Sum depends on women's own recognition of themselves and of one another as legitimate cultural—and therefore political—agents. This is what makes their cultural praxis truly autonomous. It is the individual author and bookmaker herself who consecrates her work as valuable, and that consecration is only further validated and solidified by her fellow workshop participants, who also recognize her as an artist and her work as an object of art. Furthermore, this method exploits the distinction between literature as a seemingly intellectual endeavor and everyday objects as lacking artistic or intellectual value. Ergo Sum book-objects, in contrast, encourage us to understand ordinary objects as symbolically meaningful. Likewise, these objects motivate us to see literature as an ordinary object that is not the domain of cultural elites but that can and should be created by any and all members of society.

3

Cartonera Publishers

Artisanal and Industrial Book Production in Neoliberal Chile

"Things have a life of their own," the gypsy proclaimed with a harsh accent. "It's simply a matter of waking up their souls."
—Gabriel García Márquez, *One Hundred Years of Solitude*

Chilean book historian Bernardo Subercaseaux argues that the political ideologies and economic policies of the military dictatorship altered the ontology of literature as both a social and material good. He writes that during the dictatorship period "either the book becomes incorporated into the mechanisms of the culture industry or it runs the risk of being a marginal cultural product and of even having to be recycled into raw materials."[1] What Subercaseaux means by the first scenario is that the kinds of books that have best survived Chile's neoliberal restructuring are those that meet the commercial needs of the global free market economy. As we have seen, these are most often books that belong to the genres of self-help, how-to, cookbooks, sentimental literature, and nostalgic historical fiction. These genres have a more "practical" use value—especially how-to and cookbook genres—and so they produce greater capital value, whereas those books whose use value lies in their contribution to society as a social good find little commercial worth within Chile's postdictatorial political economy.

The lack of capital value in noncommercial books leads to Subercaseaux's second scenario in which books cease to be books at all and undergo a material transformation from work of art into raw materials. Subercaseaux writes that these books "are destined to be cut up, pulverized, and converted into raw materials. . . . We are talking about a kind of reverse resurrection, in which the book's soul dies in order to resuscitate its body, a body that is transformed into kraft paper, napkins and envelopes."[2] When the souls of books die, their bodies continue to live but are resurrected as other kinds of nonartistic objects-commodities.

Luis Cárcamo-Huechante also invokes the metaphor of death in his description of Chile's postdictatorship literary market. He references the capitalist invention of the market niche to explain certain "deaths" within literary culture, such as the death of the author and the death of certain genres for which the market finds no use. Cárcamo-Huechante describes how the concept of the market niche originated from evolutionary biology, which defines the niche as the environment in which species fight for space and their function within that space.[3] The literary market, like environmental ecosystems, pits literary genres against one another in a competition to the death for survival of the fittest. Moreover, Cárcamo-Huechante pointedly notes that in Spanish the word *nicho* (niche) has a strong connection to death in the sense that it denotes cemetery crypts where remains are inserted and stored, rather than being put into the ground. "This makes even more evident the petrifying effect that the concept of market niche has as a method of *encasing* the author-work-product as a lifeless, motionless entity."[4]

We have already seen how Pía Barros responded to this editorial environment in its early phases under dictatorship. Not only did her underground literary collective, Ergo Sum, make book-objects out of the remnants of literature's "dead body"—kraft paper, paper bags, and envelopes—but it also crafted those materials into objects that directly cited the theme of death. Whereas Barros herself describes *Ergo Sum,* the collective's first book-object published in 1985, as a box of "women's things," Ergo Sum scholar Resha Cardone interprets it as a handkerchief box. She argues that the handkerchief motif symbolizes a state of mourning, that the tan color of the kraft paper trifolds found within the box recalls the color of human flesh, and that the black band binding those trifolds together represents the cultural tradition of wearing a black band around one's arm in honor of a deceased friend or relative.[5]

Similarly the book-object *Ensacados: 26 cuentos ilustrados* (Bagged: 26 illustrated stories) is a hand-sewn miniature burlap bag that contains individual kraft paper trifolds. As previously mentioned, the burlap bag is a direct citation of the known military practice of discarding disappeared bodies wrapped in burlap bags into Santiago's Mapocho River. Cardone argues that Ergo Sum's editorial practice and feminist philosophy embodies living and dead bodies in such a way as to make both women and the disappeared "participants in political and literary life."[6]

Like Ergo Sum, Chilean Cartonera cardboard publishers also overtly invoke the metaphor of death and resurrection into their method of book production. Whereas Ergo Sum's use of kraft paper and burlap bags was a direct critique of the economic policies and human rights violations of Chile's military state, the Cartonera method of hand-making books out of cardboard trash critiques global capitalism at large and Chile's postdictatorship literary market in particular. Cardboard is both a product and a symbol of global industrialization, and cardboard trash especially is the material trace left behind by completed transactions of global capitalism; it is the carcass of goods exchanged across the globe. As a vehicle of transportation of object-commodities throughout the global economy, cardboard is incredibly useful to capitalism but in itself contains no social value and is not what we would consider a social or aesthetic good. The choice by Cartonera publishers to make books only out of cardboard trash thus draws our attention to the ways in which social goods find it increasingly difficult to establish their use value in the current globalized marketplace.

On a national level, cardboard publishing in Chile draws our attention to the ways in which the military regime devalued books to such an extent that they were literally pulverized and turned into cardboard; Subercaseaux reports that during the dictatorship books were "acquired by paper collectors, in order to be resold to paper and cardboard industry manufacturers by the kilo."[7] The Chilean cardboard press La Fonola Cartonera puts forth an even sharper critique by citing one of the military regime's social services in its very name; during the dictatorship the word *fonola* was used in reference to cardboard materials that the state gave to shantytown residents in order to help them fix their leaky roofs.[8] In taking *fonola* as its name, this cardboard press critiques the military's contempt for poor people (cardboard is not a good water repellent) and books at the same time.

Some Cartonera publishers explicitly express that their editorial project is an effort to resurrect cardboard as the discarded remains of global capitalism and to infuse within this material substance the social, humanitarian, and artistic spirit that is so often lacking in the global exchange of object-commodities—most of which travel the globe wrapped in cardboard. For instance, Santiago-based Cartonera editor Kika Valdés claims that her press, Meninas Cartoneras, is committed to "infusing life" into the cardboard with which they make books, and her coeditor, Carolina Espinosa, describes cardboard as the press's "medium and message of protest. It is exquisitely and revindictively diverse."[9] Likewise, Calafate Cartonera editors Amanda Espejo and Karen Peñaloza explain that their choice to work with cardboard is an attempt to give value to something commonly seen as valueless or, like the literary text itself, as rendered valueless once it no longer serves a purpose in the global economy.[10] The theme of reanimation was even present at a meeting of eight Latin American cardboard bookmakers in Madison, Wisconsin, in 2010; together these eight cardboard presses held a bookmaking workshop at the University of Wisconsin, where they handmade bilingual posters that read "Cartón es Vida / Cardboard is Life."[11]

In the Christian construction of resurrection the material body dies and is then brought back to life and reunited with the soul, which, although temporally separated from the body, never itself dies. What has happened to literature in postdictatorship Chile is that the soul of the literary work, its social value, not only dies itself but its death also prefigures that of literature's material body: the paper book. Once Pinochet's repressive cultural and economic policies, in conjunction with the global publishing market, have rendered the book valueless as an artistic object, the materiality of the book is brought back to life by being recycled into other material objects: napkins, kraft paper, envelopes, and so forth. The difference, of course, between what Subercaseaux calls a "reverse resurrection" and the Christian concept of resurrection lies in the trajectory of the soul; when the material body of literature is brought back to life, it is not reunited with literature's artistic spirit in the way that the Christian body is reunited with its soul. In the global market scenario, the death of literature's soul is a permanent loss. Napkins, kraft paper, and envelopes are not art objects because their symbolic value is purely economic and determined by their practical usefulness and not their ability to facilitate reflection on aesthetic beauty, the social condition, individual existentialism, political freedom, or cultural identity.

Cartonera cardboard book publishing attempts to reverse this "reverse resurrection" and infuse life into cardboard by turning it into art, by giving it a social spirit that it does not contain in its function as physical support for industrialized capitalist exchanges. What is most important about this resurrection, however, is not that cardboard as a raw material is brought to life but that the social spirit of a people is brought back to life through the resurrection of cardboard as a literary object. This, according to Chilean blogger Felipe Almazán, is what is "fantastic" about all the Cartonera presses, that they "re-valorize" principles of "solidarity, communal work and, to be sure, the search for the book's relative independence."[12] Almazán's use of the word "revalorization," as well as Espinosa's use of the word "revindictively," echoes the idea that Cartonera presses are reviving something that has been lost, that has died, but that is coming to life again through the Cartonera mode of book production.[13]

One Chilean Cartonera press intentionally conjures the theme of death and resurrection beyond its mere use of cardboard trash as the *materia prima* of its bookmaking process. Animita Cartonera, the first Cartonera press established in Chile, cites the concepts of death and the soul in its very name. In Spanish, the word *animita* signifies roadside shrines erected to memorialize individuals who have lost their lives in car accidents. Animita Cartonera's logo, inscribed in all its books, is a picture of a roadside shrine. The word *animita* derives from the root word *ánima,* the Spanish word for "soul."[14] The word *animita* thus references soul and death at the same time, making it a more than appropriate choice as a name for Chile's first cardboard publishing house. Furthermore, both Ergo Sum and Animita Cartonera make a connection between the loss of life in literary objects (books) and the loss of life in human bodies, thereby ascribing a Benjaminian view of artistic objects as possessing an "aura" similar to that of the human soul.[15]

In the Cartonera model of cultural democratization, the social power of literature lies in an aura, or *ánima,* that is brought to life through non-industrial modes of book production, or what I call artisanal book craft. This model of cultural democratization did not originate in Chile and is not at all unique to this country; rather, it is a fast-growing trend of Do-It-Yourself (DIY) book production found in almost two hundred countries across the globe. Chile stands out within the large and ever growing global network of Cartonera presses because it has more of them per capita than any other country in the world. Chilean *cartoneros* (cardboard bookmakers) believe that the social value of literature is not primarily produced through the act of reading, but rather through the literary work's formation as a material object and, more important, through artisanal, non-industrial, and collective processes of bookmaking as a social activity.

Chile may have more Cartonera publishers per capita than any other country in the world because of the way the military regime so forcefully and quickly restructured all Chilean society. But perhaps most important, Cartonera publishing has grown so quickly in Chile because its artisanal method and its reliance on cardboard produce an effect that is widely considered a key ingredient of Chilean cultural democracy: equal accessibility. Cartoneros, like other minority literary producers in Chile, conceive of literary equality as not only access to books for reading, but also as access to material modes of production that make it possible to create books to be read. Their particular model of providing such access is to bypass all industrialized forms of book production, since industrialization inherently limits what kinds of social actors can access material modes of cultural production and objects of material culture.

This non-industrial stance places Cartonera bookmakers not only in opposition to global publishing magnets, but also to Chile's local publishing industry and the state's cultural infrastructure that supports it. As we have seen, leaders of Chile's local editorial industry and state officials have argued that the best way to fight global capital's monopolization of Chile's literary market is to economically and politically strengthen the local editorial industry.[16] The ethos of Cartonera publishing seems to disagree. The Cartonera critique of industrialized bookmaking is not just that it restricts equal access to material modes of literary production, but also that it necessarily defines the literary work as private property, which thus greatly restricts its ability to circulate through the public sphere; this in turn limits the work's ability to produce social value through its consumption by individual readers.

Such a critique has led many Chilean Cartonera publishers to directly challenge the state's newly written copyright legislation and increased policing of intellectual property. Some Cartonera presses have gone so far as to intentionally violate state copyright laws, qualifying their books as illegal publications—a distinction that forces us to recall the illegal nature of autoediciones. The choice to create a work of art in defiance of government approval is thus not a political strategy that ended with the dictatorship, but rather one that has remained relevant and—as some Cartonera editors believe—even necessary within Chile's postdictatorship era.

Cartonera Publishers: A Global Family of Cardboard Bookmakers

Cartonera publishing is by no means a Chilean phenomenon, but its presence in Chile proves exceptional. The origins of the international "cartonera explosion" are by now a well-known story within the Cartonera family and its followers.[17] The technique originated in Argentina in 2003 during that country's dire economic crisis. Faced with the immediate problem of scarce material recourses, but also inspired by the opportunity to prove that book production and consumption could be both cheap and a source of economic and social empowerment at the same time, Javier Barilaro, Washington Cucurto, and Fernanda Laguna decided to start making books out of cardboard trash. Their project centered on the common Latin American figure of the *cartonero*—a person who makes a living scavenging *cartón* (cardboard) on the street and then selling it to recycling centers or other buyers. The Argentine economic crisis of the early 2000s resulted in an increased number of citizens turning to this form of work, and Cucurto, Barilaro, and Laguna used this unfortunate situation—a result of Argentina's own military dictatorship in 1976–83—to economically uplift cardboard trash collectors while giving them a sense of artistic purpose at the same time. The idea was to buy cardboard trash from cartoneros at a higher-than-market price and then invite the trash collectors to participate in the process of handcrafting and artistically decorating books out of that same trash.

Cucurto, Barilaro, and Laguna named their cardboard press Eloisa Cartonera, and thus the Cartonera family was born. A little over ten years later, as of 2015, there are nearly 200 Cartonera presses world-wide, with 154 in

Latin America, 34 in Europe, 2 in Africa, 4 in the United States, and 1 in Asia.[18] Chileans have taken an exceptionally keen interest in Cartonera publishing and have opened a total of 23 cardboard presses since 2005.[19] Meninas Cartoneras editor Kika Valdés believes that so many Cartonera presses have been founded in Chile because the price of books is exceptionally high there, which is due to the high cost of paper in Chile as well as the 20-percent VAT tax on all books that was inherited from the dictatorship.[20] Indeed, many Chilean Cartonera editors in addition to Valdés cite these factors as reasons for why they started a cardboard press.

The family metaphor works well in describing this global network of book publishers for many reasons. The first is that every Cartonera press comes into being as a result of its relation to another, "mother" Cartonera, with Eloisa being the founding matriarch of the entire family.[21] Cartonera publishing has become organically reproductive: all Cartoneras can be traced back, in one way or another, to Eloisa Cartonera. While the spawning of new Cartoneras was not part of Eloisa Cartonera's original artistic or social mission, breeding has become a fundamental aspect of this editorial model. To cite their connection to and inheritance from the matriarchal Eloisa, almost all cardboard publishers worldwide intentionally take the name "Cartonera." The name of these presses functions in the same way that Western family names function, with the surname "Cartonera" denoting kinship ties and the given first name marking individuality and distinctiveness from the group. One hundred forty of these presses have taken "Cartonera" as their surname, the grand majority of which have also chosen a feminine first name for their cardboard press (even when the editors are all or mostly men); eighteen other cardboard presses use "Cartonera" as their first name.[22]

However, in direct counter distinction to the Western patriarchal tradition of naming and inheritance, the Cartoneras are without a doubt a matriarchal clan in which familial identity and inheritance descend solely from female reproduction, that is, from birthing. The concept of the feminine is also perfectly encapsulated by the techniques of this editorial practice. Cardboard publishing most often takes place in the domestic sphere of the home and includes craft practices that have traditional ties to women across cultures: cutting, sewing, and the piecing together of recycled materials, much like the *arpillera* patchwork tradition in Chile, and also extremely similar to Ergo Sum's production of feminine book-objects.[23] Also like feminine handicraft, and especially similar to arpillera production, Cartonera book production is almost always a social activity that is accompanied by conversation, storytelling, and other forms of communal sharing. Meninas Cartonera, for example, refers to the process of binding its books as "sewing and singing."[24]

From a theoretical standpoint, Cartonera presses inhabit the feminine subject position with regard to their subjugated relation to power as expressed through the global publishing market and postdictatorship Chilean cultural policies. Although the founders of Eloisa Cartonera did not give their press a female name because they anticipated that it would produce offspring or because its editorial practice shared common techniques with traditional feminine domestic arts, they did intentionally assume a marginalized position within the globalized field of cultural production.[25]

One final reason why "family" is such an apt way of thinking about this global network of publishers is that, like family members, all Cartonera presses share common characteristics that bind them together while they also differ significantly enough from one another to remain unique and independent. As in most families, the differences between Cartoneras far outweigh their similarities. The biggest differences are more material than ideological in nature. For instance, only one Chilean Cartonera, Animita Cartonera, buys its cardboard trash from cartonero street collectors in the original style of Eloisa Cartonera.[26] And none of the Chilean presses include cartonero trash collectors in the process of book production, although Animita Cartonera has paid young, economically disadvantaged women to make a large portion of their cardboard books, which they do on their own schedules and out of their own homes.[27]

The editors of the other Chilean Cartonera presses all collect cardboard trash themselves—often from their places of work, from their neighbors' trash, or simply off the street—and make the books themselves or with the voluntary help of friends and family. This change in the material practice of book production has caused the word *cartonero* to experience a semiotic alteration: no longer does the term simply denote poor men and women making a precarious living from the collection and sale of cardboard trash; now it also describes a certain type of bookmaker. Anyone who makes books out of cardboard trash is a *cartonero,* even middle-class Santiago residents working in professional fields. Chilean bookmaking cartoneros have even started using the word in verb form, *cartonear,* to refer to the process of making books out of cardboard trash.[28]

Chilean Cartoneras also differ in their styles of book production. Most follow Eloisa's trend of making the decorative cover of each book wholly unique, while others choose a single design that repeats itself on the cover of all books in a given print run.[29] Some, like Calafate Cartonera and La Joyita Cartonera, are fundamentally concerned with the aesthetic quality of the physical book object and include intricate illustrations both on the external body of the book and throughout its interior pages, aiming to create ornate art books. Another major difference in their material production is the editorial information they choose to include in their books, such as the date of publication, the individual number of each copy in a given print run, ISBN registration, intellectual property registration, copyright or copyleft, and so forth. The absence of a uniform method for how to treat bibliographic information speaks to the anti-institutional spirit of Cartonera publishing.

Editorial choices such as which authors to publish, how to organize catalogs, and how to reach readers also vary among Chilean Cartoneras. Animita Cartonera and Meninas Cartoneras follow the model of commercial presses and have different editorial lines structured around categories such as Chile's national canon, international writers, children's literature, fiction, and poetry. Quite a few Cartonera presses publish classic works that have passed into the public domain, but there are those who knowingly publish third-party texts to which they have no rights or permissions. A somewhat new trend among Chilean Cartoneras is to seek out unknown writers from the general public by creating writing contests, typically based on particular themes or literary genres; editors publish a selection, or sometimes all, of the texts they receive from the public in anthology form.[30] Then there are those Chilean Cartoneras that specialize primarily in self-publication and publish the writings of the press's founders, who are also its editors and book manufacturers.[31]

Most Chilean Cartonera presses circulate their books by hand, but some also sell them in bookstores, boutiques, cafés, bars, or restaurants while still others selectively digitize some of their titles and make them available on the web. (Although the digitization of selected texts and their publication on the Internet may appear to contradict the artisanal nature of Cartonera book production, this practice is in keeping with Cartoneras's attempt to massify Chilean literary culture, as discussed below.) Some Chilean Cartoneras specialize in working with particular populations of the Chilean society, such as school children (Animita Cartonera, Benicia Cartonera, Helecho Cartonera, Isidora Cartonera), prison inmates (Canita Cartonera and Fugitiva Cartonera), university students (Isidora Cartonera), working professionals, and poor people (Benicia Cartonera).

Despite their differences, all of the Chilean Cartoneras share three characteristics: the first is that they are all noncommercial enterprises, meaning that none of them attempt to make a monetary profit from their editorial endeavors and that no one works for these presses professionally; the second is that their production is non-industrial, meaning that all books are individually made by a human person and not a machine; and the third is that they all rely on cardboard trash as the base material from which their books are made.[32] The third characteristic predetermines the previous two since the noncommercial and non-industrial ethos of Cartonera publishing is made possible by its use of cardboard.

The use of cardboard trash is primarily practical: it is equally available to everyone almost anywhere on the globe, which is certainly one reason why this publishing trend has spread to so many different locations around the world and why it has been overwhelmingly more popular in developing regions than in developed countries.[33] This allows agents who would otherwise not have the material means to start a literary press to be able to do so. Using cardboard allows people to make books by hand without having to rely on the industrial machinery required of traditional publishing, meaning that they can circumvent the financial limitations that restrict them from editorial production. In fact, many Chilean cartoneros admit that they chose to begin a Cartonera press instead of a different kind of cultural project (or no project at all) because of its economic viability.[34]

The lack of a requirement for material investment to start a Cartonera press is also why so many Chilean cartoneros use the term *auto-gestión* (self-sustaining) to describe their editorial enterprise. Canita Cartonera, for instance, explains its method of auto-gestión as transcending from the punk rock philosophy of *hazlo tu mismo,* or what is referred to in English as Do-It-Yourself (DIY).[35] Isidora Cartonera defines auto-gestión as "turning a project into something that comes from the depths of one's self," which is to say that the individual possesses all the necessary means for producing works of art and need not rely on external factors, such as financial investment.[36] For its part, La Vieja Sapa Cartonera relates auto-gestión to anarchism, which also has direct ties to the punk tradition, and defines it as a vehicle for rejecting profits and the capitalist system.[37]

Despite the desire to exist independently of the market, however, cardboard book production does require some material investment in the form of purchasing paper, paying for photocopying, and buying the materials needed to assemble and decorate each book: tape, staples, yarn, string, glue, and, most important, paint, which is by far the most common material used in the decoration of individual cardboard book covers. This is why almost all Chilean Cartonera presses do charge money for their books, but only enough to recuperate production costs; some also believe in the symbolic power of paying for a cultural good, believing that the Chilean public does not value what is free.

La Fonola Cartonera believes so strongly in its commitment to auto-gestión that its editors do everything they can to acquire the materials required for cardboard book production for free, whether that means receiving donated supplies from friends and family, recycling and repurposing as many used goods as possible, or sometimes even gathering materials without permission.

Selling Cartonera books at cost does not impede the noncommercial spirit of this publishing trend because, in the words of Animita Cartonera editors, "whatever money we earn is for making more books."[38] Even if readers were willing to buy cardboard books at the prices necessary for presses to turn a profit, Cartonera presses would never to be able to produce the amount of books needed to make a press commercially sustainable. Because it is non-industrial, Cartonera publishing is an extremely time-consuming process, and typical print runs average between twenty to fifty books. Olga Cartonera, for instance, limits its print runs to the number of books it can make with one ream of store-bought photocopy paper.[39]

Ingrained within the Cartoneras' social mission is an attempt to democratize literary culture. For instance, even though Animita Cartonera charges money for its books, its editors are clear that this money is strictly used to "preserve the idea of bringing culture to the people, because Animita is a social project."[40] Other Cartonera editors agree with this sentiment, insisting that their editorial projects are not hobbies because hobbies are purely selfish and done only for the enjoyment of one's own self, whereas Cartonera book production is fundamentally a social project that is meant to bring people together, to "generate humanity."[41] In the words of La Vieja Sapa Cartonera editors, this means "to carry literary creation to the farthest points possible."[42] Roberto Toledo, editor of La Gata Viuda Cartonera, makes the explicit connection between these social projects and democracy by arguing that even "in democracy, people are left out"; it is his goal as a cardboard editor to include more people in the processes of literary production and consumption.[43]

Scholars, critics, and members of the popular press agree with Cartonera editors that their democratizing artistic mission is, in the words of journalist Heidi Schmidlin Moore, "based on solidarity and in which the predominating value of exchange is the idea of transforming trash into art."[44] What makes this kind of book publication a social, politically committed, and community project is that it is realized through living human bodies rather than industrialized technology.

Artisanal Book Production

There are manifold reasons why artisanal cultural production is a logical choice as a means of democratizing postdictatorship Chilean literary culture. The history of artisanry is the history of pre-industrial and pre-capitalist production in which not only were objects made by hand, but there was also no differentiation between objects of utility and objects of art. Raymond Williams points out that the onset of industrial capitalism separated "cultural production" from the "general productive order"; the former is understood as containing a symbolic function while the latter has a utilitarian one. This in turn led to a differentiation between the "artist" as producer of "objects of art" and the "artisan" or "craftsman" as producer of "objects of utility."[45]

The arrival of industrial capitalism did not mean that culture lost its anthropological definition as a "shared way of life" but that it also came to be defined through individual material objects that are the private property of their producers and users. Because artisanry formed before industrial capitalism, it historically has not exhibited these differentiations; material objects of utility also communicate aesthetic meaning, which is the "shared way of life" of the people by whom and from whom artisanal objects are made. Thus artisanal objects are equally material (utilitarian) and symbolic (representing the collective traditions and aesthetic sensibilities of a social group).[46]

In Latin America, artisanry originates from the region's pre-Columbian communities. The present-day preservation of artisanal practices in Latin America is understood as the preservation of Native people's particular cultural traditions, spiritual practices, and collective identities; in other words, artisanal objects in Latin America have historically been understood as the material embodiment of the collective spirit of indigenous peoples. The historical association between artisanry and Latin American Native communities has made artisanal production attractive to present-day individuals looking to challenge the free-market economics of global capitalism. There are a number of reasons for this, one of which is the importance of the utility of the artisanal object.

Many actors within Chile's postdictatorship literary culture critique market capitalism for its inability to value the aesthetic or intellectual merits of a literary work as "useful" at all. For example, Roberto Toledo, editor of La Gata Viuda Cartonera, describes a conversation he had with the president of La Cámara Chilena del Libro (The Chilean Bureau of Books) about a best-selling cookbook. When Toledo asked why a cookbook sells so well in Chile, the answer he received was that it has "use value" and publishers need to sell books of "use value" in order to finance their production of books of social worth. The example given to Toledo of a book containing social worth, in contrast to one containing use value, was *Don Quijote de la Mancha,* by Miguel de Cervantes.[47] Independent editor María Sol Vera describes a similar situation: Vera claims that sales from a popular day-calendar allowed her press, Editorial Cuarto Propio, to subsist during its early years and publish other works of literature and cultural critique that made virtually no money.[48]

Because the artisanal object has historically been an object of utility that simultaneously possesses sophisticated aesthetic qualities, the artisanal production of books redefines their utilitarian function. Whereas Ergo Sum book production points to the fact that everyday, useful objects can also be works of art, Cartonera cardboard publishers attempt to establish art, in this case literature, as useful, with books functioning as objects of utility. Both projects challenge the distinction between art and everyday objects of utility as mutually exclusive categories.

More important, Latin American artisanry is historically an anti-industrial, anti-capitalist, and, therefore, anti-foreign form of cultural production. Just as industrial capitalism arrived in Latin America as a product of European colonization and imperialism, so too is neoliberalism a foreign import. This is perhaps nowhere more evident than in Chile, where Pinochet's junta consciously invited U.S. economist Milton Freeman and the University of Chicago's School of Economics to apply a free-market "shock doctrine" to the Chilean national economy.[49] Capitalism at large and specifically the latest version of global capitalism known as neoliberalism are—at least in their origins—not natively Chilean. The act of hand-making books in an artisanal mode is thus an act of solidarity with a centuries-old Latin American tradition of non-industrial, noncapitalist, and nonforeign material and symbolic creation.

Chilean Cartoneras make this connection explicitly. La Vieja Sapa Cartonera, Olga Cartonera, and Calafate Cartonera, for example, all qualify their books as "artisanal" precisely because they are not productions of industrial capitalism and they do not circulate within capitalist circuits of economic exchange.[50] Moreover, Nuestra Señora Cartonera claims that "cartonera projects come into being as a form of resistance to the maximizing market of publishing houses."[51] In conjunction with their oppositional stance against market capitalism, Chilean Cartoneras, like most independent publishers working in Chile's postdictatorship literary culture, make a point of defining themselves in opposition to foreign presses. Their artisanal practice is a means of further solidifying their autochthonous identity.

Consequently, Chilean Cartoneras make use of the historical traditions of artisanry in Latin America by fostering feelings of local and national belonging. Some have intentionally chosen names for their presses that directly cite iconic Chilean narratives, characters, or historical references.[52] Perhaps the best example of this is Calafate Cartonera, whose name derives from an indigenous legend about the *calafate* flower found in southern Patagonia; the press's editors chose this name because they wanted to associate themselves with Chilean national traditions.[53] Other Chilean Cartoneras ground their editorial activity in the localized space of the neighborhood by organizing literary events in the communities in which they live and work and by editing anthologies centered on the theme of the neighborhood. For instance, Benicia Cartonera hosts writing and bookmaking workshops for members of the community in which it works; it has also organized cultural encounters directly intended to cultivate neighborhood belonging and identity. A good example is the event "Feria del Trueke," which the press has described as "using autogestión to recuperate neighborhood identity, encounter and exchange."[54]

The most powerful demonstration of the connection between artisanal book production and the construction of local social bonds is the Cartoneras' use of the home and the workshop as privileged sites of bookmaking. The home is of course a collective and shared space where the spiritual belief system of a family is practiced and reproduced; it is also the traditional site of Latin American indigenous artisanal cultural production.[55] Many Cartonera editors invite family, friends, and often the authors they publish to participate in the collective process of artisanal bookmaking, which takes place at the kitchen or dining room table and over friendly conversation and sharing.[56] Calafate Cartonera defines its editorial production as artisanal precisely because it takes place in the home.[57] Using the private home as the headquarters of Cartonera publishing also clearly distinguishes this form of book production from that of multinational presses that, according to Cartonera scholar Ksenija Bilbija, have transformed from "*casas* editoriales" (publishing *houses*) to "*empresas* editoriales" (publishing *companies*).[58] Chilean Cartoneras reverse this transformation by constructing a literal notion of the publishing house as being centered in the home.

The *taller*, or workshop, has become an indispensible characteristic of Cartonera publishing in Chile and all over the world. According to Cartonera scholar Craig Epplin, Eloisa Cartonera originally based its production in the workshop setting because the press's founders conceived of the literary act as a collaborative performance—as an encounter—and the workshop as the physical space of that encounter, as a stage on which to question authority through the redistribution of roles and the formation of an egalitarian social life.[59] Chilean Cartoneras have retained that commitment to sharing the technique of cardboard bookmaking with the public, and in particular with marginalized communities within the public through the workshop setting.

Animita Cartonera's description of the taller and its function within its editorial project echoes Eloísa Cartonera's original intent; Animita editors believe that their press creates "a sense of community that services the interests of different people since we believe that art is a tool that generates spaces of dialogue and the exchange of experiences and ideas."[60] Therefore, while Chilean Cartonera presses have not maintained Eloisa's tradition of inviting cartonera trash collectors into the workshop to participate in book production, the spirit of collective literary production and a shared sense of community are ever present in the Chilean version of Cartonera publishing, evidencing yet again the artisanal qualities of this editorial practice and the commonalities it shares with cultural practices of the dictatorship period.

Latin American artisanal culture shares much in common with Walter Benjamin's concept of the "aura" of a work of art. Benjamin's notion of aura is synonymous with pre-industrial forms of cultural production in which human hands, rather than machines, make the cultural object. "Authenticity" is a concept that Benjamin uses almost interchangeably with the notion of "aura" in his essay "The Work of Art in the Age of Mechanical Reproduction," and it is also key in understanding how artisanry represents cultural traditions in Latin America.

In her article "Walter Benjamin: Traces of Craft," Esther Leslie argues that Benjamin sees the "authentic experience" in the work of art as marked out by human hands; crafts, such as pottery and sewing, are embedded in authenticity and human experience because they are made by hand.[61] Leslie believes that the reason why Benjamin conceives of writing as craft is that it stems from the author's first-hand experience of touching the world, and like artisanal utility, Benjamin believes, "good stories relate a practical knowledge."[62] It makes sense to handcraft the book since the story inside it is also handcrafted, woven together, sewn in the same way that the pages of Cartonera books are often sewn together by hand (fig. 6).[63] The handcrafting of Cartonera books, therefore, interlaces the multiple acts of crafting, storytelling, and book production as forms of "practical knowledge" with use value.

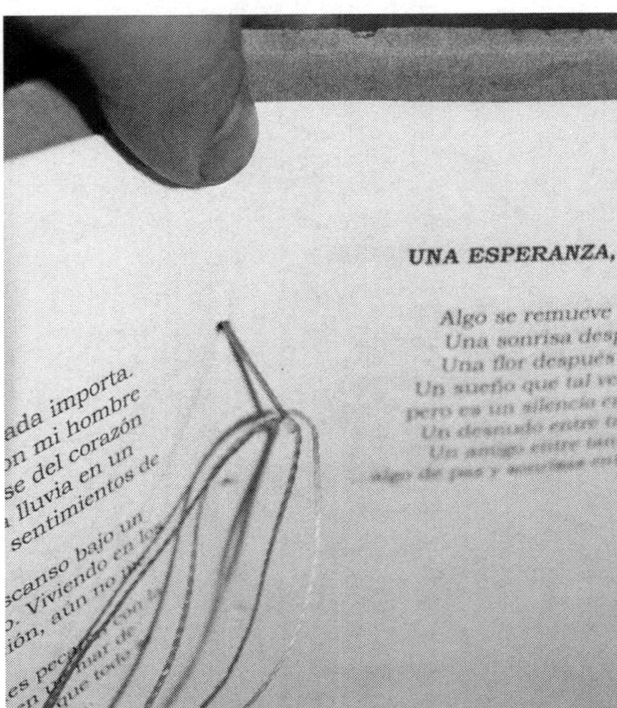

Figure 6. The hand-sewn binding of an Olga Cartonera cardboard book. Photograph by Miguel Araya. Reproduced by permission of Olga Cartonera.

Chilean Cartonera publishers share Benjamin's belief that the act of handcrafting a work of art is the source of its uniqueness, authenticity, or aura. Cartoneros employ multiple practices to show the *cariño* (care) that goes into every book through the process of being touched by human hands.[64] For instance, Olga Cartonera prints the following statement on the inside cover of all of its publications: "This book is unique, original and unrepeatable and it is made by hand by OlgaCartonera."[65] Animita Cartonera employs a similar tactic, printing on the inside covers of all its books, "Art object made and painted by hand with the help of trash collectors and young people."[66] Another common practice is either to hand stamp or write a number in each book indicating its place in the production order of a given print run.[67] This does not happen in industrial book production because all books of the same edition are exactly identical; whereas in Cartonera publishing, even if all books of one edition share the same aesthetic cover, their individuality is marked by a number that registers the book's place in time—its "presence," to use a Benjaminian term, or its "birth" to continue with the metaphor of life and death.

Chilean cardboard bookmakers likewise believe that a trace of the bookmaker remains present in each book. La Vieja Sapa Cartonera, for instance, purports that everyone who participates in its bookmaking workshops leaves a part of their own identity in the book itself, in its material composition.[68] Cartonera scholar Ksenija Bilbija agrees, arguing that the individuals who make cardboard books "inscribe their identities into the books."[69] Cartonera publishing thus conceives of the book as the material body that houses not only the "soul" of literature but also the human soul of the bookmaker.

In this sense, the technique of hand-making books out of cardboard trash is a form of testimony. Benjamin writes, "The authenticity of a thing is the essence of all that is transmissible from its beginning, ranging from its substantive duration to its *testimony* to the history which it has experienced."[70] Thus testimonial practices can take place on a narrative level, as they do in Latin American literature and cinema, drawing from a variety of postdictatorship traditions. They do this as well on a material level: just as the narrative of a testimonial text leaves traces of its historical moment of production, so too do Cartonera books leave material markers of the moment and time that they came into being.

Because global publishing conglomerates have taken almost full control over the production and circulation of literary representations of Chilean national identity, the cultural capital of testimony as a material and symbolic practice has remained strong throughout the newly democratic period.[71] Artisanal bookmaking techniques, like testimonial literature, present the possibility of grounding Chilean literary production—both writing and bookmaking—in the reality of the everyday lived experiences of Chileans and can be understood as an act of protest against the global publishing industry's colonization of Chile's national literary culture.

Benjamin's concern with the mechanical reproduction of art and artisanal practices of cultural production stands in juxtaposition to the very idea of a "culture industry." Yet within postdictatorship literary culture there is not one monolithic publishing "industry" but rather two seemingly different industries struggling for space within the field of literary and book production: the national industry, made up primarily of independent presses, and the global industry, made up primarily of transnational corporate conglomerates. The independent publishing movement, both in Chile and elsewhere around the world, criticizes the global publishing industry for the same reasons that Benjamin and his contemporaries at the Frankfurt School criticize capitalist culture industries: they see the global publishing industry as killing the soul (aura) of cultural products in the name of turning a profit. The independent press's response to such a problem is not to do away with the industrial production of books wholesale, but rather to localize, that is, to nationalize its book production by creating material objects of economic worth without sacrificing their unique cultural spirit.

Articulating this view is Octavio Getino who, at the 2004 international symposium titled "Industrias Culturales: Un aporte al desarrollo" (Culture Industries: Supporting Development) hosted by Chile's Consejo Nacional de la Cultura y las Artes (National Council on Culture and the Arts, CNCA), proclaimed that industrialized cultural production, when enacted by Chile's *national* culture industry, would not "kill" the spirit of art at all, but rather bring it back to life. As he explained, "The great importance of the [culture industries] cannot be measured by their economic dimension . . . so much as *by what the symbolic values that they produce support, or can support, in terms of improving the national and regional public space.* That is to say, their support of information, education, culture, and knowledge, accounting for what is needed for their equal and democratic development."[72] Thus culture industries function as productive agents in the democratization of Chilean and Latin American culture and not as part of a foreign monopoly that threatens the economic livelihood and aesthetic autonomy of individual cultures and local peoples. Here Getino is referring to and endorsing Chile's *national* culture industries: businesses that produce symbolic goods and that are owned and operated by Chileans. The belief represented by Getino and others at this symposium is that national culture industries work to diversify culture from the bottom up while global culture industries tend to homogenize it from the top down.[73]

The ever-growing number of Cartonera book publishers in Chile invites us to question this presumption, however; their opposition to industrial book production at large—whether by national or global businesses—highlights the similarities shared between national and global publishing industries. For instance, Chile's national publishing industry still functions according to a traditional exclusionary model in which the editor serves as a cultural gatekeeper, access to cultural products is regulated by intellectual property rights, and the work of art is consecrated by institutionalized notions of taste and—although to a much lesser degree than in the corporate publishing industry—market sales. The smallest and most independent Chilean publishing houses that have entered into the field of postdictatorship literary production have done so with the purpose of giving voice to Chile's next generation of writers who, according to Calabaza del Diablo editor and writer Jaime Pino, are not currently represented by corporate publishing houses. Independent houses such as Calabaza del Diablo hope to design the future of Chile's national literary canon in ways that they see the commercial industry failing to do.[74]

A very small number of Chilean Cartoneras are also interested in helping to give voice to the next generation of great Chilean writers (Animita Cartonera most of all), but most of them are not; instead, they are committed to a fundamentally inclusionary practice of publishing *anyone* and *anything* they can. To this end, some Cartonera editors use the word *masificar* (massify) to describe their editorial mission, but they do not use it in reference to mass culture or to an increased number of cultural products in the public sphere (best achieved by industrialized print production). For Roberto Toledo, founding editor of La Gata Viuda Cartonera, cardboard publishing "is born from the need to take to the streets and massify a message that is trapped in the clutches of the bad faith of market publishers."[75] Likewise, editors of La Vieja Sapa Cartonera believe that it is the capitalist literary market that detrimentally limits the range of people able to participate in literary culture whereas renegade presses like their own open up the circuits of literary participation to more people.[76]

There are varied ways in which Chilean Cartonera presses put these theories of public inclusion into practice. One is through open calls for submissions of original writings based on a particular theme; yet, rather than selecting a group of texts for publication out of all the works submitted by the public, more often than not Cartonera editors choose to publish all submissions they receive in anthology form. Inclusion, or what Cartonera editors refer to as massification, also takes place through Cartonera writing and bookmaking workshops that instruct participants on how to write narratives and then how to publish them in handmade book form. Through their participation in Cartonera workshops, members of the public with no prior writing experience or established talent are able to become published authors and bookmakers.

These practices "massify" literary production in the sense that they contain virtually no filter whatsoever between an individual who wants to write and publish a literary work and her ability to do so.

This lack of filter is what distinguishes Cartonera book publishing not only from the commercial industry that it openly opposes but also from Chile's local independent publishing industry. Like Ergo Sum, Cartoneras reject the hierarchical contingencies on which literary consecration is achieved—either by the market, the academy, or other institutions—whereas the independent publishing industry believes in the process of consecration but wants to take control of that process back from multinational publishing corporations. We are therefore dealing with two different forms of cultural power: one that is derived from the process of selection (independent presses) and another that is derived from the process of creation (Cartonera publishers). The former is made possible by preconceived and institutionalized notions of taste, whereas the latter is made possible through the act of craft whose own etymology stems, according to Leslie, from the notion of power, force, or strength.[77]

Ultimately what establishes the connection between independent and corporate literary publishers is that their use of industrial modes of production guarantees their role as cultural intermediary whereas artisanal modes of cultural production, such as those employed by Cartonera publishers, attempt to create a direct relation between the artist, the work of art, and the world. Raymond Williams's own definition of artisanal cultural production is one in which the artist has a direct relation to the modes of production and circulation. "The producer is wholly dependent on the immediate market but within its terms his work remains under his own direction, at all stages, and he can see himself, in this sense, as independent."[78] In contrast, what Williams refers to as "post-artisanal" cultural production creates a mediated relationship between the artist and her work of art. "First, the producer sells his work not directly but to a *distributive* intermediary, who then becomes, in a majority of cases, his factual if often occasional employer. Then, second, the producer sells his work to a *productive* intermediary, and typically capitalist social relations begin to be instituted. The intermediary invests in the purchase of a work for the purpose of profit; it is now *his* relations with the market which are direct."[79]

In the post-artisanal phase, the artist's relationship to her artistic production changes in that the artist herself no longer owns her art. Williams cites the evolution of book distributors into book publishers as the prime example of this post-artisanal shift in the social relations of capitalist production. For Néstor García Canclini, this mediation between the artist, the work of art, and the world also creates social hierarchies among different types of cultural labor and laborers. He explains that the move from artisanal to industrial cultural production created a technical division of labor that "goes alongside the much more blatant social differentiation between those who provide manual labor and intellectual labor and those who contribute capital and appropriate the product."[80] In artisanal cultural production there is only one single agent responsible for both the intellectual (aesthetic) and manual production of the object and, as we learned from Williams, this agent has direct control over the object produced. By contrast, industrialized cultural production not only creates a division—and a hierarchy—between symbolic labor/laborer and manual labor/laborer, but it also inserts a third actor into the process who then appropriates the work of art for legal and economic purposes. This is as true for the independent press in Chile as it is for corporate multinational publishing houses working there, and it has serious implications for the political import and democratic mission of Cartonera artisanal book production.

Policing Literary Production and Distribution in Postdictatorship Chile

Both Chile's local independent publishing industry and the global publishing industry abide by legal mandates that regulate the production and circulation of literary texts. In Chile, these mandates have changed throughout the dictatorship and into the postdictatorship period, and the local publishing industry has directly shaped those changes. The first legislation passed in Chile regarding intellectual property and copyright was the Literary and Artistic Property Law in 1834, but it is the 1970 Intellectual Property Law that has shaped the current condition of copyright protection in contemporary Chile.[81]

The Intellectual Property Law has been modified three times, once under the military regime in 1985, again after democracy's return in 1992, and most recently in 2010. Each of these modifications has increased the protections of copyright and intellectual property, expanded the definitions of cultural piracy, increased the sanctions for infringement of intellectual property and copyright law, and increased the state's power to regulate and protect cultural products as private property as well as the public's access to those products. The motivation behind the latest reform was specifically to make the prosecution of copyright and intellectual property infringement faster and more efficient.[82] While the 2010 modification was passed under the right-wing presidency of Sebastián Piñera, it was first proposed in 2007 by the leftist administration of President Michelle Bachelet. It therefore received support from both conservative and progressive governments.

These modifications in copyright law have come about because the state, in partnership with local industry leaders, has identified the illegal copying and unauthorized reselling of books—that is, cultural piracy—as a serious threat to the democratization of Chilean literary culture. Despite low literacy rates and the fact that Chile's local publishing industry has been steadily increasing its production and distribution figures throughout the postdictatorship period, there has still been an increase of illegal literary circulation (typically by photocopying) and the unauthorized sale of published works in recent years.[83] Agustín Squella, who led the formation of the state's new cultural institutionalization under President Ricardo Lagos, reports that in 2005 piracy represented 25 percent of the book market in Chile.[84] While admitting that the "copyright industry" has become one of the principle sources of wealth in the era of globalization, the leaders of Chile's local editorial industry argue that anti-piracy policies do more than serve their own private economic interest; they also serve the greater public interests of protecting the integrity of creative production, helping empower small, local businesses and fighting neoliberalism.[85]

The participation of Chile's national publishing industry in writing the state's new cultural policies explains why it focuses so much on copyright protections and piracy. Williams explains that "professional societies," such as those helping the Chilean state draft its new cultural policies—specifically the Asociación de Editores de Chile (Association of Chilean Publishers)—emerge as a result of the need to protect copyright and anti-piracy laws, and he uses the example of editorial and literary industries as typical in this respect.[86] Print culture has a unique historical relationship with piracy due to the fact that print technology developed more quickly than did other cultural media, thus making copying a problem for printed media before it became a problem for other art forms.[87]

In addition to intellectual property and copyright laws, Chilean government administrations of the postdictatorship period have implemented other pieces of legislation that increase the state's ability to regulate literary and editorial production and discipline cultural piracy. The 1993 Promotion of Books and Reading Law mandates that all books (and many other printed and published materials) register themselves with an International Standard Book Number (ISBN).[88] Article 8 of this law requires that "in every book printed in the country there will be proof of an International Standard Book Number that will be listed in a public record under the direction of the public or private entity that represents the International Standard Book Number."[89]

Since 1987, the Chilean Bureau of Books has been the agency in charge of administering the ISBN in Chile. Founded in 1950, this not-for-profit organization is a professional association that unites book publishers and distributors, bookstores, and direct-sales organizations.[90] While the organization's functions are not restricted to the commercialization of books, most of the work accomplished by this agency relates to the commercial book industry. The bureau describes its objectives as "defending the freedom to publish, import, commercialize and circulate books, the right to intellectual property in all its manifestations; to foster the development and dissemination of the Chilean book, both in country and abroad; to create and support all initiatives destined to train people working in the editing, publication, commercialization, and distribution of books."[91]

While its purpose is obviously geared toward industry professionals, the bureau's services and mandates extend to non-industry literary producers, such as writers who self-publish their own works, or books that will never enter the capitalist market. All noncommercial publications are required by the 1993 law to register themselves with an ISBN through the bureau. In guidelines provided on its website, the bureau states, "It is important to highlight that the ISBN is applicable independent of the end to which the publisher intends to use a book, whether it be for sale, donation or internal circulation."[92] Therefore, as part of Chile's new cultural institutionalization, all books, even autoediciones produced by groups like Ergo Sum, are expected to adhere to this internationally standardized system of book identification.

There is no coherent practice among Cartonera publishers regarding whether or not to register their publications as intellectual property, assign them ISBNs, or respect copyright. Some Chilean Cartoneras boisterously reject these norms for political reasons, while others choose to loosely abide by them or sometimes conform to them but not always, and a small few make a concerted effort to formalize their production by adhering to copyright norms. Animita Cartonera is one of the only Chilean Cartoneras to register its publications with an ISBN and as intellectual property and, along with Calafate Cartonera, to print a copyright symbol in the inside covers of its books. Some Cartoneras print their publications under a Creative Commons and Copyleft license; some acknowledge the names of illustrators (in addition to authors) who have worked on individual handmade books, but many others do not—principally because the production is collective and cannot be attributed to a single person.

In lieu of copyright or intellectual property registration, many Cartoneras simply publically thank the author for giving the press the right to publish her work.[93] It is also common for Chilean Cartonera presses to "pay" their authors by giving them a certain number of published books rather than paying them in money since the books earn only enough money in sales to pay for the raw materials needed to make them (La Gata Viuda gives each author five copies of the book as payment). A few cardboard presses, including

Calafate Cartonera and Olga Cartonera, justify their choice not to register their publications with an ISBN precisely because of the artisanal nature of their books and the fact that they are never going to be sold for profit.[94] A practical reason why most Chilean Cartoneras do not register their titles with an ISBN or as intellectual property is that the monetary fees required for those legal formalities are prohibitive.

Many Chilean Cartonera book publishers see intellectual copyright protection as impeding their attempts to "massify," and thereby democratize, postdictatorship literary culture. As a result, they explicitly encourage the public to make and distribute unauthorized copies of their publications. For example, La Vieja Sapa Cartonera prints the following on the inside cover of all its books: "Any copy, reproduction or falsification is fully permitted, and even encouraged by this press. What is more, after reading, it is recommended that you carefully fold this book and make it into a paper airplane. Hopefully by giving it wings it can fly where we ourselves have not yet arrived. Property is theft."[95] Sharing this sentiment is Roberto Toledo of La Gata Viuda Cartonera, who also comments that he does not care if anyone pirates his books, even though he respects intellectual property; he is opposed to people stealing his ideas or those of his authors, but he has no problem if others reproduce and distribute his books without permission.[96]

In the same vein, Canita Cartonera makes some of its publications available for download on its website, where it instructs the public to print them out and photocopy them as much as possible in order to "free voices that no one would otherwise hear," and it even urges readers to leave copies of its publications in their own neighborhood bars.[97] Beyond its copyright politics, the fact that Canita Cartonera is run out of a state penitentiary and its authors and bookmakers are prison inmates further invokes a spirit of defiance of state laws (both cultural and other). The act of liberating books from their confinement by copyright protections is also a symbolic act of liberating, if not the inmate authors of those texts themselves, at least their creative voices.

Perhaps the most blatant act of disregard for copyright protection is La Vieja Sapa Cartonera's unauthorized 2012 publication of Jorge Tellier's *Crónica del Forastero* (Chronicles of a Foreigner). This text was originally published in Santiago in 1968 by Arancibia Hnos.

These are just some examples of the ways in which Chilean Cartoneras both passively ignore and actively violate laws regarding copyright and intellectual property that have been implemented by the state and that have been strongly supported by the national publishing industry during the postdictatorship period. By ignoring these mandates, Chilean Cartoneras join the company of Chile's most widely and forcibly criminalized cultural producers of the postdictatorship period: cultural pirates. While this may seem a dubious association, Chilean Cartoneras themselves tend to see their literary production as sharing much in common with the spirit of cultural piracy. In the first sense, all but one (Animita Cartonera) are not legal businesses, meaning they do not pay taxes to the government—specifically the infamous VAT tax on all books—and when they do take money in exchange for books, they do so "informally."[100] It is precisely for these reasons that Calafate Cartonera editors Espejo and Peñaloza have identified themselves as "pirates."[101]

While the reasons behind the state's implementation of stricter copyright laws seems logical, the general refusal by Cartonera presses to strictly abide by them invites us to question the ethical ground on which the newly democratic state disciplines the cultural sphere in the name of democracy. Copyright protection has gained much criticism in recent years—and not only in Chile. One problem that critics frequently cite is that laws such as these reproduce the problematic logic of nineteenth-century liberal political theory and, by extension, contemporary neoliberalism. Specifically, international intellectual property and copyright laws (on which Chile's 1992 modification of its own copyright law is modeled) directly depend on problematic liberal definitions of "property" and "the individual."[102]

Former CNCA director José Weinstein employs these definitions in explaining how intellectual property requires a concept of the individual as the precondition to political rights. He claims that "the need to establish copyright is solidified by initiating a process of affirming individual rights that, since the far-off time [of the eighteenth century] have progressively expanded to the present day."[103] The liberal notion of the individual makes it possible for culture to exist as private property, but it also establishes a social structure in which individuals relate to culture not as equals but according to social differences, determined primarily by wealth and property accumulation but also by race, gender, age, and other social distinctions. We know from feminist, race, postcolonial, and queer theory that the individual of Enlightenment liberalism is not universal but a decidedly Western and patriarchal historical construct. Carole Pateman, for instance, is well known for her argument that women are not granted the inalienable rights guaranteed to the individual as defined by Enlightenment political philosophy, which Pateman exposes as a patriarchal enterprise.[104] Others have critiqued the liberal notion of the public sphere for the same reason, arguing that it denies access to certain kinds of individuals over others and claiming that the very demand for absolute equality is itself an exercise of hegemony.[105]

Historically, the definition of culture as the private property of only certain individuals emerges at a particular moment of capitalist development; Williams locates this moment as the "post-artisanal" phase in which we first see the appearance of the artist as "market professional."[106] Not surprisingly, it is this emergence of the artist as professional that, Williams tells us, coincides with the emergence of intellectual copyright campaigns and the separation of "artist" from other kinds of laborers, such as "craftsmen."[107] Paul Steidlmeier, scholar of international economics and management, agrees with this view, arguing that the importance of intellectual property is a relatively new development in human history and that traditionally "intellectual ideas have been treated as part of the public domain."[108] Cultural policies designed to protect intellectual copyright thus interpellate citizens as "artists" only if their relationship to their artistic production is meditated by the market and the intellectual property laws that regulate it. Likewise these discourses determine the kind of cultural production and consumption in which citizens may engage. It is not hard for us, then, to see the ways in which intellectual property, copyright, and anti-piracy discourses produce both a certain definition of culture and correlating types of cultural producers that conform to the neoliberal economic structure of postdictatorship Chilean life.

The productive disciplinary power of the newly democratic state evidences a number of characteristics similar to those of the authoritarian regime. Specifically, the newly democratic state and its civil society partners, like the military regime before them, have increased the state's authority to discipline areas of social behavior that have not traditionally fallen under its direct control. Lawrence Lessig, one of the most critical scholars of copyright law in recent years, has argued that this is indeed one of the effects of contemporary intellectual property law. "For the first time in our tradition, the ordinary ways in which individuals create and share culture fall within the reach of the regulation of the law, which has expanded to draw within its control a vast amount of culture and creativity that it never reached before. . . . The consequence is that we are less and less a free culture, more and more a **permission** culture."[109]

While Lessig's comments reference the legal context of copyright law in the United States, they are equally applicable to the situation in postdictatorship Chile. His use of the word "permission" immediately reminds us of the state's censorship policies that produced illegal autoediciones, described by self-published author Horacio Eloy as circulating "without anyone's permission."[110] Similarly, Agustín Squella, an advocate of Chile's recent anti-piracy discourse, describes pirated culture in such a way that would equally describe the autoedición, explaining that the latter employs strategies of street vending in order to conceal its hidden merchandise from the police.[111] Laikwan Pang's research on intellectual copyright policies in Asian cinema makes this connection explicit when she argues that intellectual property policies are modern forms of state censorship.[112]

The similarities between the newly democratic state's increased defense of copyright and intellectual property and the cultural censorship of the military regime make us question the democratic ethos of Chile's new cultural institutionalization. On the one hand, there are those officials within the state's cultural infrastructure, such as Squella for instance, who cite civil society's participation in the state's cultural reform as evidence of Chile's democratic development. This makes sense in comparison with the dictatorship period in which authoritarian regimes throughout South America's Southern Cone viewed civil society as an enemy rather than an ally and directed their censorship policies at private institutions and as well as individuals.[113] On the other hand, the increased power of the newly democratic state to discipline Chilean culture has occurred as a direct result of Chilean culture industries' public outcry for greater intellectual property enforcement and their alliance with the state to write and enforce laws that do just that. Roberto Ampuero and Luis Martín-Estudillo support this interpretation, arguing in the introduction to their edited volume *Post-Authoritarian Cultures: Spain and Latin America's Southern Cone* that the cultural initiatives of the democratic transition "maintain their regressive social tendencies, as they complacently reproduce the power structures postulated from above."[114] As was true under the military dictatorship, the private economic interests of those in power are privileged over the public interest in making artistic production and consumption equally available to all.

Speaking to this point, in *Las políticas culturales en América Latina* (Cultural Policies in Latin America), José Joaquin Brunner ultimately defines cultural policies as formal structures of control and "social closure." As he explains, "Democratic cultural policies are—in the most general sense—formal policies. They follow institutional agreements more than applying cognitive content to society. They intend to create structures of opportunity (markets, systems of choice, a plurality of offerings, variety) and, at the same time, they prevent (through counterbalances, proceedings, forms of control, measures of open and closed competition, etc.) that those structures of opportunities be objects of social closure, of ideological closure or of any other form of monopolistic manipulation."[115] The question of interests sheds light on many contradictions inherent in Chile's new policies of cultural reform. The emphasis on defining and defending culture as private property presents a serious deterrent to one of the state's fundamental goals, which is to increase the equal access of culture to all citizens. Indeed, this contradiction between private and public interests is a tension that has plagued the history of international copyright law: the desire of copyright owners to expand the protection over the ideas and information contained in their works conflicts with the democratic notion that those ideas and information be free for others to use.[116]

The policies of Chile's new cultural institutionalization attempt to satisfy both desires simultaneously. It would seem then that the desire to protect private interests applies primarily to the production of ideas and information whereas the desire to protect public interests applies primarily to the consumption of ideas and information that have already been copyrighted. This reproduces the hierarchy of production/consumption that restricts cultural production to a relatively small group of elites while relegating the masses to the position of passive cultural consumers.

More concerning than this, however, is the way in which the focus on intellectual property presents a contradiction to the pro-nationalist stance embodied by the state's new cultural institutionalization and its efforts to create and protect autonomous Chilean cultural industries. This is because throughout its history, intellectual copyright law has been used by global industry powers as a means of ensuring their economic and cultural domination over the developing world.[117] Many scholars typically describe the international debate on intellectual property as emblematic of the North/South global divide. For instance, Pang writes that "copyright is clearly one of those Western legal concepts regulating the current global hierarchy, allowing only the 'legal' circulation of ideas and creativity and criminalizing those evading the capitalist order—all in the name of protecting cultural diversity. In other words, copyright echoes the concerns of both the WTO [World Trade Organization] and UNESCO [United Nations Educational, Scientific, and Cultural Organization], proposing a 'top-down transcultural structure' to promote one's 'right to culture.' . . . [C]opyright levels culture in the name of culture.[118]

Pang recognizes the irony in criminalizing certain kinds of cultural practices in order to preserve the "diversity of culture"—a concept that has become so pervasive in our discussion of global culture that its exact meaning is difficult to pin down and we forget its political significance.

Like Pang, economists James D. Gaisford and R. Stephen Richardson argue that intellectual property laws divide the world into an antagonistic binary. They conclude that it is nearly unavoidable that "Less Developed Countries as a group will tend to lose from the worldwide standards on intellectual property protection."[119] Those countries will not benefit from copyright laws, according to communications scholar Ronald Bettig, because international intellectual property laws increase the hegemony of the global cultural industries (which own the majority of copyrights), leading to the further homogenization of cultural products worldwide. Bettig claims that this, "in turn, fosters the erosion of national, regional, ethnic, and group autonomy, undermines democratic participation in cultural expression, and increases inequalities between people and nations."[120] Through this lens we can see that the cultural policies Chile has adopted to economically strengthen its local literary industry and defend national difference have the potential to actually endanger local identity and reinforce global homogenization.

This wider perspective also provides new insight into why so many Chilean Cartoneras have chosen to resist institutionalization and the structural inequalities and contradictions it causes. By not registering their books with an ISBN, Cartonera publishers violate current Chilean law. Still, these presses' choice to produce illegitimate—and in some cases illegal—cultural products is as much a form of political action in the postdictatorship period as the work of Ergo Sum and its contemporaries was under dictatorship. This leads us to question whether other illegal cultural producers of the postdictatorship period, for example cultural pirates, might be similarly motivated by political incentives rather than purely economic ones. Chilean Cartoneras as well as underground self-publishers such as Ergo Sum provoke the question of whether or not cultural pirates can be political revolutionaries.

The logic of intellectual property discourse forecloses this possibility since it conceives of cultural copying in particular and cultural production in general as primarily economic, rather than aesthetic or social, activities. According to this logic, economic gain is the only, or at least a primary creative inspiration, and, therefore, must be protected in order to ensure the symbolic diversity of cultural production. Bettig writes that "the exclusive right to exploit a copyrighted work is meant to supply the motivation for intellectual and artistic activity. . . . If the copyright system works this way, it is functional in terms of the social good since it stimulates intellectual creativity."[121] Bettig's research, however, shows that the copyright system does not in fact operate according to this ideal. One of the ways in which he proves this is by showing that copyright laws produce a conflict of interest between creators (the author, translator, or inventor) and industry institutions (publishers, printers, distributors, and vendors). His research shows that it was industry institutions and not cultural creators that pushed through what is considered the first modern copyright law, the United Kingdom's 1710 Statute of Queen Anne. "The protection afforded was against the piracy of printed works. There was nothing in this Statute that touched upon the creative or moral rights of the author. The right protected was a property right."[122] From its origins, then, the function of copyright law has been the preservation of economic wealth and not the proliferation of artistic freedom or creative diversity. These laws are more responsible for stifling artistic creativity than for preventing cultural piracy.[123]

Pang stands out for her ability to recognize culture's inherent body/spirit divide as paramount to the intellectual property debate. While Pang argues that copyright discourse is more concerned with policing the material reproduction of cultural products than it is with policing symbolic copying, she also strongly defends the notion that these two aspects of culture cannot be separated from each another. She claims that restricting the reproduction of cultural goods as material commodities equally limits our ability to copy ideas, which, according to Pang, is the driving force of individual creativity and cultural heritage. This supports the idea that the social value of art, what Subercaseaux calls "spirit," what Bettig terms "social efficiency," and what Benjamin calls "aura," depends on copying, imitation, intertextuality, mimesis, and repetition, all of which are criminalized by contemporary international copyright discourse. Bettig writes, "It is clear that *social* efficiency, in terms of access to and use of informational and cultural products, is indeed threatened by private intellectual property rights. Social efficiency stems from the social nature of intellectual and artistic creativity."[124] What Bettig is saying is that intellectual property laws threaten the definition of culture as a "spiritual way of life" created and shared by all. And yet it is in defense of this definition of culture that the Chilean state justifies its implementation of stricter copyright protection.

These claims explain how cultural piracy can function in contemporary Chile as a form of political resistance and democratic activism. Cultural pirates challenge the definition of culture as private property; they weaken neoliberal hegemony, not through state laws such as those initiated by Chile's new cultural institutionalization, but by direct and unmediated action through which local citizens reclaim the right to cultural production. As communications professor Kelly Gates explains, cultural piracy creates a "crisis of legitimacy" that challenges whether or not the culture industries truly are the "rightful proprietors and purveyors of culture."[125] However, while cultural pirates successfully defend the equal and democratic access to culture as a public good, they still do so in order to exploit the material value of cultural commodities. A more tenable alternative is found in the editorial practices of Chilean Cartoneras, which equally challenge the community's alienation from material modes of cultural production, distribution, and consumption but do not do so in the spirit of capitalist accumulation.

4

Libros de Mentira

Fake Books, Digital Matter, and Cultural Democracy 2.0

A book is a machine to think with.
—I. A. Richards

We are the little people who turn the pages while you read.
—Libros de Mentira

Until this point, our investigation into postdictatorship Chilean literature has focused predominantly on experimentations in print culture. Not only are Ergo Sum book-objects and Cartonera cardboard books made out of paper, but the use of unique kinds of paper in the production of these objects is also fundamental to the aesthetic meanings and political statements they create. There is no denying that literature today is still mainly dependent on paper as the medium through which it comes into the world, but it is also true that the twenty-first century presents the first real possibility for literature to exist independent of paper.

This is especially true in Chile, which has led the Latin American region in Internet readiness and usage for years. According to the CNCA, between 2003 and 2010, the number of Chileans connecting to the Internet increased by 263.6 percent, meaning that over half of the country's citizens were online during this period.[1] In 2014 the World Economic Forum (WEF) ranked Chile 35 out of 148 countries in Internet readiness (down one position from its 34th ranking in 2013), and 39 out of 148 in Internet usage.[2] In its analysis, the WEF stated that Chile "relentlessly continues to develop its ICT [Information and Communications Technologies] usage across stakeholders, with the highest rates of Internet users . . . , e-commerce . . . , and online government . . . services in the region."[3] Within the global index of Internet preparedness, no other Latin American country ranks in the 30th percentile, and Chile directly trails the European countries of Portugal and Spain, which rank 33 and 34 respectively.

However, even though Chileans are using the Internet and information technologies far more than their Latin American neighbors, they are not necessarily as readily incorporating literary and cultural activities into their Internet usage. In a 2011 report, the CNCA found that 44 percent of the Chileans it surveyed read newspapers and magazines on digital reading devices, and 30 percent read books on digital reading devices.[4] Another poll conducted in 2010 by Fundación la Fuente (The Source Foundation) found that 73.8 percent of those surveyed claimed not to be familiar with e-books; 15.7 percent claimed they knew of them by name only; 5.3 percent had heard a little bit about them; 3.8 percent had read extensively on the topic and knew a good deal about it; and only 1.4 percent of those surveyed actually used e-books.[5]

Because of these low figures, the CNCA has made digital reading a top priority of its cultural campaigns and policies in recent years. The state laid out its goals to support the production and distribution of digital texts and to make them more accessible to the general public in its *Plan Nacional de Fomento de la Lectura: Lee Chile Lee* (National Plan to Promote Reading: Read Chile Read). This 2011 publication demonstrates the state's commitment to bringing Internet access and digital reading materials to more Chileans, primarily through public community and school libraries; it also shows that the state strongly supports the publication and distribution of digital texts as a necessary area of growth for the nation's commercial book industry. Toward this end, the CNCA has committed to investing monies into research and training to explore how the national publishing industry can take advantage of digital technologies while still preserving the intellectual property rights that authors hold over their texts.[6] Consequently, it has identified intellectual property rights as a principal concern in the area of digital publishing.

However, it is not just the state and private industry that have shown increasing interest in digital publishing in Chile in recent years. Despite the fact that on the whole Chileans are not overly active in using digital technologies for literary production and consumption, there are a small number of cultural organizations and individual citizens working hard to do so. For instance, the website Escritores y Poetas en Español, Página Chilena al servicio de la Cultura (Writers and Poets in Spanish, Chilean Culture Page) offers an extensive source of works by Chilean and foreign writers published in Spanish.[7] The Escritores (Writers) website also has a large catalog of Chilean literary works available for reading on the web in addition to offering digital publication services to authors. From this group of online literary producers,

I have chosen to focus on the website Libros de Mentira, which I translate into English as Fake Books.

Libros de Mentira is many things: in its online existence it is a digital press, a platform for self-publication and digital bookmaking, a literary community and social media website, a blog, and the self-proclaimed first "virtual bookstore" in Latin America. On this site readers can browse texts belonging to a variety of genres and deriving from a variety of national traditions—from European philosophy, to Japanese manga, to "karaoke" literature, to new Latin American fiction.

The website's description of itself as an online "bookstore" is ironic considering that nothing on the Libros de Mentira site is for sale; readers can open and read any digital book they want for free.[8] If readers wish to do more on the site than simply browse through and read its digital catalog, they can set up a free membership, which requires choosing an avatar and username, and selecting a country of residence. Having become members, users can actively engage with others in this online literary community by commenting on and discussing particular digital publications on the site and, most important, by uploading and publishing their own works to the site. In addition to the online press, Libros de Mentira also maintains a blog where readers can read articles pertaining to Chilean literary history as well as learn news of current Chilean literary culture. Offline, Libros de Mentira publishes a small number of books in paper, and it organizes writing and book-making workshops (for both paper and digital books), book fairs, book launches and readings, and other literary events happening primarily in and around Santiago de Chile.

Libros de Mentira began in 2008 when it was formed by three college students studying journalism at the University of Santiago: Mauricio Sanhueza, Gabriel Oyarzún, and Luis Cruz. The three young men wanted to share their own original writings with the public but felt frustrated by the lack of opportunities available to them on the commercial market; they therefore set out to create their own means of literary publication and dissemination.[9] Taking advantage of the most common technologies available to their generation, the group of college students turned to the Internet, where they set up a website and, using originally designed software, began publishing what they referred to as "digital books." In its first year of operation, the press released a collection of fifteen narrative works written by "distinguished authors"—all pertaining to Chile's national literary canon; the following year it published a poetry collection, which also contained fifteen works by "prestigious authors"—all of whom were also esteemed Chilean poets.[10]

Once it released these titles, and with its website up and running, readers almost immediately requested that the press accept open submissions from the general public.[11] The website's creators responded by providing members with software tools that allowed them to upload their own texts and publish them as digital books on the website. With these tools, and the web space provided by the press, members can publish works for free and without having to pass through a process of editorial selection that is typical of print publication. However, Libros de Mentira does have an editorial board that selects books by third parties for digital publication in a way that is similar to the practice of traditional print presses; this board selects acclaimed works of global literature to publish on the website as well as unpublished works written by consecrated authors of the Chilean canon. The editorial board also determines which of the user-uploaded digital books will appear on the site's homepage, and it determines which of the press's digital books it will publish in paper form.

Despite some similarities to independent print presses, Libros de Mentira shares many qualities in common with the Ergo Sum writing collective and press. Even though not all Libros de Mentira books qualify as self-publications, the raison d'être of the press is rooted in that spirit: anyone can upload a work of writing and publish it on the site as a digital book without editorial approval. But rather than self-publishing hand-made books on mimeographs and photocopy machines, as was the trend under dictatorship, Chile's contemporary youth have relied on technologies specific to their generation: computer software and the Internet. Yet in spite of the innovations in technology that have occurred between the dictatorship and postdictatorship periods, much remains the same in the world of Chilean self-publication: there is still a serious emphasis on creating and maintaining a spirit of community built around shared literary activities and a commitment to making every aspect of literary production—from writing to editing to book manufacturing—available to those individuals and groups most frequently denied access to them.

For Ergo Sum during the dictatorship period, this meant publishing books without the approval of military authorities, who attempted to function as cultural gatekeepers. In the twenty-first century, the role of gatekeeper has passed to professionals of the literary industry, namely editors and publishers but also critics, who employ their own standards of quality to determine which texts will circulate among the public. Whereas military personnel made editorial decisions in accordance with their capitalist and politically conservative ideologies, corporate publishers now follow global sales trends and marketing formulas to determine what kinds of text to publish.

A central commonality between Ergo Sum and Libros de Mentira is that both presses, to varying degrees, work independently of either of these models of cultural mediation. For Libros de Mentira, this means bringing books to readers independent of the commercial market. As the press plainly states on its website, "This is a collaborative and independent initiative, and as such it does not function according to market interests."[12] Like Ergo Sum book-objects, Libros de Mentira's digital books do not carry ISBNs, and the press holds no intellectual property rights over any of its publications; these rights remain the sole domain of individual authors, who can lawfully republish the same texts without asking Libros de Mentira for permission. In addition, authors receive no capital gains when readers consume their works on the Libros de Mentira website because readers are not charged to consume those works.

In order to avoid traditional regulatory processes of literary production, circulation, and consumption, both Ergo Sum and Libros de Mentira have strategically manipulated the book form as the privileged material vessel through which a text's discursive content arrives in the hands of its readers. Both presses intentionally play with the materiality of their books in ways that throw the very definition of the "book" into question. Ergo Sum does this, as previously discussed, by producing books in drag. At first glance the drag performance of Ergo Sum book-objects appears to mislead readers—we might even say to *lie* to them—about what the object is. Libros de Mentira books follow directly in this tradition by presuming to "lie" (*mentirar*) to their readers. Without a doubt the very name that its founders chose to give this press claims that the literary materials it produces are books (*libros*) and not books at the same time (*de mentira,* fake); we can thus interpret the name of the press, Libros de Mentira, as "books that lie."

Yet, like Ergo Sum book-objects, these digital publications are only lying about their identity in terms of our preconceived expectations of what books should be, what they should look like, and what material form they should take. Ergo Sum book-objects are not so much books *disguised* as feminized object-commodities as they are *both* feminized objects *and* books at the same time. Likewise, Libros de Mentira digital books are both fake and real at the same time: they are "fake" presumably because they are digital and have no physical embodiment such that we historically expect books to have; yet they are real because even without a physically material form, they are still books in the sense that they consist of narrative and poetic formations of language that we can read and enjoy. In the sense that they are both books and not books at the same time, Ergo Sum book-objects and Libros de Mentira digital books redefine what constitutes the book as an art object within their respective historical moments.

One significant difference, however, between these two presses is that Ergo Sum's book production depends solely on manual labor whereas Libros de Mentira's method employs mechanical reproduction. Libros de Mentira's use of digital technologies, specifically the Internet, allows it to incorporate more people into its editorial practice than Ergo Sum could ever possibly do. It also, therefore, requires more capital investment, which it receives from sponsorship by the state, private educational and cultural organizations, and the commercial sales of books in print.

But even more than its institutional affiliations and dependencies, Libros de Mentira's technical reproduction of the literary work is a key concern in determining the press's democratizing potential. Central to Libros de Mentira's editorial philosophy—reflected in the design and structure of its website—is the belief that advancements in the technological reproduction of the literary work of art, specifically digital technologies and the Internet, have democratizing potential. On its website, the press openly states that it has a democratic agenda and connects this agenda with its strategic use of the Internet to produce and distribute noncommercial literature: "This is a free and open access initiative, founded on pluralism, integration and a concept of democratizing publishing that utilizes the Internet as a scaffold of literary and creative content."[13] Like many other alternative literary producers in Chile, Libros de Mentira equates the democratization of literary culture with literature's ability to exist as a non-economic good. Consequently, it attempts to provide Chilean citizens with equal access to material modes of literary production, distribution, and consumption. It believes that the Internet, especially in its Web 2.0 iteration, is uniquely equipped to facilitate this process.

Libros de Mentira's editorial model attempts to harness the participatory nature of Web 2.0 by inviting Internet users and literary enthusiasts to directly engage in every aspect of literary production, from writing, to editing, to book manufacturing; it also empowers readers to determine what kinds of texts to upload and publish on the site, and it encourages them to comment on, critique, and discuss texts with one another and with the text's author through onsite dialogue. The press's model of cultural democracy parallels the structure of Web 2.0 in the sense that both seek to provide users with tools necessary for empowering them as creators of cultural content rather than as mere consumers.

The Internet does indeed possess the potential to democratize literary culture, as the example of Libros de Mentira demonstrates, but that does not mean that this potential is always realized. This is in part because of the differences between how Libros de Mentira members use the site compared to how the press designed the site to be used; but it is also due to the politics of the Internet itself and the increasing power that state governments and multinational corporations possess in controlling the ways in which individuals are allowed to use this supposedly global and egalitarian public space. Furthermore, and perhaps most surprisingly, Libros de Mentira's editorial practice shows us that the Internet's ability to democratize literary culture does *not* include undermining or eliminating print culture by any means. Rather, we will see various ways in which Libros de Mentira's online form of publication somewhat ironically reifies the hierarchical quality of print culture as part of its democratizing mission.

Digital Matter: The Book Is a Machine to Think With

The question of literature's material form takes on new significance in the age of electronic literature and digital publication. This is because many people see electronic literature as quintessentially *im*material, as a form that exists without any material support.[14] Representing this view, Sven Birkerts argues that "the printed word on the page is a *thing* [. . . whereas t]he configuration of impulses on a screen is not. . . . The former occupies a position in space—on a page, in a book, and is verifiably there. The latter, once *dematerialized* . . . cannot be said to exist in quite the same way. . . . The same sign, but not the same."[15] Similarly, in his article "The Body of the Text," Raffaele Simone argues that the book is a "graphic materialization" or "physical container" of language, whose own existence is separate and unique from that of the text. For Simone, the discursive body of the text is composed according to laws that do not correspond to the material construction of the book: "The two entities (the book and the text therein contained) are quite separate."[16] In the case of electronic literature, the material "container" of the text becomes, in Simone's words, "immaterial."

Scholars such as these critique the "dematerialization" of literature by digital technologies as, in the words of Ted Striphas, the "toppling of a whole tradition of textual authority."[17] These critics see textual authority as residing in the power of the author who has dominant if not total control over the creation of the text. According to this logic, electronic literature radically deconstructs the very notion of the author and the authority and privilege this subject-position has established throughout the modern period. Once dematerialized, the text becomes open and vulnerable to change by agents who are not the text's original authors. Without a material form to protect it, the text is exposed.

It would be more than easy to read Libros de Mentira books in this way, as "dematerialized." We could read their "fakeness" as evidence that material reality and physical objects are ever more being replaced by simulacra; books no longer exist in our hands as three-dimensional objects that we can touch and smell, but rather as two-dimensional, antiseptic images on computer screens, in the ether. We could understand Libros de Mentira as the epitome of our postmodern condition in which there is no "real" thing, only a copy (of a copy of a copy) of something that was once real but is now obsolete because all we need is the copy. In the early years of the Internet the very vocabulary we used to talk about cyberspace established online activity as a "virtual" world and, therefore, decidedly not "real."[18] Within this conceptualization, the virtual itself is a lie—*una mentira.*

In contrast to these opinions, there are ways in which to read all electronic literature and Libros de Mentira digital books in particular as pointing toward a renewed importance of the material in our postmodern age rather than a retreat from it. Let us start first with the very name of the press, *Libros* de Mentira, and its emphasis on the book form. If we agree that the book is only the material body through which literature reaches its audience, then it seems logical that advances in technology would allow us to bypass what the previously cited critics understand to be the symbolically inconsequential form of the book in favor of a more evolved and less material means of getting literature's artistic content to readers. In other words, there is no practical reason that Libros de Mentira needs to hold on to the concept of the book at all. This fact is evidenced by the many different genres of electronic literature that exist independent of the book form and make no reference to it.[19] Certainly e-books intentionally invoke the memory of "real" books, but this is often because they also exist in paper form. Other forms of writing on the web, including blogging and the many different genres of electronic literature, do not retain the notion of the book for the simple reason that they do not need to because they are not books but rather something else.

And yet this is not what we see happening in Libros de Mentira. Rather than using digital technologies to leave the book format behind in the proverbial dust, Libros de Mentira conceives of this particular graphic materialization of the text as still relevant, even in its reference to books as a "lie." There are many reasons for this. One reason for the ongoing relevance of the book format, according to electronic literature scholar Katherine Hayles, is that readers come to digital works with expectations they already have based on their experience with print media, meaning that digital works must be created with these expectations in mind.[20] Libros de Mentira does this by intentionally exaggerating the embodied experience of reading a paper book while simultaneously creating an experience that is unique to the consumption of digital media.

For instance, all Libros de Mentira digital books look like two-dimensional paper books. Upon selecting a book to read, the first thing a member of the site sees is the book's cover; this typically looks like a paper book cover, except that the cover is slightly open and it moves up and down, almost as an invitation to the reader to open it and see what lies inside. When the reader opens the book, the cover flips over with a "thump" sound, as if it has landed on a table or desk where it virtually sits. Each time the readers turns the page of a Libros de Mentira digital book with the click of a cursor, there is the overt accompaniment of a "swishing" sound that intends to mimic the sound that pages of a paper book make when we turn them. While both of these sounds, the thumping and the swishing, are recognizable to readers, it is obvious that they are exaggerated; opening the cover of a paper book would not make any sound at all if we were holding the book in our hands or if the book did not have a hard cover, and many times turning a paper page makes no sound at all. Design techniques such as these directly connect the experience of reading electronic literature to the act of reading a paper book; in other words, they work to define these digital texts as "books."

But, like most other kinds of electronic literature, Libros de Mentira digital books are influenced by other forms of digital media, such as video games, films, animations, digital arts, graphic design, and electronic and visual culture; as such they engage the senses in ways that are different from the experience of reading a book in print form. This happens primarily through the use of audiovisual media and hypertext. Many Libros de Mentira books stimulate auditory and visual senses through their use of musical accompaniment and/or voice recordings, sometimes performed by the author herself, and almost all of these books contain colorful illustrations and photography. The website also encourages its book makers to think about the length of their books in ways that are specific to web publication, since readers tend to spend less time reading an electronic text than they perhaps would in reading printed material.

The experience of reading online is therefore decidedly different from the experience of reading printed materials, even when the online experience is intentionally designed to mimic the offline experience. Yet rather than establishing the online experience as more or less embodied, these differences remind us that *all* reading practices rely heavily on the body and its relationship to and experience with the text: how we hold it, see it, hear it, and so forth affects the way we think about it and what kinds of feelings and emotions we gain from the act of reading. This understanding of reading stands in direct contrast to the viewpoint of Simone and other critics who see the book form as wholly disassociated from the meaning produced by the text.

Libros de Mentira's decision to make digital "books" rather than some other form of online literary publication (from which there are many to choose) is also a reminder that printed books are equally the product of digital technologies. This point may not be immediately obvious since authorities on the subject of electronic literature often differentiate it from print precisely because of the way in which digital technologies participate in the writing of the text. For example, various electronic literary genres use computer code to write the text, in some cases allowing computer code to determine outcomes of the narrative that the author did not herself conceive, or allowing the reader to use computer code to collaboratively write the text with the author and/or with other readers.[21] It is true that what distinguishes electronic from print literature is that computer code is, as Hayles argues, part of the work.[22] Hayles goes as far as to consider "networked and programmable media as the *material* basis for artistic innovation and creation."[23]

It would be a mistake, however, not to recognize that technology participates in authoring texts produced in print as well. Ever since the invention of the typewriter, authors have strategically used technology to craft the shape of words on a page in a way that contributes to the meanings they present. This is true of choices as seemingly insignificant (but of course not insignificant at all) as font, type size, section headings, chapter titles, and a multitude of other typographical options that technology offers authors as they write the text.[24] Furthermore, Hayles argues that in today's writing and publishing world, almost *all* texts are first created in electronic format and only enter into the printed form once completed.[25] But whereas the presence of technology is most often taken for granted in print, it is impossible to ignore its function in electronic literature, which fuses multimedia and hypertext with discursive language. Perhaps the biggest difference then between electronic and print literature is not that the former allows technology to play an active role in writing the text, but rather that the materiality of electronic literature does not allow this role to be ignored or glossed over as typically happens with print.

This whole discussion is complicated even further when we question what is meant by literary "creation." The Electronic Literature Organization (ELO) distinguishes electronic literature from other forms of writing by its use of technology, arguing that "the confrontation with technology at the level of *creation* is what distinguishes electronic literature from, for example, e-books, digitized versions of print works, and other products of print authors 'going digital.' "[26] Thus electronic literature differs from other forms of digital literature, such as the e-book, in the sense that it uses technology to participate in the writing of the text in ways that are beyond the author's own control. Such works are considered to be "born digital" and are distinguished from texts that were originally created for print culture but that have also been digitized to exist electronically. Thus for both print and electronic literature, the definition of literary "creation" refers solely to the act of writing the text.

Libros de Mentira counters this logic by defining literary creation as both the writing of the text and the making of the book that houses it. Here, the book form does not become immaterial so much as it becomes part of the text itself, and the creation of both requires the use of digital technologies that play a decisive role in the finished literary product. On the website, the act of writing the text and making the book are often the same process because in the creation of the book, members use technology to add media that are part of the both the book and the narrative at the same time. This is both similar to and different from the creation of printed literature. It is different in the sense that it is more dramatized, but it is true that even in traditional print publishing, what we consider to be nonliterary or non-artistic material actually does play a part in how the text constructs meaning. What truly differentiates Libros de Mentira from print culture is that it exaggerates the creativity of bookmaking and its relation to the literary text to the greatest possible extreme. The purpose behind the creation of the website is to enable both writers and bookmakers—the site imagines them to be the same person—to use technology in the creation of a literary text; in other words, the process of writing and the process of bookmaking both count as literary creation.

Libros de Mentira is thus a perfect vehicle through which to think about the book, both the printed codex and the digital book, as a machine. In his essay "Material Matters: The Past and Futurology of the Book," information scholar Paul Duguid reminds us of I. A. Richards's proclamation that "the book is a machine to think with."[27] Duguid uses this concept to oppose what he describes as a "liberationist" theory of literature in which technology can "free" the text from the "imprisonment" or "incarceration" imposed on it by the material constraints of the book form.[28] Instead, he maintains that the book form does not impose material constraints on the text at all but rather provides it with "social resources" that, if removed, must be "reconstituted in some way if the status of the text is to be maintained."[29]

According to this logic, both computer technology and the print book (also a machine) are not separate entities from the discursive text but rather integral components of it. As Duguid explains, "The implication that technologies are just conduits for information produced elsewhere both denies the material role technologies play in producing information and . . . assumes that information has an inherent shape and integrity independent of the system in which it is produced and consumed."[30] Libros de Mentira's reference to its publications as "books" only makes this point more salient. The design of its website and the kinds of activities and services it offers its members invite them to make books with machines, to make books *as* machines, and to conceive of both writing and bookmaking as intimately related processes that rely on the creative use of digital technologies.

Creating a Platform for Cultural Democracy 2.0

Libros de Mentira believes that the Internet and digital technologies are especially adept tools in the democratization of literary culture, and it is not alone in this belief. The invention of new communications technologies has always been tied to democratizing initiatives. Communications scholar Kristin Sorensen has argued that "the development of new media outlets . . . allow[s] narratives to be told from fresh and different points of view, including the perspectives of people whose voices have been marginalized and silenced in traditional media outlets."[31] This is as true of the invention of the printing press as it is of the invention of the Internet: both were originally founded in order to make communication more democratic than earlier technologies would allow. Internet scholar Robert W. McChesney has claimed that "by no means did the printing press generate modern democracy . . . on its own, but it was a precondition for [it to] exist," and digital technologies scholar Ithiel de Sola Pool has famously written that "the printing press was without a doubt the foundation of modern democracy."[32] But scholars such as McChesney, Sola Pool, and Lawrence Lessig, among others, have also noted that as much as the printing press has done to contribute to democracy's development worldwide, it also has been directly responsible for the invention of copyright laws that, over time, have resulted in anti-democratic effects that severely limit the use of cultural products everywhere.[33] Thus while the origins of the printing press are tied to the spirit of free speech and democracy, print culture has evolved into a top-down structure based on limited access and controlled participation.

One of the main purposes for the invention of the Internet was to offer services very similar to those previously provided by print culture, but through a bottom-up model that would grant freer access and participation than the print industry provided. Sociologist David Gauntlett argues that the inventor of the Internet, Tim Berners-Lee, "imagined that browsing the Web would be a matter of writing and editing, not just searching and reading," placing the emphasis on production rather than consumption alone.[34] Despite these intentions, the first version of the Internet, now known as Web 1.0, did not allow for pedestrian participation, and it was not until the emergence of Web 2.0 in the early 2000s that the web's participatory potential became truly radical. Gauntlett claims, "Rather than just seeing the internet as a broadcast channel, which brings an audience to a website (the 1.0 model), Web 2.0 invites users in to play."[35] This invitation to anyone and everyone to use the Internet as a tool of creation is what constituted its democratizing potential and what set Web 2.0 apart, at least initially, from print culture.

While there are critics of the Internet who denounce its democratizing potential, they are far outnumbered by those who see it as a radically democratic tool.[36] Scholars have a number of reasons to justify this latter point of view, the most important of which is that the Internet functions as an egalitarian structure of communication. The printing press, on the other hand, like broadcast media, creates a center-periphery, or one-way street structure of communication in which middlemen, mediators, and gatekeepers filter what information reaches the public and when.[37] This structure assigns the recipient of information the passive role of reader, listener, or viewer.[38] In contrast to this model, scholars describe the Internet as an egalitarian, point-to-point, or horizontal structure in which independent units communicate directly with one another and without the filter of middlemen gatekeepers.[39]

In the spirit of Web 2.0, Libros de Mentira has designed its website as a platform where users can upload whatever they want without the mediation of editors. The idea is inclusive and participatory. Besides providing the digital tools required for electronic book production and the web space needed for publication, the only other intervention that Libros de Mentira editors make in this do-it-yourself process is to ensure that all books published on the site adhere to the press's online "Terms of Use." Even the decision of genre classification is left up to the individual author/bookmaker. This approach strives to democratize literary culture by equalizing the hierarchical structure of the print world, giving individuals the opportunity to act as productive agents rather than as passive recipients. The ability of members of the general public to share their literary creations with other members of the public without having to obtain the permission of authorities to do so is a democratic gesture in any society.[40] In light of Chile's recent history, when citizens had to ask for state permission to publish literary works, the opportunity that Libros de Mentira offers Chileans to publish works without permission from anyone is an advance in cultural democratization.

The website is designed in a number of ways that encourage readers to transform their relationship to literature from that of passive recipient to that of productive agent by acting as literary critics, editors, archivists, and bookmakers rather than readers alone. One way it does this is by allowing members to determine at least some of the press's marketing decisions based on their own reading preferences. The site's homepage features two "readers' choice" titles, one determined by the number of times a book has been read and the other based on the amount of reader votes a book has received (readers have the option to vote on every title, and all titles display the number of votes they have received).

By showcasing books with the highest number of votes on its homepage, the website lets readers know that their preferences and personal literary tastes matter and have practical consequences to the operation of the press. This strategy is by no means unique to Libros de Mentira or even to the Internet (on the contrary, it is now commonplace in today's mediatized cultural marketplace), but it is especially common on the Internet because of its ease in facilitating collective participation on a large scale. What makes Libros de Mentira slightly different is its motivation for using such a strategy. Commercial cultural producers incite audience participation as a way of keeping users on their websites as long as possible, which can lead to increased sales of products or increased sales of advertising on the site. Libros de Mentira has no such economic motivation since it does not sell anything, including advertising space (at least not yet). Allowing audience votes to partly determine what books the press will promote on its homepage proves to the reader that her personal literary tastes matter and that she does not need to rely on cultural authorities to tell her what to read or what definitions of literary taste she should adopt. Instead, she can look to her peers for this kind of guidance or decide for herself.[41]

The press also invites readers to act as literary critics through the comment box that is attached to every book published on the site. Members can leave comments and critiques on any digital book they read, and other readers, including the book's author, are free to respond and engage in conversation or debate. The press strategically uses the Internet to break down the social differences separating amateur readers from professional critics, and any member of the website can simultaneously act as both. The result is a restructuring of the hierarchical divide between professional and amateur that is inherent in commercial print culture.

Just as Libros de Mentira works to dissolve the distinction between "reader" and "critic," so too does it work to weaken the barriers that print culture has established between "author" and "book manufacturer." The website offers writers the digital tools to make their own books for web publication, meaning that the person who writes the text is also intended to be the same person who turns that text into a book that can then be consumed by readers once it is published. The press conflates the work of author and bookmaker by referring to both as "author." In reality, the website goes even further than that, compounding the multiple subject-positions of reader, critic, editor, author, and bookmaker all into the single signifier of "author."

Such a move is an attempt to alter the modes of literary production that have been firmly set in place since the onset of industrial capitalism. As LOM Ediciones directing editor Paulo Slachevsky has commented, "Since the nineteenth century we've talked about the alienation of capitalist production. And it doesn't cease to be comical that in an environment in which we could create different experiences, we reproduce a form of work marked by segmentation: the author writes, the editor selects and edits, the printer prints, the distributor distributes, the bookseller sells and the consumer reads. Each one is limited to doing only that which they are assigned in their part of the chain and that kills the book, both in terms of its possibility and its reality."[42] Libros de Mentira sees the Internet as precisely the kind of environment that Slachevsky refers to here, in which the possibility to conflate these separate tasks and their laborers is finally upon us. Thus, just as Cartonera presses use artisanal modes of literary production in an attempt to deconstruct the hierarchical divisions that capitalism has imposed within the field of cultural production, so too does this press channel the egalitarian potential of the Internet for the same purposes.

Anyone who creates a Libros de Mentira account and becomes a member of the site appropriates the title of "author" regardless of whether they publish anything on the site or not, and regardless of whether they publish something they originally wrote or a text written by a third party. For instance, when creating a personal account on the site, new members are asked to identify themselves in a number of different ways, including by age, gender, nationality, name, username, photo, or avatar. Most important, members are asked from what subject-position they will be sharing information on the website: as a "reader" or as a "writer." The dropdown box reads "I write as (*Escribo como*)," and then members can choose to publically declare themselves as either a reader or a writer—the two options given by the website. Yet despite this choice, all users are eventually interpellated as "authors."

For instance, when I created my own Libros de Mentira account, I self-identified as a reader (*lector*) named Jane Griffin from the United States. Thus when any other member of the site goes to my member profile page, they see my avatar (I chose one of the options provided by Libros de Mentira although I could have uploaded a photo of myself or any other image of my choosing), my username, and my status as a "reader" from the United States. Yet my page, like all member pages, displays two main sections: the first, "About the Author," provides a space where I can write a self-description; the second, "Books Published by the Author," includes a list of all the works I have published with the press.[43] These subject headings do not change even when the member has, as in my case, self-identified as a "reader" and not a "writer."

Users who are not sure if they want to upload their own writings for publication on the site (an action that requires membership) may still wish to become members of the site so that they can leave comments on digital books they read (an action that also requires membership). A large number of Libros de Mentira members choose to make and publish books on the site that they themselves did not write, and these books still appear under the heading "Books published by the author." Whether or not we can or should refer to members as "authors" if they themselves did not write the discursive content of the digital book they publish is a topic worthy of discussion. What is certain is the democratizing potential that this label offers; it is an affect that is similar to Ergo Sum's attempt to empower women by getting to them to think of themselves as published authors.[44]

Of course the Internet has everything to do with why Libros de Mentira can claim so many authors, and not only because it uses template software to do so. Print publishing must work within certain material constraints that limit the number of books a press can produce and distribute and, consequently, the number of authors it can contract to publish. Internet publishers do not have to pay for any of the raw materials required for print production, nor do they pay warehousing or shipping costs for physical distribution. An online press only needs to make one copy of a digital book because that one book can be read an infinite number of times by any of the billion people currently on the Internet.[45] This means that online publishers can support a larger number of authors, since the more books they publish, the more authors they can claim. As Lessig argues, "Digital technologies have inspired an extraordinary range of creativity in part because they lower the media market's barriers to entry, which in turn invites a much wider range of participation."[46] The technology of the Internet allows presses like Libros de Mentira to massify the political impulse we saw Ergo Sum initiate on a more limited and grassroots level; it also provides a notion of massification that is similar to the one articulated by Cartonera publishers.

Libros de Mentira further increases the range of participation by not paying authors any capital gains for the distribution of their texts. It is actually an economic incentive for many Chilean writers to have their works published online for free, given that independent presses in Chile commonly charge authors to publish and distribute their works—an effect of the neoliberal restructuring of Chile's editorial industry.[47] Not only does Libros de Mentira not charge members for publication or distribution fees, but it also provides them with the tools needed to publish a digital book without charging a fee. Other options of creating electronic literature require authors to become intimately familiar with using and writing computer code—a skill they most likely would have to pay for through education and/or training.[48] Libros de Mentira offers authors an alternative for which they need no such education or training but instead are provided a free template for making and publishing their own digital books. Granted, this template is limited in its features and the final product is wholly distinct from electronic literature written with computer code, but it is freely available to the public. Another advantage for authors publishing with Libros de Mentira is that they are not responsible for buying server space on which to publish their works, since that is provided by the press for free.

Readers also benefit from the website's free platform. Libros de Mentira is able to give its digital books away for free in part because it does not have the overhead costs of paying for the kinds of material production and distribution associated with print publication, and it does not pay its authors. As a result, the press can reach a greater number of readers, especially those who might not be able to afford the cost of paper books.[49] This is of special importance in Chile, where print books are notoriously expensive for a number of reasons, not least of which is the 20-percent VAT tax inherited from the Pinochet regime. By giving its digital books away for free, Libros de Mentira makes literature equally available to all Chilean Internet users, which is over half of the nation's population.[50]

At least one user of the website praises the press for making literature so accessible. In a comment box on the press's "Who We Are" page, Jenny Maturana writes, "I had never been able to read anything by [Alberto] Fuguet before, [but] today, thanks to your help, I was able to read one of his books, so thank you."[51] We cannot know for sure if Maturana had never been able to read anything by Fuguet because of economic barriers or other circumstances, but what is certain from this comment is that Libros de Mentira gave her access to a text that she did not have access to before, and that she was grateful for this. Alberto Fuguet is a prominent figure in the Nueva Narrativa Chilena (New Chilean Narrative), and by reading his work, Maturana becomes more literate in her own national culture and gains cultural capital.

Through analyzing Libros de Mentira's website design and the kinds of services it provides to its members, we can see that the press adheres to two fundamental principles that structure its use of the Internet as a tool in the democratization of literary culture in Chile. The first of these is the legitimation of the amateur. We have seen how the press encourages everyday readers to act as literary critics and how it values and respects their reading tastes, allowing them to at least partially determine how the press will promote its catalog. Toward a similar end, the website classifies all its members as "authors," even those individuals who themselves do not write the text of the digital books they publish. Both impulses work to erode the social disparities that the capitalist field of cultural production has established between professionals and amateurs and between cultural producers and consumers. In addition, the website's method of book design involves aesthetic choices, thus encouraging the bookmaker to see herself as an artist and encouraging readers to see her book as an art object.

The second principle at the heart of Libros de Mentira's democratizing ethos is its commitment to giving away its books for free. In doing so, the press challenges the neoliberal business model of the global publishing industry and defines the value of literary works not in terms of their monetary worth—which we know is so often determined arbitrarily—but rather by its social significance within a definitive community of readers and writers. For much of the time, the social significance or value of Libros de Mentira digital books lies precisely in the reconfigured social relations that members of the website establish for themselves and with one another through their activity on the site. The site prompts amateur writers and readers to recognize their own intellectual and creative skills and encourages others in their communities (both on and offline) to recognize them too.

Before moving on, it is important to recognize the limitations and possible contradictions inherent in these democratizing practices. The first of these relates to the readers' choice categories of "Most Read" and "Most Votes" books on the site. In the first place, the "Most Read" qualifier is not an accurate gauge of how many users have actually read a piece of work but only of how many have clicked to open a particular digital book and perhaps even flipped through its pages; in this sense the "Most Read" registry serves the same purpose as the sales ratings of commercial books: anyone can buy a book without reading it. The only real indicator of the reading practices and preferences of Libros de Mentira users is captured in the comments left on individual books.

A second consideration is that tracking user preferences and habits of behavior on the Internet is problematic. One of the most dangerous aspects of the Internet is that corporations and governments use it to track users' every move and gather data regarding virtually everything about them.[52] There is no reason to believe that Libros de Mentira is using or would use this information for commercial gain, but it could decide to at any point. Moreover, if pressured by authorities, Libros de Mentira might release details about readers' activity to a third party, which in turn could be used against members of the site. We saw earlier how interested Chile's military government was in citizens' reading preferences and practices and how it strategically sought out and then used that information to classify individuals as threats to national security. It is not at all inconceivable to think that this could happen again, even under a democratically elected government. However, it is possible for users to create an anonymous account with Libros de Mentira, and since no one ever uses a credit card to pay for anything on the website, authorities would have to go to greater lengths to match user data to actual people, in contrast to the easier access to personal data that commercial websites permit.

A third concern is the lack of options available through Web 2.0. For instance, as Jaron Lanier points out, Web 2.0 limits the ability of users to express themselves creatively on the web. Lanier's problem with Web 2.0 is that although it allows more people to produce creative content, it does this primarily through the use of templates that reduce self-expression to a limited number of pre-fixed options, including martial status, nationality, gender, and so forth. This almost perfectly describes what is happening on my own Libros de Mentira member profile page. I have chosen to describe myself as a "reader," which is a marker that the site itself offered me; but the site refuses to accept this identity, insisting instead on constantly referring to me as an "author" through the subject titles on my member page. Libros de Mentira thinks of me as an author and, more important, suggests that other members of the site do so as well, even when I myself have chosen a different identity.

It might be, however, that the progressive possibilities of interpellating all members as "authors" outweigh the problems associated with limiting individual choice. For one thing, the author label lends credibility to novice writers hoping to get their start at a professional writing career. Since its inception, Libros de Mentira has always sought to provide a venue for unknown authors to gain public visibility in the hopes of launching literary careers in print and with commercial publishers. The founders of the press established this goal precisely because they did not see print culture as openly accepting of unknown or unpublished writers.[53] Another possible benefit pertains to novice writers with no ambitions of launching a professional career but who nonetheless wish to share their artistic tastes and literary creations with the public. Having appropriated the title of "author," most amateur writers are more likely to consider themselves as such, as someone with a public voice who possesses a certain measure of cultural agency, who deserves to have her creative voice be heard, and who is heard by a public audience. For Chilean members of the website, the symbolic significance of such a title is no small thing considering that only a few decades ago, the military state retained full control over who could claim this title and who could earn the social privileges it provided.

One final caveat concerning this model is that although it attempts to elevate the amateur to a social status on par with that of the professional, it does not in fact displace or even replace professionals or cultural elites from the field of literary production. This is evidenced by the fact that Libros de Mentira has an editorial board that makes decisions about what to promote on the site's homepage, as well as which of the digital books published on its site it will produce in paper book form. It is true that the majority of Libros de Mentira members who publish books on the site do so without editorial mediation; however, it would be inaccurate to say that the press's web platform is a purely horizontal communicative structure. The editorial staff does read through each book published on the site and selects what it considers to be some of the best books, which it then posts on the site's home page. The website states: "The press will make periodic selections from material that users upload to the site. Chosen works will go on to form part of the DISTINGUISHED BOOKS section on the homepage. Librosdementira reserves the right to edit and/or modify the works to be included in this section so that they meet the quality requirements demanded by the press."[54]

This selection and modification process only affects a small number of titles, but it does mean that the press's website is something halfway between a hierarchal and horizontal structure of communication. Such an in-between model has its benefits for amateur authors; selected works appear on the site's homepage alongside those of professional authors, most of whom belong to Chile's national literary canon.

Furthermore, the press invites commercial book publishers to use its online services in the same way that it invites literary novices to do so. On the "Terms of Use" page of its website, Libros de Mentira states that other presses may use the press's platform to "publish and promote commercial works, provided that they subscribe to our specific agreement for these types of entities. The sale of books (in physical or digital format) outside the channels that Librosdementira has established for this kind of labor remains strictly prohibited."[55] Libros de Mentira also explicitly prohibits commercial entities from providing their contact information on the website; if they wish to publish this information, they must do so through the website's administrators. In this way, commercial presses can use the website in much the same way that the music, film, and television industries (among others) currently use YouTube and other free media-sharing websites: as a mode of free advertising.

Thus Libros de Mentira's online press and social media website is not simply a space for amateur literary enthusiasts to communicate with one another without the mediation of content gatekeepers. It is also a place where amateurs and professionals can meet and engage in dialogue with one another and where professionals can further their own public prominence. We heard scholars above describe the Internet as an egalitarian space where individuals can communicate directly with one another rather than through cultural gatekeepers. Internet scholar Jeff Jarvis also believes that the Internet allows everyday citizens to speak to and be heard by institutional authorities rather than simply communicate with their peers, which is why he sees the Internet as a democratic public space: "Publicness is a sign of our empowerment at their [institutional authorities'] expense. Dictators and politicians, media moguls and marketers try to tell us what to think and say. But now, in a truly public society, they must listen to what we say."[56] Jarvis's coupling of "dictators" with "media moguls" is more than appropriate within the context of post-1973 Chilean literary culture. While it is not the implicit intention of Libros de Mentira that members use its site to speak back directly to their government officials, it is one of the press's goals that commercial publishers will take note of what is published on the site and take an interest in its authors.

Using a Platform for Cultural Democracy 2.0

It is clear that Libros de Mentira has designed its website to be used as a platform for democratizing literary culture, but it remains to be seen whether or not members themselves actually use it this way. Our demographic knowledge of Libros de Mentira users is limited by the fact that readers can consume texts anonymously without leaving any trace of their own identity. However, we do know that users must contain at least reading competency in Spanish since the site's administrators and members alike use Spanish as their principal language of communication. The only real indication of the number of people accessing reading materials on the site is the list of books singled out as "Most Read." For instance, at the time of writing, the "Most Read" book on the site had been viewed 68,025 times, the second had been viewed 18,948 times, the third 12,862 times, the fourth 10,430 times, and the fifth 3,169 times. We cannot be sure that the 31,942 times a text has been viewed means that it was viewed by 31,942 different readers, since one person could read a digital book multiple times. But in comparison to the low print runs of Chile's independent print industry, which tend not to exceed two thousand at a time, these figures seem to indicate that a relatively large number of people are using the Libros de Mentira online platform to access digital texts.

Although we have limited knowledge of the category of people who just read books on this website, we do know slightly more about people who actively contribute to its content in the form of publishing a digital book or leaving a comment about one. Both of these activities require membership on the site, which in turn requires individuals to claim a national identity. When we look at the nationality of members who publish books on the site and those who leave comments on books they have read, we realize immediately that the majority of people using this site are Chilean. Those few members not from Chile are almost always from other Latin American countries (including members from Columbia, Guatemala, Mexico, Peru, and Argentina), and still others are Chileans living in the diaspora (such as in New Zealand and Japan).[57] The Chilean majority is somewhat ironic considering that the very inquiry into members' nationality suggests that the press anticipates members from all over the globe—an expectation that is more than appropriate given the commonly held assumption that the Internet is a global village. In an e-mail to its members, Libros de Mentira administrators highlight community-building as a "principal interest" of the site;[58] from its active members we can see that this community, despite inhabiting a global stage, is constructed primarily along national lines.

The predominance of *la chilenidad* (Chileanness) on the website suggests that individuals' use of the site is, at least to a large degree, dependent on what we might call "real world" social relationships; members find the site by hearing about it from someone they know personally (which is indeed how I first found out about Libros de Mentira), or by coming into contact with Libros de Mentira offline through the many literary activities it organizes in and around Santiago de Chile. Another possible reason for the high number of Chilean members is that the press's editorial project specializes in Chile's national literary cannon. The press has two "collections" of works that it compiles independent of members' voluntary submissions, and all of the works included in these two collections are written by Chilean authors who hold established positions in the national literary canon. The press's ability to build community online is thus inseparable from its own situatedness, and that of its members, in *off*line communities, preventing us not only from conceiving of the Internet as different from "real" life, but also from thinking of it as something that weakens feelings of national belonging in favor of building global communities.

Within Libros de Mentira's online community, users act in two different ways: as literary consumers and producers. In thinking of how members consume literature on the website, the first and most obvious question relates to what type of digital texts readers like to read the most. One indicator of the most popular texts is found in the site's listings of "Most Read" and "Most Votes" titles. These listings serve as an up-to-date register of the texts that users read and vote on the most. One of the most striking characteristics of these registers is that (at the time of writing) the top five winners of the "Most Votes" are all unknown and nonprofessional writers. One of these amateur authors is responsible for four of the five books that have received the most reader votes. This tells us that members spend more time reading works by amateur writers and editors than they do reading and voting on works written by professionals.[59]

Another important indicator of how members use the website is the "comment box" attached to each Libros de Mentira publication. The comment box has become a staple feature of Web 2.0, and Internet users commonly use it as a means of debating with one another over something they have read or seen on a particular site. Libros de Mentira members seldom use the comment box for this purpose, preferring instead to use it as a space to communicate directly with the text's author who sometimes, although rarely, responds to the comments posted. In the congregate, members' comments to authors are overwhelmingly positive and congratulatory; readers almost never use the comment box to express anything negative or overly critical of a digital book they have read.

There are many possible reasons for this, the first being that politeness is a principal aspect of the Chilean national character. Because the majority of members leaving comments are Chilean, their respectful demeanor is consistent with their national identity.[60] Even more likely, however, is the fact that members comment more on texts written by amateur writers than they do on works written by authors whose literary careers are already established. By receiving encouragement and support from their peers, novice authors will be more likely to continue exploring and refining their literary talents. The positive support from readers of amateur writers on the site suggests that members share the press's own goal of converting the public into active literary agents rather than passive consumers.

A telling example of this phenomenon is the digital book *Pandemonium,* by Argentine author Cristian M. Vázquez. In a comment to this book, Carlos Toledo writes to the author, "Cristian, I loved your book. I don't know why but there are parts that remind me of the Macanudo comic strips by Liniers. You are charming and profound, and I am grateful to you for having shared your poems with us (I speak in the plural, since to share a book on this illusionary website is an act of generosity to readers). I give you five stars and a hug. Here's hoping the administration puts you on the Distinguished List!"[61] Here Toledo publically recognizes Vázquez's work as on par with that of an esteemed professional writer (Liniers) and urges the editorial board of Libros de Mentira to validate Vázquez's work by consecrating it as distinguished.

On the other hand, the transformation from passive-consumer to active-creator only extends, in the activity of Libros de Mentira members, to the role of "author" rather than to that of "critic." As we saw earlier, the press intentionally designed its website to interpellate the average reader as a literary critic. Based on the content of their remarks in the comment box, however, Libros de Mentira members themselves do not yet seem comfortable with or ready to assume this role: their comments are far too complimentary to qualify as true literary criticism, and they are personal and emotive rather than displaying knowledge of literary history or theory. From the standpoint of artistic taste, members' use of the comment box leaves us little reason to believe that they use the website to acquire a more sophisticated definition of the literature's aesthetic value.

The question of artistic taste is central in understanding how members act as literary producers on the website, but with regard to their reading practices and use of the comment box, it suffices to say that Libros de Mentira members seem more interested in creating social bonds and artistic solidarity with other members than they do in appropriating an identity of literary authority or cultural critic. This could be because they do not deem themselves worthy of appropriating elite privilege, or it could be that they reject positions of privilege and the uneven balance of power they afford.

The comment box also reveals that the act of consuming a digital book inspires additional cultural consumption, production, and critical thought. Members frequently comment that a particular text inspired them to revisit a song, movie, or another literary text. They also use the comment box to continue a dialogue inspired by the text itself, to express their own opinions on a topic introduced by the text, or to philosophize about a theme advanced by that text. And they express how a digital book inspired them either to start writing or to continue to work on a literary piece they have already started. Consuming cultural products is an age-old method of forging social bonds and building community, and, as Benedict Anderson has shown us, written artifacts—specifically the novel and the newspaper—hold a special power in this regard.[62] What Web 2.0 changes about this process of social formation is that average citizens no longer bond with one another through their consumption of cultural products made by industry leaders and cultural professionals, but rather by consuming objects made by their peers.[63] Libros de Mentira's presence on the Internet establishes its site as a public space where amateur cultural actors meet to share, discuss, and inspire one another, which results in further creative and intellectual activity.

Finally, the remarks in the comment box reveal that members use the website not only to gain access to publications that are new to them, but also that they wish to use and enjoy those publications in ways that exceed the possibilities offered by their digital format. Over and again members use the comment box to express their desire to have a paper copy of the digital book they have read or to ask the author directly how they can obtain such a copy. Their reasons for wanting a physical copy vary, but for the most part they stem from a desire to consume and share the literary objects independent of digital technologies. For instance, María Francisca Sasso Lorca writes that the digital book she read, "creat[ed] an almost guilty desire to have a copy of this fake book in paper to share with my students. I would happily receive such a copy."[64] Likewise, Mariel Sanhueza comments, "I want to have it in my hands so that I can look at these stupendous drawings again and again without having to turn on my computer!"[65] And Carmen Gloria Salas Jara praises the digital book *Baila* (by Virginia Herrera), stating, "I loved this book! Beautiful, and without a doubt a book that I would want to have in my own small library to thumb through its pages everyday. Cheers, CG."[66]

These comments reflect what we heard Katherine Hayles describe above: namely, that reading is an embodied experience and that our ability to comprehend and digest a text is directly informed by the material object through which that text reaches us. Such a boisterous request for the printed page is a clear sign that Libros de Mentira members are open to experimenting with nonprint forms of literary production and consumption, but that they are not yet ready to wholly abandon print culture for digital technologies.

The pleasure they receive from the experience of reading is still intimately bound to the book as a physical object. In this way, and somewhat ironically, Libros de Mentira and other forms of digital publishing support and reaffirm the endurance of print within literary culture rather than supplanting it altogether.

Analyzing how members use the website to create and publish digital books is a more complicated task than analyzing their habits of consumption, and this is in large part because of the difficulty in differentiating the person who wrote the text from the individual who uploaded it and published it as a digital book. Despite the complicated question of authorship on the site, we can rightly identify various groups of producers who use the Libros de Mentira platform to publish texts. The editors of Libros de Mentira themselves create a large portion of works published on the site in the form of edited collections (namely poetry and narrative). However, the press also claims responsibility for publishing other texts on the site that are written by third parties; Plato's *Allegory of the Cave,* for example, displays Libros de Mentira itself as its "author." There are also a number of iconic authors of world literature whose works are published on the website, from Edgar Allan Poe to Franz Kafka, and their digital books list the author him/herself as the party responsible for uploading and publishing the text. Because it would be impossible for deceased authors to upload their own works or create their own member pages and author biographies, we can assume that the press itself is responsible for the uploading of these books and their authors' member pages, creating the illusion that world-famous writers have become members of the website and use it in the same way that ordinary people do.[67]

This illusion is even more powerful in the case of living Chilean authors whose place within the national literary canon is established. Because they are still alive, their membership and activity on the site seem on par with those of everyday, average users. Yet it is unlikely that this is true. As with the digital books published by world-famous writers, texts by national literary celebrities exhibit a more professional production value than those uploaded and published by amateur members.[68]

Carmen Berenguer, Alejandra Costamagna, Alberto Fuguet, Jaime Collyer, Jorge Montealegre, Ramón Díaz Eterovic, and Pía Barros are just some examples of publically recognized and established Chilean writers who have published digital books with Libros de Mentira. Almost all these authors were invited by the press to select a previously unedited work to publish as part of the press's narrative and poetry collections, and they accepted that offer in an act of solidarity with a new and experimental publishing house and as an expression of their support of alternative and noncapitalist forms of literary publication and distribution.[69] Their willingness to publish with the online press may also be an attempt to connect with new audiences or to publish works whose content lends itself to digital publication. More important, the inclusion of works written by critically acclaimed Chilean authors on the website grants legitimacy to all the other digital books and authors published by the press.

But again, we should be wary of assuming that the presence of their publications on the site levels the playing field between professional and amateur cultural producers. The activity of Ernesto Langer as a Libros de Mentira member exemplifies the divide that continues to exist between professional and amateur literary agents on the site. Langer is an interesting case because his own literary credentials fall somewhere in between those of an acclaimed national author and those of an amateur writer, and his behavior on the Libos de Mentira website reflects this midway cultural position. Langer is not as well known or established as some of the other professional writers who publish with Libros de Mentira (most of his works have been self-published and he does not list any awards in his writer's biography), but he has published with the esteemed LOM Ediciones, has written for some national newspapers, and is currently the editor of the Chilean literary website Escritores.cl, where he has published extensively.

As opposed to Langer, none of the national authors who were invited to publish works as part of Libros de Mentira's narrative and poetry collections have participated in any other capacity on the website: they have not responded to other members' comments to their work (which are few, but they do exist), nor have they commented on any other digital book on the site—demonstrating that they use the platform differently than does the average amateur user. Langer, on the other hand, frequently comments on other members' writings. Yet unlike amateur members, Langer is only one of two Libros de Mentira participants I have found to comment negatively on a piece of writing published on the site. This is surely because his publications with commercial presses, namely LOM, consecrate him as a more legitimate author and grant him literary authority to express his critical opinions more freely than the average member may be comfortable doing. Langer's activity on the site shows that despite the illusion of equality that the member profile establishes between professionals and amateurs, the two groups use the website in very different ways and seldom, if ever, interact directly with one another or assume the cultural and social position of the other.

A third category of individuals publishing works on this site is made up of independent Chilean print presses, cultural and academic institutions, and government agencies. Libros de Mentira's editorial team intentionally designed the site for the purpose of being used by such organizations, and it openly encourages other literary producers to publish their own works through its platform. Not surprisingly, many of the presses who have accepted this invitation are also small, independent, and even alternative literary producers, including Editorial Viceral and Olga Cartonera. Like the established Chilean writers who publish with the press, these small publishers most likely participate on the Libros de Mentira website in an act of solidarity with the press and its noncapitalist cultural politics; and rather than lending cultural legitimacy to the online press vis-à-vis their own established reputation, as is the case with award-winning national writers, their collaboration with Libros de Mentira strengthens their shared commitment to local and anti-corporate literary production in Chile. That does not mean, however, that these presses do not publish digital books with Libros de Mentira in order to advance their own individual interests, including commercial gain. They most certainly do. These small print presses take advantage of the free and wide-scale distribution provided by Libros de Mentira's Internet platform to promote themselves and drum up business.[70]

Free advertising is also the reason that larger institutions that are not necessarily as progressive in their cultural politics as Libros de Mentira also publish their texts with this online press. Perhaps most surprising in this regard is the presence of Chile's Consejo Nacional de la Cultura y las Artes (National Council for Culture and the Arts, CNCA), which used the web platform to promote its 2013 book *El fútbol también se lee* (Soccer is also for reading). This collection of stories about soccer served as an advertising tool to promote a writing contest co-created by the CNCA and the Federación de Fútbol de Chile (Chile's National Soccer Federation). Contest winners received free tickets for themselves and invited guests to attend professional soccer matches in Santiago.

It is not surprising that the CNCA would have partnered with Chilean professional soccer while it was under the administration of President Sebastián Piñera, which privileged corporate culture. Rather than proliferating the idea of literature as a social good capable of inciting intellectual development, social formation, and/or political consciousness, this book constructs the acts of reading and writing as advertising tools used for the purpose of strengthening Chile's highly corporate and incredibly lucrative professional soccer industry. Thus while the cultural politics of Libros de Mentira itself attempt to weaken corporate hegemony within Chilean literary culture, its platform is still used by other entities whose own goals stand in counter-distinction to those of the online press.

Another group of literary producers publishing digital books on the Libros de Mentira website is exactly the type of cultural actor that the online press seeks to target most directly: amateur writers looking to launch or advance a professional career in the arts. These members almost always self-identify as such by using their member profile pages to direct readers to their own personal web pages, where more of their artistic production is available to the public.[71] Without a doubt, Guillermo Uribe P. stands out within this group as proof that the Libros de Mentira platform does indeed advance the writing careers of unknown authors in a way that is comparable, if not superior, to what is possible through the means of traditional print publishers.

Uribe researches and teaches pedagogy, specializing in the high school level, and he published his book *Educación Tecnológica Primero Medio Guías y Experiencias en borrador* (Technical education for high school: Guides and experiences in progress) with Libros de Mentira on September 22, 2011.[72] At the time of writing, this digital book has been read 18,948 times, making it the second "Most Read" book on the website. Uribe acknowledges that he created the book in the hopes that instructional materials would become "more enjoyable"; its enthusiastic reception by the Libros de Mentira online community seems to prove that he has succeeded in this regard.[73] In addition to its high rate of circulation, it is one of the most talked-about books found on the Libros de Mentira website. Almost all the members who left comments on this book are themselves educators; they praised Uribe for his contribution to their field of pedagogy, expressing their desire to use the book in their classrooms and asking where and how they could get hard copies for their students.

Even though Uribe is not writing literature, but rather pedagogical practicum, he is still using the Libros de Mentira platform in the way for which it was intended. And it is having an impact. Not only are readers consuming his text in large quantities, but they are also applying it in a "real world" context with their students (or at least expressing the desire to do so in their comments about the book). Conversely, the Libros de Mentira platform is giving readers access to a text that they themselves claim they need and want and that they are seemingly not finding through other venues. The press's administrative team also left a comment on this book, reaffirming Uribe's use of the website as the essence of the press itself, writing that "works like yours give meaning to our day-to-day toils."[74] Both Uribe himself and everyone else who left comments on his book self-identify as Chilean, thus proving that, at least in this one case, Libros de Mentira is succeeding in providing Chileans with greater access to modes of publication and circulation and in giving readers greater access to reading materials in the postdictatorship period.

One of the most interesting groups of individuals publishing books on the Libros de Mentira website consists of people who write as a hobby and who are not interested in parlaying their amateur status into a professional career. We can divide this group into two separate categories: amateur writers and amateur archivists. The first category is different from the amateur writers we described above in that its members write only for pleasure and use the Libros de Mentira platform to share their creativity with others, rather than as an attempt to gain notoriety and professional credibility. On their member profile pages, they often qualify their dilettante status by listing their nonliterary career first, and then go on to describe themselves as "an amateur writer/fan," as a "frequent reader and occasional writer," or as using "writing as a form of expressing my view of the world."[75]

The way in which these amateur writers describe their work also gives us reason to believe that were it not for the Libros de Mentira platform, they might not have attempted to publish their literary works. For example, Jeanette González says that her digital book *Al arrogante pájaro* (To the arrogant bird) is her first publication, and goes on to say, "I began writing this text around the middle of 2008 . . . in 2009 I gave it up as done and forgotten, until now, when I have decided to edit and publish it. I hope you enjoy reading it."[76] González admits to giving up on the book "until now" when she decided to publish it on the Libros de Mentira website, suggesting that had it not been for the opportunity this site provided her, she might never have made her writing available to the public, which has viewed it 328 times.

Within this subcategory of amateur writers, two stand out as particularly exemplary because of their success in grabbing the attention of Libros de Mentira readers. The first of these is Rosemarie Brand H., who wrote the digital book *Poemas cortos* (Short Poems), which was uploaded and published by "Romy" on January 10, 2012. Besides Romy's Chilean nationality, we know virtually nothing about either Rosemarie Brand H. or Romy, except that the two could very well be the same person, since "Romy" would be a reasonable nickname or username for "Rosemarie." *Poemas cortos* is a book of very short poems whose simplicity seems to be the work of a novice poet. Despite the plainness of the text, or perhaps because of it, it has been viewed 7,603 times (at the time of writing). The second outstanding example in this group is Roberto Rabi, whose self-description on his member profile page consists of only three words: "Simply for pleasure."[77] Rabi has uploaded and published five original texts, four of which fall into the "Most Votes" category; the fact that Rabi's texts occupy four of the five spots within the "Most Votes" category means that Libros de Mentira readers have given more votes to Rabi than to any other author on the site. Because of their lack of experience and layperson status, both Rabi and Romy would most likely not find publishing opportunities in the traditional literary market. But on the Libros de Mentira website, they are both incredibly successful with this large online literary community.

The second category of literary amateurs publishing digital books with Libros de Mentira is what we might consider archivists. These are members whose primary literary interests reside in reading rather than writing and who publish texts that they themselves did not compose.[78] In their selection of which texts to upload and publish, these members act as curators and editors, using their own judgment and literary taste to determine which parts of their own personal libraries to share with the public in digital form. This style of literary publication is common on the Libros de Mentira website and, therefore, is a much better gauge of members' literary taste than the less frequently used comment box. Moreover, the fact that many of these types of publications have become some of the most widely viewed and voted on digital books on the site demonstrates that readers appreciate and value the archival work of other members and share similar aesthetic sensibilities.

There are a number of members specializing in this kind of curatorial activity on the site, but two in particular stand out as noteworthy. The first is Patricio Meneses, whose 2011 publication of a Spanish-language translation of *Evangelion,* an internationally popular Japanese comic book series, is the fifth-most viewed digital book on the Libros de Mentira website (at the time of writing). Meneses has published volumes 1 through 13 of this series with the online press and describes himself as a compulsive comic book reader whose preferences lie in the Japanese tradition but who also enjoys other international comic franchises. Libros de Mentira readers share Meneses' love of comic books and graphic literature, specifically Japanese manga and animé genres, as is evidenced not only by the number of times Meneses' *Evangelion Vol. 1* has been viewed (3,852 times), but also by the number of other digital books published on the website that belong to this genre.

Were Meneses simply to collect this series without sharing it publically, he would be acting as merely a private collector or hobbyist, but in making his private collection public in digital form, he seeks to impart his literary tastes to others. His Libros de Mentira member page, where all his digital publications are catalogued, serves as something of a self-created canon of what are, according to him, the most important texts to read within this particular genre. Whereas we saw earlier that Libros de Mentira members are reluctant to accept the role of active literary critic that the press extends to them vis-à-vis the comment box, the example of Meneses and of many others like him proves that members are much more comfortable critiquing literature from the position of archivist or editor. Such a position transforms these members' passive role as literary consumer into a more authoritative position of expert autodidact. Indeed, within the Libros de Mentira online community, there is no doubt that Patricio Meneses has established himself as the leading authority on Japanese comics.

In using the Internet to publish texts written by third parties, Libros de Mentira members are also able to diversify the variety of literary texts available to Chilean readers, a latitude that stands in contrast to the dictatorship years, when circulation was controlled by the state. An excellent example of a member who has contributed to this diversification is Francis Villegas, a Chilean who has uploaded and published eight pieces of writings that all fall squarely within a Marxist philosophical tradition. One of those texts, *The Part Played by Labor in the Transformation from Ape to Man,* by Frederick Engels, has long held the place of "Most Viewed" title on the website and has been viewed close to seventy thousand times (at the time of writing).[79]

The fact that Villegas uses this site to disseminate Marxist writings, and the fact that at least one of them has been viewed more times than any other Libros de Mentira publication, is an undeniable indication of how far Chilean literary culture has come since the days of the military dictatorship. Villegas's listed publications are precisely the kind of books that military personnel of the 1970s and 1980s were looking to destroy when they forcefully entered private homes, raided personal libraries, and publically burned books that did not meet with their approval. Keeping in mind that the majority of Libros de Mentira members are Chilean, it is more than noteworthy that one of Villegas's texts, which would have been outlawed thirty years ago, is now one of the most widely read books produced and distributed by this Chilean press.

Thus, to answer the question of whether or not Libros de Mentira members use the website toward the democratizing ends for which it was created, it is clear that to a large degree they do. Transcending the divide between amateur and professional would be a major advancement in a project of cultural democratization in postdictatorship Chile, and while Libros de Mentira has not fully bridged the distance between these different social categories within the cultural field, the press and its users have all made significant strides toward this end. Even if the talents and expertise of amateur readers and writers are not recognized by anyone outside of this online network, there are still ways in which we can read the literary activity of an amateur community as democratically progressive.

From comments made by Libros de Mentira members on the website, we see that not only do they decidedly seek the opportunities provided by this online press, but they too, like the press's administrative and editorial team, believe that such opportunities are capable of altering the hierarchal nature of Chile's commercial literary industry. Take Roberto Rabi's comment on Marko Torres's digital book *Los Pituflaites:* "There are not enough people with your kind of talent currently in circulation; hopefully people will come to know your work."[80] Here Rabi is stating a desire for talented works such as *Los Pituflaites* to find public recognition despite the selective nature of Chile's current literary market. The fact that Rabi was able to gain access to this text is evidence that his hope is already being realized and that Torres's book is attracting the kind of public attention he thinks it deserves.

A member who calls himself Gato voices a more direct critique of traditional print culture when he writes openly to the Libros de Mentira administrative team: "Hopefully you will make room for previously unpublished authors. Because even small, independent presses continue to be saturated by insider influence, favoritism, and other forms of corruption. As of yet, there is no escape valve to get us away from all of that, but I hope you will end up being that escape valve."[81] In light of such comments, it is no wonder that so many Chileans are using the Libros de Mentira website as an alternative to a literary industry that they see as corrupt and exclusionary.

Finally, "Charol" expresses perhaps an overly idealistic belief in the revolutionary potential of Libros de Mentira to overthrow the elitist structure of the literary print industry; she writes to the press's editorial board and website administrators, "I am grateful that with your words those in the cultural elite will be brought down to the level of the average citizen with just one click. Thank you. Thank you. Thank you."[82] Libros de Mentira does not so much work to bring the cultural elite down to the level of the average citizen as it does to empower the average citizen with tools and opportunities to gain cultural capital and exercise cultural agency; what is evident from Charol's comment, however, is that Libros de Mentira has connected with a significant sector of Chile's literary community that feels excluded from the general modes of local production and circulation. Digital literature has by no means procured the cultural legitimacy that printed texts have long held. But the way in which the Internet allows unknown, inexperienced, and therefore excluded literary producers to circulate their works among the general public is something that many Chileans have shown they want and value.

What happened to the printing press, at one time the "foundation of modern democracy," could also happen to the Internet: namely, that the "flood of publishing" it brings forth could lead to as much censorship as it does freedom.[83] This is, in fact, what Lessig fearfully predicts will happen very soon in our age of increasingly punitive international copyright law. As opposed to printed media, which can be *used* multiple times without being *copied,* "it is the nature of digital technologies that every use produces a copy."[84] Lessig thus imagines a digital future in which "every use [would] presumptively require permission."[85] That possible future would seem hauntingly familiar to those Chileans who, not so long ago, had to ask permission from an illegitimate government for the right to publish books, magazines, newspapers, and any other printed materials. But, in accord with our current neoliberal reality, permission is now granted by private industry, rather than the state. This leaves us asking the same question as posed by Henry Jenkins and David Thorburn: "Which is the greater threat to free speech: government censorship or corporate ownership of intellectual property?"[86] For now, Libros de Mentira has devised a way to function independently of either threat. It will be interesting to see how long that model can last.

5

Santiago en 100 Palabras

Mass Literature, Cultural Sponsorship, and Globalization

We believe in a plural and heterogeneous society in which the spaces that permit citizens to express themselves creatively prove indispensable in the democratization of culture and its visible diversity.

—Plagio

On April 23, 2007, Chilean citizens, writers, editors, school children, press, and state officials gathered in Santiago's Plaza de Armas (Central Plaza), the historical center of the nation and heart of its capital city, to celebrate World Book and Copyright Day.[1] The celebration revolved around a book fair, where scores of local and international publishing houses were selling their titles and where two representatives of Chile's institutional literary culture addressed the crowd: Paulina Urrutia, then state minister of el Consejo Nacional de la Cultura y las Artes (National Counsel of Culture and the Arts, CNCA), and Eduardo Castillo, then president of the Cámara Chilena del Libro (Chilean Bureau of Books).

These two figures, and the public and private cultural institutions for whom they spoke, represented the predominantly market-based model of cultural democratization that the Chilean state, in partnership with civil society, has developed since democracy's return in 1990. Both Urrutia and Castillo spoke of the important role that literacy, literature, and publishing played in Chile's continuing democratic development. They identified the need to diversify literary production, strengthen the nation's publishing industry, and extend literary access to the nation's marginalized social sectors. Central to these goals, and in the spirit of World Book and Copyright Day, they denounced the nonsanctioned production and circulation of books on the black market and emphasized the need for stricter state regulation of intellectual copyright laws.

After her speech in the Plaza de Armas that April 23 morning in 2007, State Minister Urrutia descended the stairs into the Plaza de Armas subway station where another, subterranean literary event was taking place. In the Plaza de Armas subway station, literally under the site of the book fair above, the state-owned public transportation corporation Metro, along with the foreign-owned Chilean copper conglomerate Minera Escondida and the independent cultural collective Plagio, were celebrating World Book Day in a very different way. For the seventh consecutive year, these three unconventionally and unexpectedly partnered literary producers had organized and sponsored what they and others claimed to be the country's most massive literary contest: Santiago en 100 Palabras (Santiago in 100 Words).

The contest came into being at the turn of the millennium, when then university students Sylvia Dümmer, Ignacio Arnold, and Carmen García were looking for ways to finance an independent literary journal they had cofounded and named *Plagio.* The group modeled its magazine after a Spanish cultural journal of the same name, which translates into English as "illegal copy," or something that has been plagiarized. The print magazine *Plagio* eventually evolved into a purely digital online magazine, which then developed into the cultural agency Plagio that organizes multiple artistic and literary projects throughout Chile, and, more recently, in Mexico and Hungary as well.[2]

Like almost all other independent cultural projects of Chile's postdictatorship period, the Plagio team has faced serious challenges in finding ways to finance its creative endeavors. It has solved this problem by securing financial sponsorship from private businesses outside the culture industries. The first corporation Plagio solicited for financial support was the state-owned transportation corporation Metro Santiago, which already had its own thriving cultural program, titled Metro Cultura. Metro itself was unable to finance the journal but was interested in recruiting the Plagio team to help create a new project for Metro Cultura. The result was the literary contest Santiago en 100 Palabras, which came to fruition when Metro brought on board the privately owned copper company Minera Escondida to donate the capital needed to finance the project.[3] Since then, Plagio has taken responsibility for the overall administration of the contest, while Metro has provided the physical space in which the contest takes place—the subway—and Minera Escondida has financed the publication and free distribution of all winning stories as well as personnel expenses required to run the contest and the monetary awards given to contest winners.

The contest rules stipulate that stories be no more than one hundred words in length; however, there is no limit to the number of entries individuals can submit, which they do either by hand-dropping stories into large receptacles stationed throughout Santiago's subway system or by submitting them electronically. Chilean citizens participate en masse in this contest and have collectively produced 389,205 original short stories since the contest began in 2001. All entries enter a two-tier selection process. The pre-selection is judged by a committee of "distinguished professionals from the national literary scene" that selects between 1,000 and 1,500 of the best stories from the total number of entries submitted in a given year.[4] From those pre-selected stories, a second and final selection committee chooses the top three winning stories of the year and any Honorable Mentions.[5]

Winning stories are published in a number of different ways and are always distributed to the public for free. Billboards located throughout the subway system—on platforms and in train cars—are the primary way in which the contest publishes winning stories, thereby exposing them to Metro's more than 2,200,000 daily passengers (fig. 7).[6] Postcards with winning stories published on them are also given out for free to subway riders every year in celebration of World Book and Copyright day, as are other "objects of everyday use" such as calendars and magnets with winning stories printed on them (fig. 8).[7]

FIGURE 7. "Los monos de Baquedano manipulan la mente," by Marietta Bravo, Honorable Mention, 2006. This story was published on a billboard in a stairwell of a subway station in Santiago, Chile. Photograph by Jane D. Griffin. Reproduced by permission of Santiago en 100 Palabras.

FIGURE 8. A collection of postcards on which are printed the winning stories from the 2005 version of Santiago en 100 Palabras. Each postcard contains an original illustration on one side and a winning story printed on the other. In the center of the photo is a small brown paper bag in which the postcards were bundled and distributed for free to subway riders. Photograph by Jane D. Griffin. Reproduced by permission of Santiago en 100 Palabras.

In addition, every two years the contest celebrates World Book and Copyright Day by publishing 100,000 copies of pocket-sized books containing the top one hundred stories submitted to the contest over the previous two years. The contest celebrated its upcoming tenth anniversary by publishing in 2010 a standard-sized, hardbound book that documented the history of the contest as well as highlighting some of its most celebrated stories. This book, along with every edition of the pocket-sized books, is available for free in PDF format on the contest's website.[8] The anniversary book, as well as three of the "best-of" pocket-sized books, is also available on the website for download as an audiobook. In all of these different forms of publication, every printed story is accompanied by an original illustration provided by Plagio's design team.

When State Minister Urrutia descended into the Plaza de Armas subway station on April 23, 2007, she expressed her public support of the contest and of its commitment to making literature more equitably accessible to citizens. The way in which the contest achieves this equitability reveals both alliances with and departures from the state's own model of cultural democratization. Santiago en 100 Palabras is capable of making literature so massively accessible to the Chilean public because of corporate sponsorship, which in turn is made possible through the Law of Cultural Donations, passed by the state in 1990.[9] Through this law, the state recognizes the need for free culture but also its inability to fully pay for that; it therefore solicits financial help from the private sector in the form of cultural donations, specifically from private businesses.

Santiago en 100 Palabras is perhaps the best example of the effects of the 1990 law due to its longevity and the massive participation of Chilean citizens in the contest as both readers and writers. Similarly, through its fourteen year sponsorship of Santiago en 100 Palabras (and its sister contests in other Chilean cities), and also through its sponsorship of a whole host of other cultural projects, Minera Escondida has taken advantage of the Law of Cultural Donations to become one of the primary donors to Chilean culture during the postdictatorship period.[10]

The contest conditions citizens to think of literature as a non-economic good and to make and consume it independently of the local publishing industry, and it does so by altering the material form of literary publications in ways that are similar to those practiced by the Ergo Sum writing collective. In terms of their editorial methods, both of these alternative literary producers target individuals with little or no formal literary training to become published authors (women in the case of Ergo Sum, and the Chilean masses in the case of Santiago en 100 Palabras). In addition, both choose everyday objects as the material form through which literature reaches its audience, converting non-artistic objects into works of art.

Both producers also employ a similar method of free literary distribution that privileges literature's social function over its economic value; to that aim, both Ergo Sum and Santiago en 100 Palabras disseminate their works for free to readers and often do so in a personal and intimate, hand-to-hand way (as when contest volunteers hand out pocket-sized books and other everyday objects to subway riders). In terms of their shared aesthetics, the contest and the feminist writing collective both specialize in the same genre of writing: the *micro-cuento,* or micro-fiction. Finally, they both combine mini-narratives with original illustrations created specifically for each individual short story.

Despite these similarities, we cannot ignore the important differences between these two nontraditional literary producers. Most important, Santiago en 100 Palabras's financial sponsorship by both national and transnational corporations stands in direct opposition to Ergo Sum's feminist politics of institutional autonomy, which not only entail autonomy from the state and the literary industry, but from other capitalist institutions as well. National and global corporate funding allows Santiago en 100 Palabras to exponentially increase the size and scope of its alternative literary project, which in turn increases the democratic impact it has on Chilean literary culture. In contrast to Ergo Sum, which constructs social identity primarily through gender, Santiago en 100 Palabras produces a social identity around the category of "the masses," which leads to the construction of a national literature and a uniquely Chilean national identity, or *la chilenidad.* What is somewhat unique about the contest's particular construction of la chilenidad is that it is produced by average citizens and not, as has been the case historically, by a small number of relatively elite and predominantly male authors.[11]

While Santiago en 100 Palabras attaches no economic value to literary works and while it functions apart from both local and global culture industries, it does constitute a capitalist enterprise. This is because the contest relies on corporate sponsorship to finance its status of independence from the literary market. In return, its corporate sponsors receive economic benefits, directly in the form of tax write-offs and indirectly in the form of cultural capital (positive public relations and national belonging), which they then use to accumulate political power and economic wealth within the Chilean and global economies. What is most important here is not necessarily the realization that global capital uses national difference as a tool toward its own economic advantage, but rather that the Chilean masses are equal participants in the usage of global capital for their own interests—be they aesthetic (pride in a uniquely national cultural identity), political (cultural democratization), or economic (aspiring writers may use the contest to gain experience and credibility that could lead to professional writing careers). Santiago en 100 Palabras allows us to see how local masses and global elites have entered into a partnership in Chile's postdictatorship period, even though it is not in the name of a mutual or shared cause but rather to further each party's individual and distinct interests.

Literature by the Masses, for the Masses

Santiago en 100 Palabras draws attention to a complicated conversation within cultural studies scholarship about the political implications of mass culture in general and about the mass production of literature in particular. Cultural studies scholars have long critiqued the culture industry's mass production of cultural commodities, arguing that its practices threaten the essence, or "aura," of art. Scholars in this field have also critiqued the elitist nature of the capitalist culture industry and its subordination of the masses into the passive role of cultural consumers. Exemplifying this view is the work of Pierre Bourdieu, which posits art as a form of hegemonic ideology whose transmission from generation to generation preserves and reproduces the dominant position of a dominant class; in other words, cultural capital serves as an instrument of political domination.[12]

The exploitative nature of mass culture has found particular relevance within the context of Latin America, in which the division between cultural elites and the masses has historically also been a division between the global and the local—a separation that subjugates the Latin American masses into a marginalized position with relation to the market and the foreign cultural elites who have historically controlled it.[13] Within this view, the Latin American masses exercise little agency over the kinds of cultural products they consume and, consequently, the kinds of cultural values those products generate. Latin American cultural and intellectual elites have also shown great skepticism and mistrust of mass culture due to its association with "low" culture. The stereotype of "mass" as "low" extends beyond literary producers and distributors and is even reiterated by Latin American cultural studies scholarship, which firmly differentiates literature from popular culture, thereby designating it as "high" art and reifying its contradistinction from mass culture.[14]

There is, however, a school of cultural studies scholarship that recuperates the value of mass culture by theorizing consumption as a symbolically productive, and even critically counter-hegemonic, activity. For instance, the work of Michele de Certeau has informed a generation of researchers who study the ways in which consumers exercise the power to produce meaning through their everyday use of cultural commodities. Within the context of Latin America, this view is represented by the authors of *Cultural Consumption in Latin America,* who argue that through their consumption and use of mass-produced cultural commodities, marginal social sectors (the masses) deconstruct and re-codify dominant images and messages according to their own symbolic lexicon and toward their own political interests. For example, Jesús Martín-Barbero argues that Latin America's history of low literacy rates and strong oral tradition commonly produce what he terms "collective interpretations," in which marginalized groups communally consume and interpret mainstream cultural products and appropriate them into their own unique symbolic order.[15]

While this theory understands the masses as actively exercising cultural agency, it also predicates their ability to act as cultural producers on their more primary role as consumers of mass culture. The theory seems to suggest two different moments of cultural production: the first is primary, or material, production, and is the process by which a cultural product takes its form; as such, this process is controlled by the culture industries. The second, secondary production, is mobilized by the masses through their consumption of cultural commodities created through the process of primary production. Secondary production differs from primary production in that it is made by a different group of producers (the masses rather than cultural industries), but also in that it is "silent" and "hidden" within the product's *use* by consumers.

As De Certeau explains, "We must first analyze [the cultural product's] manipulation by users who are not its makers. Only then can we gauge the difference or similarity between the production of the image and the secondary production hidden in the process of its utilization."[16] Martín-Barbero agrees, writing, "Very well, if the product or standard of consumption are the arrival point of the production process, they are also the point of departure, and the primary material, of another production process, silent and disperse, hidden in its uses."[17] Therefore, while primary production involves both material and symbolic construction, secondary production is almost wholly symbolic in nature, as is evidenced by its "hidden" quality.

This theory reproduces, rather than deconstructs, the hierarchal binary separating cultural elites from the masses. The fact that secondary production is "hidden" suggests one of two scenarios: the first scenario is that secondary producers—that is, the masses—are themselves not cognizant of the new meanings they produce through cultural consumption, therefore presumably relying on intellectuals for their enlightenment; the second scenario is that the masses are cognizant of the new meanings they produce, in which case the new meanings would only be "hidden" and "silent" to intellectuals and the act of "revealing" them would only bear significance to intellectuals (i.e., cultural elites). In either case, the binary between "high" and "low" remains intact.

Jesús Martín-Barbero, himself an advocate of this model of viewing cultural consumption, seems to recognize this problem. He writes that

> the educative process shifts between an active pole that deters knowledge—the elite, the intellectual, the master—and another pole, ignorant in its passivity: the people, the masses, the child, with the consequent legitimation of the division between the sphere of production and creativity on one side and that of consumption, passivity, and conformity on the other. What remains to be seen is a *social history of reading* that would allow us to break this dualism, removing us from the theoretical-political place in which it originates and in doing so be able to detangle popular reading's differentiating traits.[18]

Martín-Barbero is correct in saying that such a "social history of reading" that would break the binary separating production from consumption and the elite from the masses remains on the horizon. His own definition of consumption as secondary production, hidden and distinct in its time and place from primary production, cannot define the masses as primary producers of culture and therefore does not challenge the original hierarchy. Furthermore, the theory that cultural consumption is productive and empowering to the masses also threatens to uphold the hegemony of the neoliberal market, without which productive mass consumption is not possible.[19]

What is more, mass culture has become particularly problematic within the context of postdictatorship Chile because of its association with the global publishing industry, whose mass production of literature is seen as a threat to Chile's production of a unique local identity. The dominance of this view is evident in the 2005 document *Una política de Estado para el libro y la lectura. Estratégias para el fomento de la lectura y el desarrollo de la industria editorial en Chile* (A state policy for the book and reading. Strategies to promote reading and the development of the editorial industry in Chile), written by local editorial professionals proclaiming the need to produce a national culture that is less massive and, consequently, irreplaceable.[20] This sentiment is shared by a large number of Chilean writers and publishers who not only believe that global publishing firms homogenize local culture through the mass production and distribution of literature, but that the local editorial industry alone is capable of combating this trend through less massive forms of literary production and distribution.

These views express what many scholars, as well as some cultural producers, agree is one of the most negative effects of mass culture in Latin America today—its penchant to interpellate the masses as consumers of culture, rather than as its producers. As Cuban filmmaker and cultural critic Julio García Espinosa has claimed, "Mass art is art produced by a minority in order to satisfy the demand of a public reduced to the sole role of spectator and consumer."[21] Chilean sociologist Jorge Larraín states that culture in postdictatorship Chile has become like any other industry in that it survives according to market logic. He writes, "The culture industry converts individuals into consumers."[22] Larraín goes so far as to claim that consumption has become one of the most defining characteristics of contemporary Chilean identity: people structure their identity around how and what they consume. He argues that one of the consequences of the dictatorship is that it made collective movements less significant as markers of social identity and instead made material consumption the foundational way in which identity is formed and recognized.[23] Chilean sociologist Tomás Moulian takes the same position, characterizing postdictatorship Chilean national identity as a type of "credit-card citizenship" that is set in motion by mass consumption.[24]

While it is possible that Chileans use their desire for capitalist consumption toward progressive ends, as De Certeau, Martín-Barbero, and others suggest is possible, Larraín sees the opposite happening, and attributes mall culture and credit-card citizenship to the relative "de-politicization" of the Chilean masses since the dictatorship years—a de-politicization that he claims has continued since Chile's return to democracy in 1990.[25] Rather than seeing cultural consumption in contemporary Chile as a tool used by the people to subvert the ideological powers of capital, Larraín and Moulián give us greater reason to view this phenomenon from a more skeptical perspective.

Santiago en 100 Palabras' populist model of cultural democracy differs from both these theories of mass culture (as either exploitative or empowering) in its dependence on *lo popular* (the popular). In their equally oppositional relation to "high" culture, "mass culture" and "popular culture" are often thought to be the same thing; however, at least within the context of Latin America, their differences are subtle and often contested. Cultural sociologist Esperança Bielsa claims that "both terms have been used to describe the cultural relations, practices and products that do not belong to and are excluded from high or legitimate culture."[26] While she sees these terms as similar, she differentiates between them by explaining that "popular culture" or, lo popular, "tend[s] to express a more positive view of those cultural artifacts that are not only consumed by the working classes, but also form an organic part of their traditions, of their world vision and way of life." "Mass culture," on the other hand, "tend[s] to reflect more a view of culture as determine from above."[27]

For Bielsa, then, one of the defining differences between these two forms of culture is the group of actors responsible for their production: in the case of lo popular that would be local, Latin American masses, and in the case of mass culture it would be the elite leaders of culture industries who often are not themselves Latin American. We see another view presented by Julio

García Espinosa who, in his famous 1969 essay "For an Imperfect Cinema," identifies a greater difference between mass and popular art in Latin America; he claims that "popular art has absolutely nothing to do with what is called mass art. Popular art needs and consequently tends to develop the personal, individual taste of a people. On the other hand, mass art (or art for the masses) requires the people to have no taste."[28] From these definitions, we might think of mass culture as imposed onto the masses by cultural elites, whereas popular culture emerges from the shared beliefs and everyday customs of the people themselves.

This distinction helps explain why mass culture is often demonized within Latin America cultural economies, where it is seen as co-opting lo popular and preventing it from speaking "from below." This view is expressed by Guillermo Sunkel in *El consumo cultural en América Latina* (Cultural consumption in Latin America), in which he argues that mass culture tends to "determine" or "mediatize" lo popular in a way that appropriates its meaning for the purpose of global capitalist culture industries. He defines this process of "mediatizing the popular" as "the massive incorporation and diffusion of genres sometimes considered to be the expression of the 'authentic' Latin American. . . . [P]opular cultural manifestations [become] readapted for mass consumption and, in certain cases, for consumption by the elite."[29] According to this view, mass culture's appropriation of lo popular not only redirects the intended audience of popular culture, but it also changes the way in which its original audience interprets its content and meaning. Sunkel states that "the mediatization of the popular also implies a re-adaptation, and as such, a transformation that . . . provoke[s] changes in form and content."[30] Néstor García Canclini agrees, arguing that even though the formal structure of popular culture may remain the same, its meaning changes when it is appropriated by capitalist culture industries and sold to outside audiences.[31]

Santiago en 100 Palabras brings us closer to what Martín-Barbero terms a "social history of reading" by doing precisely that which Sunkel describes: mass-producing lo popular. But rather than co-opting the meaning of lo popular, as typically happens, according to Sunkel, through its incorporation into modes of mass production, Santiago en 100 Palabras allows popular culture to use modes of mass production to further its own interests, that is, by granting Chilean citizens greater cultural agency as literary producers and, as a consequence, greater control over the type of mass culture they consume.

It is to this purpose that the contest awards stories that critique mass culture's appropriation of lo popular. "El Negrito" (selected as one of the top one hundred stories of 2005–2006), by María Isabel Toro, is a good example. It reads in its entirety as follows:

> Every morning he wakes up at the feet of Valdivia's horse, feeling like a citizen, a Chilean. He can't go to the bathroom in the plaza because one hundred *pesos* that early in the morning is a fortune for el Negrito, as people who know him call him. His face is covered by a sheet of dirt, as are his hands. People say it's been five years since he's bathed. One day an artist in the plaza painted a portrait of him. In two more days, he finished the painting. He sold it immediately to a tourist for one hundred dollars.[32]

This type of representation of la chilenidad is a common theme produced by Santiago en 100 Palabras, which frequently awards stories that are focused on the figure of the street dweller, typically male, who comes to represent the image of the Chilean masses.[33] In this particular story, the act of selling this national image to a foreigner (a "tourist" who pays for the painting in "dollars") risks, as Sunkel warns, changing its form and content. Within a global context, the painted image of el Negrito can easily come to represent *all* of Chile, and perhaps all of Latin America, as the essentialized brown (literally meaning dirt on the body but figuratively racial inferiority), penniless, and homeless peasant. More important, the message this story sends is that the money generated by selling Chile's cultural image to the foreign market does not return to the hands of those citizens behind the representation—in this case El Negrito. The image in the oil painting becomes objectified by the gaze of the foreign cultural consumer and interpellated as the southern subaltern other.

However, the story challenges global culture's ability to appropriate local difference in this way since the narrative itself does not suffer the same fate as el Negrito's painted image. Unlike the oil rendition of el Negrito, the story "El Negrito" is not sold to a foreigner; it is not sold at all, in fact, but produced and consumed by and for the same audience: Chileans. The author, María Isabel Toro, highlights this fact through her repeated use of the quantity "one hundred." While el Negrito cannot even use a bathroom in the morning because he does not have one hundred pesos, the tourist buys el Negrito's image for one hundred dollars. Toro's choice of "one hundred" is a reminder that readers of this story consume el Negrito's representation *not* for one hundred pesos, nor for one hundred dollars, but rather simply in one hundred *words.* This example suggests that the problem of mass-producing lo popular is a problem inherent in the culture industry, not in the form of mass culture itself.

Santiago en 100 Palabras stories might provide an answer to Espinosa's question about whether or not the "conditions that will enable spectators to transform themselves into agents and co-authors of the text" presently exist in Latin America.[34] While Espinosa asked this question in the 1960s, the hegemony of neoliberalism in Latin America makes it more than pertinent today. These stories, and the contest at large, suggest one possible method for how to create those conditions. The contest allows Chileans to occupy the positions of literature's object and subject at the same time and thereby creates the possibility of replacing a structure of cultural elitism with one of cultural democracy. Espinosa confirms that "one of the most profoundly cultured characteristics" of what he calls "popular art" is "that the creators are at the same time the spectators and vice versa. Between those who produce and those who consume, no sharp line of demarcation exists."[35]

This merging of identities, between producers and consumers, is what makes Santiago en 100 Palabras fundamentally different from the kind of productive consumption Martín-Barbero and de Certeau describe. Unlike their models, in which consumers are *not* culture's primary producers, this contest conflates cultural production and consumption as a simultaneous act performed by a single actor: the Chilean masses. While Espinosa thinks about popular art in terms of Latin American cinema, we can recognize literature as an even more viable medium for the conflation of spectator and author since a short story is much easier for the masses to produce than is a short or feature film.

In a similar way, the contest conflates literary production and consumption into the single space of the subway. Contest organizers originally expected passengers to write stories while waiting for and riding on trains, which is why they strategically stationed depositories throughout the subway system where riders could submit their entries. The subway is also the intended site of literary consumption: while waiting for a train on the underground platform or sitting on a train traveling to and from work, citizens are confronted with literature's material presence as they face billboard-size publications of stories produced originally for the contest and often having been written within the same space of the underground tunnels and trains.

The intended goal of getting citizens to read and write while moving about the city, performing their everyday activities, is precisely why the contest mandates that stories be no more than one hundred words. Thus the contest attempts to weave literature into the fabric of the public sphere rather than sanctioning it off in spaces designated for literary activity. The Chilean state and national book industry have both tried to tackle the dire problem of low reading rates in the postdictatorship period by strengthening access to reading materials through schools, public libraries, and bookstores. These are certainly important initiatives, but they require that adults make time in their schedules to go to libraries and make room in their budgets to purchase books at bookstores. Santiago en 100 Palabras takes a wholly different approach. In casting the subway and the city itself as sites of literary writing and reading, the contest allows citizens to see both activities as integrated aspects of their everyday routine rather than private activities that they are to perform in designated places.[36]

In the same way that the contest reconfigures the public sphere as a site for literary creation and consumption, so too does it imagine average citizens—what Plagio founders Carmen García and Sylvia Dümmer refer to as "ordinary and common people"—rather than consecrated authors, as being worthy of producing literary works for mass distribution.[37] The contest presents ordinary men and women with the opportunity to occupy public spaces traditionally restricted to small numbers of elite cultural producers. Ángel Rama's groundbreaking research into the history of Latin American letters elucidates the social category of the *letrado,* lettered individuals who have made significant contributions to the design and development of Latin American urban topologies and, as an extension, cultural landscapes. Rama describes *los letrados* as a social group, consisting mostly of men, whose members use the power of their written words to bring the Latin American city into being. Rama also explains how history slowly expanded the letrado category to include a greater number of minority social actors. In its focus on the masses and their ability to "write" the city, Santiago en 100 Palabras offers letrado status to any literate Chilean citizen.[38]

Writing/Reading a Newly Democratic Chile

Santiago en 100 Palabras's populist strategy responds to a number of material problems impeding cultural democracy in Chile today. Despite the fact that in recent years Chile has experienced a rapid growth in information technologies, educational and public library programs, and state financing of cultural projects, there remains a high level of functional illiteracy and a depressed general interest in acquiring better reading habits. In its study "Chile y los libros, 2010" (Chile and books, 2010), the private institution Fundación La Fuente (The Source Foundation) reports five major findings relating to Chileans' reading habits: (1) more than 50 percent of the Chilean population does not read on a regular basis; (2) social class and age continue to be the two variables that most inhibit individuals from reading books; (3) Chileans continue to be unmotivated by reading as an activity, and thus do not make time for it in their lives; (4) eight out of ten people think books in Chile are too expensive (mostly because of the VAT tax); and (5) while libraries are generally thought to be a good means of promoting better reading habits, there is still a problem of how to get people into them.[39]

Santiago en 100 Palabras inadvertently responds to all of these deficiencies in Chilean reading culture. Through its use of the subway as the location of literary production, distribution, and consumption, the contest seamlessly weaves the activities of reading and writing into citizens' everyday routines and takes care of the problem of Chileans not having the time to read and of not getting into libraries. It tackles the problem of the high price of books by giving reading materials away for free, and it addresses the problem of class and age as inhibitors of reading by making literature—both its production and consumption—equally available to anyone who rides the subway.[40]

Furthermore, through the contest, readers are exposed to topics that spark curiosity and conversation, improving the public's intellectual skills in reasoning and logic and thereby improving citizens' ability to participate in the state's new democratic system. While the brevity of these stories leads critics such as María Constanza Mujica to argue that they are not meant for deep contemplation but rather give off the "sensation" of such intellectual activity, contest organizers García and Dümmer note that "writing a story of 100 words sounds easy, but it's not."[41] Not only is it not easy to write a story in one hundred words, it is also not always easy to comprehend and decipher a story of one hundred words either. The brevity of these stories allows them to be consumed in a short amount of time, but that does not mean that they are not intellectually stimulating and that readers do not continue digesting their content even after they have left the subway station. On the contrary, their brevity allows readers to more easily remember these stories in order to further contemplate them later on or, what is more, to use them as a point of departure for dialogue and debate with friends and family.[42]

Inviting any and all Santiago citizens to author and massively distribute their own interpretation of Chilean nationalism is a cultural practice that stands in stark opposition to that of the military dictatorship. Because its political authority depended on a single interpretation of what it meant to be Chilean, the military regime attempted to restrict citizens' ability to use literature as a tool with which to represent the nation symbolically.[43] Santiago en 100 Palabras thoroughly reverses this restriction by constructing every individual as an equal author of la chilenidad. Whereas the dictatorship used military force to control the public sphere, Santiago en 100 Palabras openly encourages Chilean citizens to exercise a sense of ownership over their city and, in the words of contest organizers, to verbally open "up a new space for the urban imaginary of our nation's capital."[44] The contest not only invites the masses to symbolically rewrite the geography of the urban landscape, and therefore the history of the nation, but it also suggests that average citizens are uniquely qualified for the task of constructing a national identity "from below."

Plagio explicitly states this view in its preface to the 2005–2006 pocket-sized book of the best one hundred stories submitted during those two years:

> Perhaps the question of identity lies beyond academic and other lofty discourses and is instead found in us ourselves, in the day to day, in our quotidian experiences. "Santiago en 100 Palabras" successfully recuperates and interlaces all those little histories that make up our everyday existence. . . . The third volume of the best one hundred stories of "Santiago en 100 Palabras" is a compilation of thousands of Chileans' response to the question of who we are. . . . [The writers who author these stories] are writing the history of this country on a daily basis.[45]

Citizens seem to agree with this sentiment, as they have produced numerous narratives that rewrite the story of their capital city and their national history according to their own personal experiences and perspectives.

One example of how citizens use the contest to rewrite Santiago "from below" is the 2002 Honorable Mention "Santiago of New Extremadura," by Jorge Aguilera.[46] In this story, readers find a familiar narrative, reminiscent of the Spanish "discovery" of Santiago but with a modern-day twist in which the authority of the Spanish colonizer is replaced by the cultural agency of everyday citizens. The story begins, "This is the place. This river will provide us with water and from this peak we will see our enemies approaching."[47] Readers immediately recognize geographical markers in this description that are symbols of Santiago in particular and la chilenidad in general. The river evokes images of Santiago's iconic Mapocho River, and the "peak" could very well represent the San Cristóbal (Saint Christopher) hill, which overlooks the Mapocho River in downtown Santiago. Both the Mapocho River and the Andes mountain range, represented by the San Cristóbal hill, are symbols of the capital city and, by extension, national identity. Moreover, national identities—even as represented in the country's physical landscape—are not static or fixed constructions established in the past but ever-evolving concepts shaped by a people's past, present, and future imaginings of itself.[48]

This reshaping of identities is precisely what we see happen in Aguilera's narrative; whereas Spanish conquistadores would have used the San Cristóbal mountaintop to spot their "enemies" approaching, Aguilera rewrites the national landscape according to the present-day interests, not of Chile's political or social elites, but of the contemporary masses: "We'll clear away one or two hilltops to ventilate the valley's basin and prevent smog."[49] Andean hilltops surrounding Santiago served a practical military purpose for sixteenth-century Spanish colonizers; however, today they contribute to Santiago's dire problem of air pollution by trapping smog into the valley basin where the capital is located. Recent studies have revealed Chileans' collective anxiety about urban congestion and air pollution, and thus we can read Aguilera's rewriting of the capital's physical territory as a populist representation of the kind of national space Chileans want to inhabit.[50]

The ending of the story solidifies the role reversal between elite European colonizers of the past and modern-day citizens as the architects of a new Santiago and a newly democratic Chile. The story ends, "What would Gamboa think? That I'm exaggerating? Well, then forget what I've said and let it be whatever you want."[51] The "Gamboa" to whom the narrator refers might well be Martín Ruiz de Gamboa de Berriz, the Spanish conquistador who was the royal governor of Chile from 1580 to 1583. The last line of the story is entirely ambiguous, reading: "y que sea a *su* voluntad" (emphasis added). The "su" here could refer to Gamboa, in which case the ending of the story would be rendered in English as, "let it be whatever *he* wants." But the "su" could equally refer to the audience as a plural "you" (*ustedes*), or as a singular formal "you" (*usted*), in which case the line would read as "let it be whatever *you* want." The ambiguity of subjects to which "su" refers opens up the possibility that not only Aguilera, as author of the story, but also any average Chilean citizen, as reader of the story, has the power to construct Santiago according to his or her own will.

In addition to re-creating the city symbolically, Santiago en 100 Palabras transforms the city physically by using the public sphere as the physical matter onto which literature is published and distributed: the materiality of the city becomes the materiality of literature and vice versa. The publication of stories in the form of billboards within the subway has rightfully caused critics to equate those stories with graffiti or murals. According to Mujica, these "blown-up graphics" are visions of the city created by everyday people that are then projected onto the city itself in a way that converts the literary and graphic images into "urban artifacts" that coexist alongside other similar artifacts such as commercial advertisements and the subway's directional signage.[52] The incorporation of these stories into the physical facade of the city makes them a material part of the urban infrastructure such that the symbolic images they contain become part of the physical matter that is Santiago de Chile.[53]

Such a physical presence allows the symbolic content of these stories to potentially transform the way in which citizens interact with their urban environment and with one another. Mujica describes the space of the subway as a "non-place" in which, "as dictated by the non-written etiquette of this subterranean world—no one looks at anyone, no one converses with their neighbor, everyone fixes their gaze outward, towards the dark tunnels or the brightly colored advertisements in large print."[54] In other words, the subway and the city at large have become nonsocial spaces in which citizens do not interact with one another as members of a shared community.

This lack of communal interaction is precisely what the contest organizers are attempting to change. As García and Dümmer have publically proclaimed, "'Santiago en 100 Palabras' makes it possible for people to meet one another through literature."[55] They go on to state that the contest's greatest contribution is "social integration" in the sense that these stories produce a large amount of civic participation.[56] There are many ways in which the contest realizes the kind of social interaction its organizers originally intended. One of them is the hand-to-hand distribution of some of the contest's publications: postcards and other everyday objects onto which winning stories are printed are handed out individually to subway riders with the intention that publications reach citizens either directly or indirectly through "someone they know."[57]

In addition to its hand-to-hand transference of literary writings among citizens, the contest exploits the billboard medium for its ability to give information away for free to the largest number of people possible. The billboard of course is by definition a mode of communication but typically one of unidirectional communication *from* corporations *to* mass consumers. In the same way that the Ergo Sum book-object undermines the capitalist function of the object-commodity, Santiago en 100 Palabras undermines the billboard's function as a unidirectional mode of communication and its ability to produce a desire for capitalist consumption within the viewer. As Néstor García Canclini puts it, "The uncritical eagerness of the masses, exacerbated by advertising, leads them to obsessively procure unnecessary objects."[58] The texts of Santiago en 100 Palabras replace the almost unconscious need to consume unnecessary objects with a desire for the intellectual activity of reading, thinking, and imagining. Furthermore, the knowledge that winning stories will be published as billboards within the subway influences the kinds of stories citizens produce for the contest, and, as a result, winning narratives repeatedly exploit the billboard's communicative function by altering it from one of unidirectional communication into a locus of social dialogue between Chilean citizens.

Two telling examples of stories that describe interpersonal communication are "Lo perdí" (I lost it) by María Inés Peranchiguay (selected as one of the best stories from 2005–2006), and "Escrito hallado en un respaldo de asiento de micro" (Scribble found on the back of a bus seat), by Julio Gutiérrez (Honorable Mention, 2006). In the first story, the narrator has lost her cell phone and all the contact information in it. Through its narration in the second person, the story constructs the reader as the narrator's personal friend; the protagonist thus uses the contest's public space of publication—the subway billboard—as a means of personal communication between herself and her friend, who is at once any and all subway riders. "If you call me today," she says to her audience, "it won't be I who will answer, but another. I have no way of letting you know, since all the information was there, and only there. If you read this you will understand and perhaps we will find each other in front of the billboard, me, hoping that you will read this and you, laughing at the scatterbrained woman who lost her cell phone."[59] The narrator addresses the audience in the familiar *tú* voice (you), hailing every potential reader (i.e., every subway rider) as an intimate friend, someone whose number she had in her cell phone; the narrator's subject-position can also be inhabited by literally any *otro* (other) who now possesses her phone. This story, therefore, calls upon all Chileans to equally employ mass communication, in this case billboard advertisements / literary publication, as their own private space of interpersonal communication.

The aesthetics of this story take on particular symbolic significance within the historical context of postdictatorship Chile. At first glance, we could read "Lo perdí" as a universal story that could literally take place anywhere in the world today; the feeling of connectedness is the foundation of all kinds of nationalisms and collectives identities, and we could argue that subways in cities around the world are as nonsocial as that of Santiago. However, we should not ignore the importance of rebuilding a sense of national unity in postdictatorship Chile. Dating as far back as the tenth century, conservative figures (and national heroes) such as Diego Portales used the rhetoric of "good" versus "bad" citizens to successfully establish Chile as a constitutional authoritarian republic. Pinochet capitalized on this history, using this same "us" versus "them" rhetoric to overthrow the presidency of Salvador Allende and maintain authoritarian control over the government for seventeen years.[60] The dictatorship period placed Chile in a virtual state of civil war in which every individual citizen had to choose a side, on either the political right or left, and those divisions often turned friends into enemies, children and parents into adversaries, and siblings into strangers. The sense of community produced by a story like "Lo perdí" invites all citizens to reconcile, to imagine themselves as a friend to a stranger, and to rebuild what historians Pamela Constable and Arturo Valenzuela have famously titled "a nation of enemies."[61]

Similarly, Gutiérrez's story, "Escrito hallado en un respaldo de asiento de micro," utilizes the same theme of interpersonal encounters made possible through the contest. We can read Gutiérrez's story as fashioning the family as an allegory for the nation and family healing as an allegory for national reconstruction. The entire story (far less than one hundred words) reads as follows: "I couldn't think of any other way to find you to let you know. Mom, Dad: I'm okay, and I forgive you."[62] This story is a message from the narrator to his parents; the story's title, "Scribble found on the back of a bus seat," lets the reader know the material mode of communication through which the narrator sends this message to her parents. The story therefore appropriates to public transportation a new purpose: it is no longer simply a "non-place" used to traverse the city; instead it becomes a text on which to inscribe one's most intimate feelings.

Through the perspective of this story, public transportation itself becomes a mode of mass communication, and mass communication becomes a mode of personal communication and artistic expression. And just as the previous story interpellates the reader into the narrative as the protagonist's friend, here the audience becomes the narrator's own parents, producing an allegory of the nation as a broken and dysfunctional family but one that can be reunited and healed by using public space—in this case the back of a public bus seat with graffiti presumably scribbled on it—as an artistic canvas and communicative instrument.

There are also numerous examples of the ways in which Chileans use the narrative space of the contest as a place to act out a kind of social behavior that, if imitated by readers, will improve the health and safety of Santiago as a place to live. Contest organizers and critics alike have noted the extent to which the theme of violence is prevalent within both the stories submitted to the contest and those selected as winners.[63] One prime example is the 2001 Honorable Mention, "Metro los Héroes" (Heroes Metro Stop), by Pablo Figueroa. The narrative exploits the reader's unfortunate desensitization to urban violence and constructs a scene we recognize as all too familiar: crime on the subway. The story begins: "Here comes the train, packed full of people like it is every morning. From the platform I choose my victim with my gaze while I go over my plan in my head. The doors open. The last to get off is a man, still half-asleep. 'My victim,' I say to myself."[64] What seems a typical and predictable scene of urban violence on the subway is, through a twist in the narrative, turned into one of intimacy and friendly exchange between fellow citizens. The story continues: "He looks at me out of the corner of his eye and I attack: "Hello, how are you? I ask him, as I climb on board and advance through the car. He turns. The doors close and I look with satisfaction at his stupefied face. Poor guy. He'll be wondering all day who it was who greeted him, and me, well I can't wait for tomorrow to find my next victim."[65]

This story forces us to rethink our expectations of contemporary social interaction and urban life so that instead of perceiving our fellow citizens as strangers, or even enemies, we see them as friends to be treated kindly and with respect. We can also interpret the author's choice to set this narrative in the subway station "Los Héroes" as contributing to the depiction of the protagonist as a hero, perhaps even a superhero of sorts, whose special power is to act kindly to strangers and strengthen the social fabric of the city.

Stories such as "Metro los Héroes" encourage citizens to enact the literary narrative themselves in the very same space in which the narrative, its production, distribution, and consumption also all take place: the subway in particular and the public space of the nation's capital in general. This is what Mujica means when she refers to the contest's "theatricalization" of the literary message; the line separating reality from fiction here becomes blurred as readers are encouraged to become the characters of the stories themselves and to act out the stories in their own everyday lives.[66] We can also read the expression of desire to alleviate contemporary urban violence as an allegory for the desire to heal the past violence of state terror, or perhaps even substitute it with peaceful reconciliation and national fraternity. Again, Larraín's definition of national identity as not only an artifact produced in the past but also an image projected into the future applies to this story.[67] Figueroa creates an image of what Chilean nationalism should strive to be; it is an image presumably shared by contest judges who selected this story as one of the best of 2001.

Beyond the common narrative themes that the judges reward through their selection of winning stories, the contest's administrators also create a sense of national community by providing readers with certain personal details about each winning author's identity. Since its first year of operation in 2001, the contest has published the author's name, age, and residential community alongside the text of the winning story itself. Knowing the author's gender (usually indicated by her/his name), age, and class (indicated by the community in which she/he lives) gives readers a sense that they know something about who this person is. Understandably, our knowledge of such identity markers is based on generalizations and even stereotypes, such that identity signifiers like name, age, and place of residence present assumptions about a person that are both truthful and misleading at the same time. However, by highlighting these details the contest creates a sense of intimacy between the audience and the author—a sense that although they are most likely strangers who have never met, they know something about each another based on their preconceived expectations of what different gender, age, and class identifications mean within the shared time and space of postdictatorship Santiago de Chile.

Finally, and perhaps most important for Chilean cultural democratization, Santiago en 100 Palabras has become a prominent producer of a cultural identity specific to Chile and not found anywhere else in the world. This is important because of the influence of the foreign on Chile's self-image throughout the history of the nation-state, and, more recently, with the onset of contemporary globalization. According to Larraín, Chileans have been a people obsessed with the foreign since the days of Independence—to the point that many speak of an imitative characteristic and lack of originality within the Chilean national identity.[68]

From a modern-day perspective, Larraín notes the ways in which economic development, urbanization, and cultural globalization have exacerbated for Chileans the appeal of the foreign, erasing local differences that used to define the Chilean way of life and replacing them with international tastes in everything from music, to food, to architecture, to intellectual thought.[69] The increased presence of and preference for the foreign within Chile has caused some to view globalization, specifically in its cultural dimension, as a threat to la chilenidad; the symptoms of this threat, claims Larraín, are witnessed everywhere.[70] Such symptoms are perhaps no more present in Chile than within the capital of Santiago where the urban experience takes on a universalizing tendency and becomes increasingly similar to the experience of living in other megacities throughout the world.

Santiago en 100 Palabras combats the threat of cultural homogenization by awarding stories that take Chilean national difference as their central theme. Writers are prolific in their incorporation of distinctively Chilean themes and characteristics within the narratives they submit to the contest, and contest judges repeatedly award such impulses in their selection of winning stories. One of the best examples of this tendency is "Dostoievski" (Dostoyevsky), by Ernesto Guzmán, awarded "Best Story of 2006"—a year in which 44,789 stories entered the competition.

Throughout "Dostoievski" the reader follows the hypothetical musings of an unidentified male protagonist through what would be a typical day in Santiago. The story begins: "He would have stopped to observe the people steaming out of the mouth of the Metro. He would have dumbfoundedly crossed la Moneda in the rain. Thoughtfully, he would have bought a *sopaipilla* for a hungry dog near Santa Lucia park."[71] The hypothetical journey of the protagonist—indicated by the consistent use of the conditional throughout the story—includes classic Chilean activities that take place in some of the capital city's most iconic and emblematic locales: walking across la Moneda street in downtown Santiago, feeding a hungry dog a *sopaipilla* (traditional Chilean street food typically served during the winter) in the famous Santa Lucía hillside park, and drinking a *navegado* (a traditional Chilean drink) with friends at La Piojera (a famous bar in downtown Santiago). Because of these activities, the reader is led to believe that the hypothetical protagonist is a typical Chilean commoner, an everyday man.

When in the last line of the text we realize that this figure is in fact Fyodor Dostoyevsky, this image of the everyday Chilean is not so much shattered as it is expanded to incorporate the Russian novelist into its parameters. After describing such a typical day in Santiago, the story ends, "Fyodor

Dostoyevsky would have liked Santiago in winter."[72] This story reverses the historic trend that Larraín cites of Chileans' attraction to foreign tastes and sensibilities.[73] Here we see the opposite take place, in that the protagonist is a foreigner charmed by the local flavors that only Santiago de Chile can offer, rather than being a Chilean adopting cultural characteristics that originated abroad. The story suggests that not only is Dostoyevsky equal to the common Chilean citizen but that, more important, the common Chilean citizen, specifically through her/his participation in Santiago en 100 Palabras, is on a par with one of the most internationally celebrated writers of modern times. The story's theme becomes reality through Guzmán himself who, while not reaching the heights of the story's historical protagonist, does become a respected and widely read literary celebrity through his successful participation in this contest.

Nothing Comes for Free: Institutional Support through Corporate Sponsorship

Santiago en 100 Palabras qualifies as an alternative literary producer due to the kinds of material practices of literary production and distribution that it employs. However, unlike other alternative literary producers, Santiago en 100 Palabras is not institutionally autonomous due to its sponsorship by two incredibly powerful national and multinational corporations: Metro Santiago and Minera Escondida (Hidden Mine). Such institutionalization brings with it increased cultural, political, and economic capital. At the same time that it establishes an innovative model to democratize literary culture, Santiago en 100 Palabras actively subjugates Chilean literary culture and the country's lucrative metal mining industry to the power of global capital.

Minera Escondida's full financial sponsorship of this contest undoubtedly proves the extent to which Chile's neoliberal economic structure has become increasingly dependent on foreign capital. Because Chile is one of the richest sources of copper in the world, this metal has proven attractive to foreign investors (specifically U.S. companies) who have consequently controlled copper mining in Chile for the majority of the twentieth century. In the late 1960s the Chilean government began to challenge foreign control of their mining industry by passing legislation that allowed foreign companies to retain ownership of copper mines but required them to pay the state greater portions of their earnings. This "Chileanization" of the national copper industry gained momentum under the socialist administration of President Salvador Allende, who began nationalizing many foreign-owned mines.

The military regime of 1973–90 formalized Allende's nationalization of previously foreign-owned metal mines by founding the Corporación

Nacional del Cobre de Chile (National Corporation of Chilean Copper, Codelco), while simultaneously countering this process by once again welcoming foreign investors to enter the local market—strategies that were maintained by the Concertación administrations of the 1990s.[74] The Codelco Law that passed in 1992 exemplifies privatization in that it allows Codelco to partner with the private sector—specifically foreign-owned companies—to forge new mining endeavors wherever precious metals are found across the Chilean landscape.[75]

Minera Escondida is a prime example of the kind of foreign-owned companies that this legislation has empowered. The history of Minera Escondida parallels Chile's history of political dictatorship and economic liberalization. The company was founded during the middle of the military regime in 1981, construction of the mine began toward the end of the regime in 1988, and full operation commenced in 1991, one year after the end of the dictatorship. The company's size and wealth have continued to grow throughout the newly democratic period, to the point that the mine is the world's largest producer of copper in the world.[76] A significant percentage—57.5 percent—of Minera Escondida is owned by the Australian company BHP Billiton, the world's largest industrial producer of mined metals and a true multinational corporation, with offices on every continent; 30 percent of the company is owned by Rio Tinto, a British company that also leads the world in the production of natural resources; and the final 2.5 percent of Minera Escondida is owned by JECO Corporation—a consortium of Japanese companies (including Mitsubishi Corp., Mitsubishi Materials, and Nippon Mining and Metals Company).[77]

The international make-up of Minera Escondida's ownership is not surprising, nor, given the neoliberal foundation of Chile's economy over the past three decades, is its dominating presence in Chile's industrial sector and national economy. What is somewhat surprising, though, is the extent to which this company, owned by foreigners, uses its economic and political power to fortify Chilean *national* culture, language, and identity through a host of cultural and social programs, but most specifically through Santiago en 100 Palabras. As the mining company states in the introduction to the second volume of the best one hundred stories submitted to the contest, Santiago en 100 Palabras strengthens Chilean identity and cultural diversity.[78]

Minera Escondida's interest in producing and reproducing Chilean nationality is not altruistic philanthropy, however; nor is the company primarily motivated by a desire to create a viable opportunity for local Chilean identity and culture to thrive within a threatening global cultural economy. As Arturo Navarro writes in his book *Cultura: ¿Quién paga?* (Culture: Who pays?), "Sponsorship by businesses or individuals has two characteristics: it seeks recognition and it takes advantage of tax incentives. Why deny it?"[79] According to art scholar Chin-tao Wu, tax incentives for cultural donations are so attractive that it is common to think of corporate sponsorship of the arts as a "tax-avoidance strategy."[80]

It is indeed the case that Minera Escondida receives tax breaks from the Chilean government through its sponsorship of Santiago en 100 Palabras. This is why on every copy of the contest's pocket-sized books we read the words "Free Distribution / The Sale of This Item Is Prohibited."[81] According to Chile's Cultural Donations Law (No. 18.985), in order for Minera Escondida to receive tax breaks, the public must have *free* access to the cultural projects it sponsors. Passed in 1990, this law serves as a legal mechanism to stimulate private financial intervention in cultural and artistic projects.[82] Considering the large fees that foreign-owned mining companies must pay the Chilean government as part of the Chileanization of the copper industry, it is no wonder that Minera Escondida eases this financial burden through its tax-deductible donations to the arts.[83]

Another material motivator for corporate sponsorship of the arts is free advertising, or what cultural critic Mark W. Rectanus labels as "promotional culture."[84] In this respect the state-owned transportation company Metro Santiago stands to benefit more from the promotional power of Santiago en 100 Palabras than does Minera Escondida because the Chilean masses who are exposed daily to this free advertising are not buying copper from Minera Escondida as much as they are buying train tickets from Metro.

Metro's incentive for sponsoring Santiago en 100 Palabras is that the contest will, ideally, entertain its riders during their commute, thus improving their subway experience and making them more likely to continue using the subway as their primary source of transportation around Santiago's growing metropolis. Metro's need to advertise may seem unnecessary when we consider that there are no competing alternatives to public transportation in Santiago; however, Chile's democratic reconstruction has strengthened the country's middle class and afforded more Chileans the possibility of personal car ownership. Having its name attached to stories placed on subway platforms and inside train cars is an optimal advertising strategy for Metro Santiago since cultural sponsorship is not as easily tuned out or turned off by viewers as is traditional advertising.[85] Subway riders are much less likely to overlook these literary stories than they are to skip over a newspaper advertisement or change the TV channel to avoid commercials.

In addition to these material incentives, there are also very real symbolic motivators at play. The first of these is that through its connection to a specific cultural project, a corporation is able to create a certain image or identity for itself. According to Wu, this strategy is most often employed by companies whose business is seen as controversial by the public (for instance, tobacco, petroleum, and weapons industries) and who wish to use their connection to culture to improve public relations.[86] Companies select cultural projects for sponsorship based on what kind of image the project will create for the firm: young, smart, environmentally conscious, humanitarian, progressive, moral, and so forth.

In the case of Minera Escondida, it is not difficult to discern the image afforded to the company through its sponsorship of Santiago en 100 Palabras: it is decidedly related to the Chilean national identity. The company has openly admitted that it sponsors the contest in the hopes that Chilean citizens will view Minera Escondida as "one of us," that is, as a Chilean citizen. As it states on its website, "The company is successful when it is valued by the communities of which it forms a part. Thus, one of our objectives is to be a responsible citizen and be recognized as such."[87] Minera Escondida acknowledges that its efforts to be recognized as a Chilean citizen are motivated by a desire to convince Chileans that copper mining is pertinent to the quality of their daily lives.

Carlos Gajardo, honorary director of Fundación Minera Escondia (Minera Escondida Foundation, an organization that the mine founded in 1995 to fund educational, health, and social services in Chile's northern region and Santiago) and the company's manager of External Affairs, describes why Minera Escondida originally took an interest in financing Chilean culture:

> Ten years ago no one would have imagined that a mining company would create a foundation to work with the people. Because to be honest, the purpose and the business of a mining company is to produce copper. . . . But it was also fundamental to us that we increase our **connections with the community**, which at that time saw our activity as foreign and distant to their own interests and necessities. The community didn't connect the idea of our company with the possibility of bettering their own **quality of life.**[88]

Through this statement we see that Minera Escondida donates to Chilean cultural programs because it wants local Chileans to see the corporations' mining activity as an integral and necessary component of their own lives, as something that is an inherent aspect of the Chilean shared way of life. The intention is that Chilean citizens see foreign participation in local industry as not foreign at all, but as part and parcel of their own national experience and existence.

In this sense Minera Escondida's sponsorship of Santiago en 100 Palabras differs from a common trend in corporate arts sponsorship that seeks to improve the social status of the corporation and of corporate executives through the accumulation of "high" culture (principally corporate art collections).[89] Minera Escondida uses cultural sponsorship to do the exact opposite: to move downward on the social ladder rather than upward. We can understand Minera Escondida's desire to naturalize itself as a Chilean citizen as the reason why it has specifically chosen to sponsor Santiago en 100 Palabras since, as we have seen, the contest successfully constructs the nation by projecting a populist image of the Chilean people. Minera Escondida wants to participate in this "shared experience" so that it can exchange its foreign and elite identity—established by its material wealth and foreign ownership—for a local, national identity established through its shared experience of Chileans telling themselves stories about what it means to be Chilean. The company wants the Chilean people to see it not as a distant elite, but rather as a commoner, as one of the people, as the very people the contest targets for participation: "average, everyday people."

Another way in which this model of corporate sponsorship of the arts is distinct from the norm is that Minera Escondida has sustained sole financial responsibility of the contest for more than a decade. In his study of why firms donate to the arts, Roland Kushner concludes that businesses are less likely to support cultural projects if they believe the project will not be able to survive without their sponsorship and thus will become dependent on the corporation's donation.[90] This is not the case for Santiago en 100 Palabras since the contest is 100 percent financially dependent on Minera Escondida's sponsorship; yet this economic dependency has not prevented the mining company from taking on full financial responsibility for the contest for fourteen consecutive years (as of 2015). It likely has done so because of the contest's massive popularity with citizens and its exposure not only to those who participate in the contest as writers but, more important, to everyone who rides the Santiago subway system. The seemingly insatiable appetite on the part of the Chilean people for this contest, in which they have participated for over a decade, is what motivates Minera Escondida to provide the capital necessary to keep the contest going.

Minera Escondida's sponsorship of Santiago en 100 Palabras is also unique in the sense that the image transfer it creates does not target the company's own market. Appropriating a Chilean identity is not going to increase Minera Escondida's profit sales because it is not intended to appeal to the company's clientele—who are not the Chilean masses. Why then is the company willing to spend millions of dollars to acquire this identity?

The answer to this question leads us to a discussion of many of the negative consequences of corporate arts sponsorship. Art scholars Mark Rectanus and Chin-tao Wu both argue that the increased power of corporations in the cultural sphere is an inherent product of neoliberalism and that such sponsorship thereby dissolves the demarcation between commercial and public interests. This dissolution causes an erosion of cultural democracy in that the decisions about what kinds of artistic projects will be funded are no longer in the hands of democratically elected government officials but rather in those of private business owners who represent their own commercial interests over those of the public. Rectanus has found that even when working with community partners, "corporations have a disproportionate influence in shaping cultural programing [and] exercise far greater power than their community partners."[91] It is no surprise that the postdictatorship Chilean state has created laws that encourage corporate sponsorship of the arts since one of the most remarkable features of neoliberalism is the increasing control by large corporations of non-economic social domains.[92]

Corporate sponsorship of the arts is widely seen as a means of producing cultural capital for the purpose of then purchasing political capital that the corporation uses to increase its economic wealth. Wu writes, "It is . . . an inevitable consequence of the corporate power of multinational capital that, as the third millennium unfolds, multinationals in the West should use art as a weapon to further their interests overseas as economic colonisers."[93] The colonization to which Wu refers is of course inherently economic *and* political; she argues that one of the ideological rationales for corporations in sponsoring the arts is that "the cultural capital thus created can, in due course and at the appropriate juncture, be transformed into political power, either openly or otherwise, to serve business's own specific economic interests."[94]

Another negative consequence of foreign sponsorship of national culture is that it limits art's critical nature. Colombian librarian Jorge Orlando Melo writes, "Private companies that exhibit their generosity through acts of patronage preside over art in order to weaken its critical spirit or cover up their own negative qualities that might affect their brands."[95] Just as corporations sometimes engage in cultural sponsorship to intentionally draw public attention away from a company's controversial business activities, so do they also make sure to sponsor projects that will not promulgate any negative feelings about the company or its dealings.

This tactic is more than applicable to a company like Minera Escondida, whose very existence ensures the deformation of the Chilean geography and natural environment and whose business requires Chilean workers to put their personal health and safety in serious danger by working hundreds of meters below the earth's surface.[96] The winning stories of Santiago en 100 Palabras do not discuss, nor even make slight reference to, these potentially damaging characteristics of Minera Escondida's mining activities. And while its organizers argue that the contest evidences the democratization of the city space in comparison to the situation during the dictatorship years, we must also note the extreme difference between the freedom of expression exercised through the contest and that performed by public demonstrators and protestors in Santiago in recent years. This contest is not comparable to the student protest movement that represents the most massive form of civil unrest and disobedience in Santiago since the fall of dictatorship. Nor is it an unauthorized or unlawful practice of cultural defiance such as what we saw taking place during the dictatorship. These stories are not even graffiti, although they have been described as such by some cultural critics. As a sanctioned and institutionalized cultural activity, Santiago en 100 Palabras still controls citizens' use of the city space to a large degree.

The purchasing power that multinationals possess to obtain national identity and citizenship places them at an unequal advantage to other foreigners competing to work in Chile's national economy, namely human immigrants. Because of its economic prosperity over the past few decades, Chile has become an increasingly popular destination for foreign immigrants from neighboring and regional countries seeking economic, social, and political salvation from their own poorer national economies. These individuals and families struggle to gain economic, social, and political legitimacy in Chile. The same process is immensely different for a multinational company like Minera Escondida, which has the resources of the world's most powerful mining conglomerate, BHP Billiton, behind it and all the political and cultural capital that it can, and does, buy.

CONCLUSION

Rethinking the Field of Cultural Production

Cultural Agency, Minority Literature, and Cultural Studies Scholarship

In the future there will no longer be painters, but rather men who, among other things, dedicate themselves to painting.

—Karl Marx

In 2000, Paulo Slachevsky, editor of LOM Ediciones, addressed a group of writers and editors at a meeting called the "Third meeting of writers for the promotion of the book and reading," organized by Letras de Chile.[1] In his address, Slachevsky argued that innovative forms of production have a greater impact on society than social critique. He then expanded on this idea: "It is necessary to generate . . . the ambition to make a project that intervenes in the society in which we live. I said that the idea was not to dwell in lament, since if we tend to respond with complaint in the face of adversity and the transformations taking place around us, we limit our ability to act, our ability to intervene."[2]

Slachevsky's point is valid. Pinochet's authoritarian government has been the target of well-deserved criticism from inside and outside Chile, and the leaders of Chile's political transition have received outspoken criticism for their inability to undo some of the most controversial changes that Pinochet made to the Chilean nation-state. Slachevsky's point is not that critique is not necessary, but that it alone does not initiate change; *making* things does. More specifically, Slachevsky seems to argue that if projects are going to intervene into society, they need to be made by members of that society.

Slachevsky went on to say, "We have to take the reins back into our own hands, combine conviction, voluntarism, and a grain of willfulness with a tradition of praxis and of learning new forms of communicating, producing, and organizing."[3] Considering Slachevsky's audience—members of Chile's national literary and publishing industries—it is likely that when he talked about taking "the reins back into our own hands," he was referring to a dismantling of the hegemony that foreign-owned corporate publishers have established in Chilean literary culture since the dictatorship period. The belief expressed here is that multinational corporations will not make a positive intervention into Chilean society; rather locally owned and operated cultural projects are best equipped to do that. Moreover, in order to retake control of material modes of print production, the local industry must employ "new forms of communicating, producing, and organizing." They must change their methods of material production if they are to compete against foreign corporations and positively intervene in their own local communities.

Noncommercial and amateur literary producers subscribe to a similar philosophy. Ergo Sum, Cartonera publishers, Libros de Mentira, and Santiago en 100 Palabras all originated from the belief that the global publishing industry impedes the process of cultural democratization in Chile and that alternative means of, in Slachevsky's words, "communicating, producing, and organizing" are necessary. The organizers and directors behind these projects have offered such alternatives precisely through the kind of conviction, voluntarism, and willfulness that Slachevsky describes. It is clear that both industry professionals and alternative literary publishers seek to take the reins of Chilean cultural production out of the hands of multinational corporations and back into their own; but whereas individuals like Slachevsky attempt to do so through industrial means of cultural exchange, Ergo Sum, Cartonera publishers, Libros de Mentira, and Santiago en 100 Palabras provide the Chilean public with an alternative to the literary market in general, including the locally controlled market. Precisely because these alternative publishers are not bound by market constraints, they are able to produce radically altered materializations of literary texts that break away from the traditional book form.

Most people who organize alternative literary projects and who participate in them do so because they believe that commercial cultural production and consumption should not be the only options available and that noncommercial and amateur forms of literary publication intervene in society in ways that capitalist and/or professional production cannot. Local industry professionals act as cultural gatekeepers and mediators as global publishers do, but their criteria for publication are slightly different and, as they themselves argue, are less dependent on the profitability of individual works. Amateur literary producers believe that even works that do not meet the standards of quality and value set by the market and by industry professionals still deserve public circulation and can still make a positive contribution to society.

There are those within the alternative literary community who have more radical views of capitalism and cultural institutions at large. For example, editors of La Vieja Sapa Cartonera willfully disregard copyright laws because they see them as inherently undemocratic. By extension this logic would posit the hierarchical nature of the market as incongruent with the very idea of cultural democracy.[4] Others, such as the Libros de Mentira member Gato, accuse the local publishing industries of corruption and favoritism. Gato comments on the Libros de Mentira website that "even small, independent presses continue to be saturated by insider influence, favoritism, and other forms of corruption."[5] Here he is suggesting that the very standards of artistic and intellectual quality established by local and independent publishing houses are often irrelevant or compromised by cronyism.

At the heart of the differences between alternative literary producers, the local publishing industry, and the global publishing industry is the question of artistic taste, which is to say the criteria through which we judge the artistic quality and value of symbolic goods. An overly simplified understanding of these differences would be that the global industry determines literary value based on market sales, whereas members of the local industry are not primarily interested in making money, although they do use industrialized modes of literary production and distribution, and they sell their titles on the market. They are, by their own accounts, more interested in strengthening national culture and creatively engaging with their local communities; in other words, they combine their own definitions of artistic quality with market definitions of economic worth.

Alternative literary producers are on the opposite end of this spectrum: they privilege the social value of literary publications over any economic factors. More important, their definition of literary value is that it is generated through the production process and the cultural agents responsible for that process. In contrast, both the local and global industries see quality as generated through acts of consumption—the capitalist purchasing of object-commodities for the global industry and the interpretive act of reading for the local industry. In both cases, the agent responsible for determining the value and quality of the literary object is not the individual(s) responsible for making that object but rather the consumers who are buying and/or reading it.

Eliminating or even limiting the ability of media gatekeepers—such as editors, critics, and academics—to determine artistic value is controversial. Critics of populist artistic formations argue that cultural authorities and gatekeepers are necessary to defend institutionalized definitions of artistic taste, without which there is no ability to differentiate between what is art and what is not, or between what is good art and what is not good art, or between who is an artist and who is not. Communications scholar Benjamin Barber writes,

"Mediators and gatekeepers, whether we call them editors, teachers, pastors, novelists, journalists, or philosophers, all help us make sense of the world: In a democracy, they are brought under democratic controls and are accountable to those they guide. Either we can select and replace them, or we can accept or reject their guidance at will: It is never compulsory. But to think democracy is better served by eliminating mediators is to opt not for liberty, but for anarchy and the fertile ground it proffers to the true manipulators."[6] This view understands artistic taste as something that is acquired through training and that is passed down from cultural authorities, such as publishers, critics, and scholars, to the general public (i.e., the masses). This view also seems to assume that cultural gatekeepers are trustworthy defenders of "real" artistic value and not, as Gato fears, opportunistic insiders.

Latin American cultural theorist Julio García Espinosa represents a contrasting view from Barber's. Espinosa argues that mediation does not in fact safeguard any notion of artistic quality, and he singles out mass art as the emblematic example of this. Espinosa differentiates between mass art and popular art, or what is referred to in Latin America as *lo popular,* by understanding mass art as being highly mediated by cultural authorities and popular art as unmediated cultural production made by and for the masses. Espinosa writes that "popular art needs and consequently tends to develop the personal, individual taste of a people. On the other hand, mass art (or art for the masses), requires the people to have no taste."[7]

Rather than believing that people learn from cultural authorities how to discern good from bad art, Espinosa defines artistic quality as belonging to and deriving from the people. Central to this viewpoint is the belief that material culture carries in it the common traditions, values, and identities of a people. "Good" art, for Espinosa, is that which authentically represents a particular culture, and the individuals most qualified to judge that authenticity, and therefore artistic quality, are the individuals within that culture itself. This is a view shared by many independent Chilean presses and alternative literary producers who attempt to use literature to reproduce a sense of national cultural difference that they see threatened by the global cultural economy. This belief is what motivates people like Slachevsky to argue that local literary producers need to take control over modes of material production out of the hands of multinational corporations and put them back into their own.

But once material production is put back in the hands of local cultural producers, there are still differing opinions about how creative projects positively influence local communities. Independent publishers share the belief that the art object itself positively influences society by having an effect on the individual readers/viewers with whom it comes in contact. The emphasis here is on the art object and the act of consuming it. Alternative publishers, on the other hand, emphasize the individual cultural producer as the agent that intervenes and positively contributes to society. This view does not locate artistic value or worth in the art object itself or even in the change that the art object makes on society but rather in the human subject who creates it.

The definition of cultural agency advanced by alternative literary projects like Ergo Sum, Cartonera publishers, Libros de Mentira, and Santiago en 100 Palabras is that the act of making something that we ourselves consider creative and artistic and the experience of sharing that art object with others gives us a new understanding of our own subjectivity, power, ability, and possible contribution to the world in which we live. For these alternative literary publishers, this is the transformative power of art: it gives the maker an internal sense of agency that allows her to then become an agent of change in her society.

The same logic that structures this definition of cultural agency is also a principal foundation of democracy: citizens need to believe that their contribution to the democratic process is valid and necessary in order to want to participate in that process, and when citizens are empowered as publically recognized cultural agents, they are more likely to participate. Moreover, literary producers actively contribute to building the communities in which they live as we have seen through the historic relationship between literature and the social imaginary in general, and print culture and the Latin American nation in particular. This relationship is the subject of research by Ángel Rama and Benedict Anderson, who both maintain that the nation is—at least in large part—a product of lettered constructions.

In his book *Imagined Communities: Reflections on the Origin and Spread of Nationalism,* Anderson argues that the nation is an imagined construct produced primarily through two specific forms of print capitalism: the novel and the newspaper. The synchronic historical emergence of both the book and the newspaper in mid-eighteenth-century Europe allowed the nation and nationalism to develop. His thesis is that newspapers allowed citizens to know what was happening throughout the geographic range of their national communities and thereby feel connected to other members of that community, even those separated by long distances; likewise, his thesis on the novel posits that this particular literary form helped produce a common narrative of the nation's origins, history, values, and identity that could be shared by all members of the national community.[8]

Similarly, in his book *La ciudad letrada,* Rama traces the history of Latin American cities—and by extension the region's nations—by drawing a genealogy of the region's architects, which he identifies as a group of lettered men he calls *letrados.* His thesis is that letrados circulated ideas through print culture that then came to life in the city's physical materialization, which laid the foundation for the emergence of the Latin American nation in the late nineteenth century. Rama's argument is that the modern Latin American nation is the product of lettered constructions.[9]

Like late eighteenth-century Europe and late nineteenth-century Latin America, late twentieth-century Chile once again found itself in a state of national re-imaging. Through this process, literature and print media became important tools in the rebuilding of a democratic nation. The important role print culture plays in the construction of the nation is precisely why General Pinochet commandeered the Chilean press and strictly disciplined publishing houses. It is also not surprising that during the dictatorship people used literary culture as a means through which to protest against the authoritarian state and to advance pro-democratic politics.

This impetus toward protest, as we have seen, has only gained momentum throughout the postdictatorship period, during which time people have increasingly turned to literary culture as a means of reimagining and rebuilding a democratic society. Moreover, Rama's research shows that the demographic make-up of the letrado group evolved throughout Latin American history, and he argues that the processes of national independence, modernization, and globalization have all allowed a more heterogeneous group of individuals to incorporate themselves into the letrado group. This, according to Rama, has resulted in a group of lettered elite that are further removed from centralized forces of power and more highly critical of them.

This is precisely what we see taking place in dictatorship and postdictatorship Chile—periods in which increasingly marginalized individuals are finding their ways in to the letrado group and authorizing themselves as architects of their national culture and community. This is best evidenced by Plagio's introduction to the 2005–2006 collection of winning stories from Santiago en 100 Palabras. Plagio introduces these stories by writing, "Perhaps the question of identity lies beyond academic and other lofty discourses and is instead found in us ourselves, in the day to day, in our quotidian experiences. [. . . The writers who author these stories] are writing the history of this country on a daily basis."[10]

The research of both Rama and Espinosa seems to be reflected in this statement, which argues that average citizens have assumed the power to produce the Chilean nation through literary production and that they are better equipped to do so than cultural authorities. This model for how to construct a national literature is opposed to that of multinational publishing houses, which, according to Kathrin Bergenthal's research, fill volumes of "national" literature with texts that do not represent the heterogeneous nature of the nation but instead reflect the bourgeoisie experience of their target audience.[11] Giving literature away for free allows Santiago en 100 Palabras, and other alternative literary publishers, to diversify the letrado group, making literature more representative of the diverse peoples that compose the nation through both their writings and their demographic make-up.

The ever-increasing number of individuals participating in alternative literary projects and the longevity of the four projects we have traced throughout this study both evidence a strong desire on the part of contemporary Chileans to enter into the letrado group and use literary culture as a means of participating in their nation's democratic reconstruction. Their desire to participate in alternative literary projects suggests that contemporary Chileans are unsatisfied in their roles as cultural consumers, even when the consumption practices they employ are subversive and counter-hegemonic. And because of the marginal position they occupy relative to corporate culture industries, they employ material modes of cultural production that are available to them, which most often are artisanal and non-industrial. Yet the hegemony of global culture industries means that Chileans are not alone in their marginalized cultural positions, and thus it is no surprise that practices of hand-making cultural objects have been gaining momentum in recent years across the globe, as the Cartonera publishing trend so clearly exemplifies.

In Chile and Latin America as a whole this form of cultural production has come to be known as *auto-gestión,* or self-sustaining; English-speaking regions of the world describe it as Do-It-Yourself (DIY). Auto-gestión and DIY employ similar methods toward similar ends: they combine new technologies with artisanal forms of material production in order to make and share cultural objects independently of corporate culture industries. As David Gauntlett has astutely argued, these methods introduce new forms of social relations, and their presence and political relevance are sure to grow rather than dissipate in the coming years.[12]

Cultural studies scholars are the most apt to understand and theorize on these new trends. While the field of cultural studies began with the analysis of industrial modes of symbolic production, in recent years it has turned its analytic gaze toward popular modes of symbolic interpretation. This has happened because the hegemony of global culture industries has made consumption, and not production, the primary way in which most individuals, but especially those in the Global South, make meaning out of culture.[13] Cultural studies scholars such as Néstor García Canclini, Jesús Martín-Barbero, and Michele de Certeau have helped us understand the infinite ways in which consumers use their interpretive powers to create new ways of making meaning in a globalized field of cultural production. Their research has transformed the way we think about cultural agency in the age of globalization, showing the counter-hegemonic power consumers have despite their marginalized positions relative to multinational corporate capital.

Despite these advancements in thinking about consumption as a source of cultural agency, the growing presence of self-sourced cultural production throughout Latin America and across the globe requires cultural studies scholars to shift their focus again back to modes of material production, specifically those controlled by popular rather than corporate forces. Susan Hekman helps us understand the importance of this in her book *The Materiality of Knowledge: Feminist Disclosures.*[14] Here, Hekman argues for a theoretical reexamination of material production and advocates that contemporary intellectuals bring the material back into our scholarship. Hekman argues that the turn toward linguistics in postmodernism has gone too far and that our theorization of everything as discourse and social construction renders us incapable of seriously combating social injustice.

More specifically, Hekman claims that feminism provides a major justification for the need to bring the material back in and stands at the forefront of such a methodology. She argues that while poststructuralism has been undeniably beneficial to feminism as a means of understanding gender as a social construct, "feminist theorists have a particular stake in retaining reference to reality. Feminists want to be able to make statements about reality—that women are oppressed; that their social, economic, and political status is inferior to that of men; that they suffer sexual abuse at the hands of men. If everything is a linguistic construction, then these claims lose their meaning. They become only one more interpretation of an infinitely malleable reality."[15] Hekman urges us to think about how the materiality of women's bodies and the material circumstances those bodies inhabit affect women lives.

I suggest that we think about the material form of literary publications in the same way. Literary publications are the material bodies that texts inhabit. As we have for human bodies, we have certain societal and cultural expectations of what literary publications should look like and what purposes they should serve within particular historical and geographical contexts. This is precisely why we can apply theories of drag to Ergo Sum book-objects. The form of these objects expresses a gendered identity, specifically a feminized identity. The other literary publications studied here, including billboards in subway stations, cardboard books, and digital books, are not as obviously gendered male or female as Ergo Sum book-objects are, but that should not prevent us from reading their material form as gendered. These publications are gendered feminine in the sense that they do not take the material forms that we expect from literary texts. Just as the category of woman is dependent on a relationship of difference to dominant symbols of power (the phallus), so too are literary objects feminized in relation to mainstream forms of literary production and circulation.

This line of thinking is consistent with the research of Chilean book historian Bernardo Subercaseuax, who claims that within "the economic and socio-cultural conditions brought about by the dictatorship, either the book becomes incorporated into the mechanisms of the culture industry, or it runs the risk of being a *marginal* cultural product."[16] The literary objects we have studied occupy a marginalized position within Chile's post-1973 cultural landscape due to the fact that they been produced independently of local and global cultural industries. If we understand the feminine as a category of marginalization that is based, at least in part, on the body's material form, then we can rightfully understand alternative literary texts as feminine cultural products.

This definition of marginal literature is somewhat different from established notions that circulate in academic scholarship. Typically "marginal" or "minor" literature is defined by the subjectivity of the author. For instance, Gilles Deleuze and Féliz Guattarri define minor literature in just this way, as derived from the racial, gendered, ethnic, or other minority subjectivity of the person writing the text.[17] According to these theorists, the author's minority identity allows her to use language in a counter-hegemonic way, thus making minor literature subversive and politically charged. Alternative literary producers require that we extend this definition to include not only the language of the text but also the modes of material production through which the text becomes an object consumable to readers. Those modes and the material objects they produce can both be minor in the same way that the subjectivity of the author is. Subercaseaux uses the word "marginal" in this very way, to describe the minority subjectivity of the literary text as material object. And just as Deleuze and Guattarri argue that minor uses of language are subversive, so too do minor forms of Chilean literary production challenge the hegemony of the political and economic institutions that structure the cultural field in which they are produced and circulated.

By defining minority texts in this way, cultural studies scholars can bring the material back into our scholarship in ways that Hekman argues have important political consequences. Moreover, by defining texts as marginal or minor based on the modes of material production that have brought them into being, we come to realize how literary texts make political and aesthetic meaning in ways that exceed the linguistic composition of the text itself. Consequently, a materialist definition of minority literature also broadens our understanding of how individuals use culture as a form of agency: they do so by writing and reading literary texts, but they also do so by making physical objects that house those texts. And just as Hekman argues that feminist scholars have a particular stake in bringing the material back into our scholarship, cultural studies scholars have a particular stake in thinking about the material body of the art object as performing subjectivity in a way that is similar to the human bodies that make them.

Not all of the producers of the minor literary objects we have studied are themselves minorities in the way in which Deleuze and Guattarri use the term: their gendered, sexual, racial, and/or class identities are often not minor in any way. But by engaging in minor material modes of cultural production, these individuals call attention to the minority subjectivity they occupy as producers within the global cultural economy. In relation to multinational culture corporations, the individuals who make alternative literary objects occupy minority subjectivities. They use that subject position to enable a form of critique, one that they realize through creative projects.

While minority forms of literary production have and are evolving in Chile, they are simultaneously erupting all over the globe. Digital technologies and the Internet have increased people's abilities to make and share creative products in ways that inspire others to do the same. We are living in a new age of cultural production in which amateur forms of art pass through increasingly more global and often noncapitalist circuits of exchange. In so doing, they remind us of Luce Irigaray's hypothesis of what would happen if women's bodies "refused to go to market" as capitalist commodities. She speculates that they might maintain " 'another' kind of commerce" among themselves. As she argues, "Use and exchange would be indistinguishable. The greatest value would be at the same time the least kept in reserve."[18] Like Irigaray's female bodies, the minority literary texts we have studied in this book have refused to go to market. The greatest value these objects create is the cultural agency of their producers; it is also that which is least kept in reserve.

AFTERWORD

Feminist Research and Pedagogy as Forms of Craft

As a twenty-year-old college student from the United States studying abroad in Santiago de Chile, I was invited one day to have lunch in the home of Pía Barros and Jorge Montealegre. At the time I had no idea who Pía and Jorge were, other than the host parents of one of my fellow study abroad classmates from the University of Wisconsin. I had no idea that decades earlier, under a patriarchal dictatorship, Pía had clandestinely founded a feminist writing collective that she named Ergo Sum. I also had no idea that Jorge had begun an underground literary and graphic arts magazine, *La Castaña* (The Chestnut), under that same dictatorship. What I did know, staring at the cigarette smoke billow out of Ms. Barros's mouth as she spoke about politics, human rights, literature, and, of course, feminism, was that I needed to know more. My need to know more launched me on a path that has not only resulted in the publication of this book but in an entire career.

My path has not been a straight line. When I started this research I wanted to write about Pía Barros's own literature and the place of women's writing within postdictatorship Chilean culture. I soon realized that those who had come before me had already done this work. Scholars such as Raquel Olea, Eugenia Brito, and Alice Nelson had already written the books that I had hoped to write as a young doctoral student. My mentor and friend, Resha Cardone, who also studies the work of Pía Barros, helped me to see Pía's work from a different perspective, pointing out that Barros's work as an editor and bookmaker was as artistically and intellectually charged as her short-fiction narratives. I thus shifted my focus from reading and analyzing literature, to reading and analyzing literary culture, or what Pierre Bourdieu refers to as the sociology of literature. Through this framework I quickly began to see what were for me exciting similarities between the editorial practice that Pía Barros had created through the Ergo Sum group and other forms of literary production that had emerged in Chile after the end of the dictatorship.

It was not until I was well advanced into this new methodology that I realized the serendipity of my altered research approach. One day it occurred to me that I come from three generations of printmakers. My great-grandfather, Carry Griffin, moved our family to Glendale, California, from Montana in 1922 and opened a printing press. Griffin Printing supported my family for three generations before it was converted into an employee-owned cooperative in 1975. I made my entrance into this world just after my family had left the printing business, but my childhood was steeped in memories of Griffin Printing.

What impressed me more than family lore was a single material artifact that has hung in my parents' home my entire life: a large composite of old printing tiles taken from the press, all individual letters of differing sizes and fonts glued together in a large rectangular frame. As a young child I stared in wonder at those tiles, contemplating their rustic beauty, the sense of industrial power that they seemed still to hold inside them even as their use value had evolved from factory production to aesthetic decoration in my family living room. For me those letters held a history of my family's labor, of our material subsistence, and of a trade that my great-grandfather had passed down to my grandfather and that my grandfather passed down to my father.

As a young aspiring scholar interested in Latin American literature and feminism, I always assumed that I had drifted far away from my family's legacy of entrepreneurship, which I associated with the printing company. About halfway through my research for this book, though, I realized I was very wrong. With no conscious intention, I have come to work in print culture as well, albeit in a much different way than my relatives before me.

I tell these stories because my personal, invested, and subjective relation to my object of study is one of the ways that I qualify my work as feminist. Feminist researchers have long fought to debunk the notion of pure scientific objectivity, demonstrating how cultural beliefs and biases as well as personal histories affect what we choose to study, the questions we ask about our objects of study, and how we interpret the data of our investigations. Instead of assuming that our personal subjectivities can remain independent of scientific discovery or of political life, or that individual biases will dangerously taint our work in those fields, feminism urges us to openly identify our personal histories and harness their power as a constructive agent rather than a contaminant.

This sentiment is shared by Gesa E. Kirsch and Liz Rohan, editors of *Beyond the Archives: Research as a Lived Process,* who argue that "personal connection can make all the difference in our scholarly pursuit: it brings the subject to life and makes us more likely to pursue hunches, follow leads, and spend extra time combing through archival materials than we would without a 'personal attachment.'"[1] This research methodology is opposed to the patriarchal tradition of seeing the investigator as a powerful agent of change and the world as a passive recipient, waiting to be acted upon. Rather, it allows the research process to foster a dynamic relationship in which the investigator and her subject collaborate in the mutual production of knowledge.

Over the years, Pía and I, in conjunction with a whole cadre of other Chilean and U.S. writers, scholars, and translators—most specifically Resha Cardone—have organized and hosted seminars, symposiums, undergraduate and graduate classroom visits, writing workshops, literary readings, and conferences in Chile and all across the United States. Pía, Resha, and I have also worked closely together on the English translation of two of Pía's collections of short stories, one of which is now in its second edition.[2] Resha describes her experience of our co-translating Barros's literature as an example of the same feminist project Barros began with Ergo Sum in the late 1970s:

> In the process of co-translating these texts, Barros created an opportunity for us to take part in reversing those paradigms she feels disenfranchise women within literary and academic establishments, where competition among writers and thinkers, exclusion, and the market tend to limit opportunity. . . . Unbeknownst to us at the time, the co-translations enacted her principles by placing more value on the process of literary co-creation than on their products, on teaching and learning rather than on perceived literary quality, and on the creation of affective, social and professional bonds among women rather than on competition.[3]

When Pía agreed to collaborate with Resha and myself in translating her works of fiction, Resha and I were both junior scholars who had studied literary translation but had published little in that area. Our lack of pre-established reputations as literary translators did not prevent her from offering us that opportunity, and it was precisely that opportunity and that experience that gave us credibility to grow a reputation in this field. This is why Resha is right to point out the way in which Pía applied the same political and artistic philosophy to her collaborations with us that she has been applying to the Ergo Sum project for over thirty years: it is a philosophy founded on the principle that individuals gain agency and legitimacy through acts of making.

Elizabeth Birmingham has thought about the ethics involved when scholarship about a particular person results in the career advancement of the researcher. In thinking about her own relationship to her deceased object of study, Mahony Griffin, Birmingham writes,

> It is difficult to say a woman like that is dead, as she helps me shape my tenure case, write this article, teach my graduate research methods class, and secure funding to work with others. . . . As scholars who work with historical

> figures, we always know that we owe those figures some sort of debt, as we mine their lives (and their deaths) to build our careers. But sometimes, when we are very lucky, . . . the relationship becomes reciprocal, and the work we do together leads to friendship and collaboration. That is the story that I have to tell.[4]

That is also the story I have to tell, except that the woman whose life I have mined to build my career, and with whom I have subsequently collaborated and formed a meaningful friendship, is not dead but alive, which only expands the possibilities of our collaborative friendship. Birmingham's ethical concern about whether we owe our human subjects some sort of debt is a crucial one. Building a career on the life of another person could be exploitative, were it not for the fact that the dynamic nature of the collaborative research relationship produces the scholar as academic expert, teacher, or translator in the same way that it produces the subject as artist, pedagogue, and, to use Birmingham's word, "historical figure."[5]

Pierre Bourdieu's work is helpful in explaining how scholarship constitutes an object as a work of art and its maker as an artist. He writes, "The production of discourse (critical, historical, etc.) about the work of art is one of the conditions of production of the work."[6] Bourdieu claims that any material object can be a work of art if it is publically recognized as such, and scholars are important agents in the discursive production of an object as a work of art. This is another way of articulating Cardone's argument that our collective scholarship about Barros's work, including our translations of her literature, forms a part of her larger artistic oeuvre. We have become collaborative agents in Barros's cultural production just as she has participated in our professional development.

This political and artistic philosophy is equally shared by the other three alternative literary producers I study in this book, who all believe in the creative power of amateur and minority writers and of the marginal cultural practices they employ. All of them work to make literary publication available to individuals who would otherwise have limited access to it, and they all work to expand consecrated definitions of who counts as an artist and of whose work should be taken seriously by the rest of society. This philosophy explains why pedagogy is at the heart of all four alternative literary projects, just as it is at the core of my own professional practice.

Pía Barros, Cartonera publishers, Libros de Mentira editors, and the Plagio team from Santiago en 100 Palabras all offer a variety of writing and book-making workshops in addition to their primary editorial projects (in the case of Ergo Sum, the workshop is the primary editorial project). Sometimes they offer these classes for free; sometimes an institution or organization sponsors these workshops; and other times individuals themselves pay enrollment fees to participate. The purpose of these classes is not to make money, but rather to spread artistic and literary know-how and teach the craft of writing and bookmaking to the general public. Pedagogy thus becomes a principal component of the democratizing model practiced by these literary producers. Through teaching, these groups empower individuals with tools that they can then use to exercise their own cultural agency and actively participate in public life.

These are precisely the same reasons I myself teach. The tools and skills I try to pass along to my students are somewhat different, but the motivations behind that act of teaching are the same. Have I chosen to study these projects because they reflect my own professional philosophies and passions? Or have I acquired those professional philosophies and passions because I learned them from the artistic projects I study? I am sure that I was originally attracted to these projects because of a particular definition of cultural agency that we all share, and I believe, in accordance with the editors and contributors of *Beyond the Archives,* that this personal connection has improved the quality of my work both as a scholar and also a pedagogue.

The definition of cultural agency that I share with the literary projects I study understands craft as a creative process that enables all individuals to exercise cultural agency as artists. Walter Benjamin's definition of craft is a process through which the crafter expresses her authentic experience of "touching the world" through the creation of material objects, which for Benjamin includes literary writings.[7] Because all individuals touch the world in a unique way, all have the power to express their own lived experiences through crafting. I understand my scholarly writings and pedagogy as forms of craft according to this definition because both are born out of my research, which is, as I have attempted to describe it here, a personal experience of touching the world.

Christine Mason Sutherland, in her contribution to the volume *Beyond the Archives,* has written that feminist research practices produce polythetic meaning, by which she means that they are derived from the personal experiences we share with our objects of study and that subsequently inform and influence our research.[8] My research for this book has produced polythetic meaning in the sense that it is the result of my own personal experiences with the subjects and objects I study. As a result, my own experiences, my scholarship, and consequently my pedagogy, are forms of craft, just as the processes of cultural production that I study are. This book is not made of cardboard trash or a burlap sack; I did not sew its pages together at a kitchen table or on my home sewing machine, as was the case with *Tenemos pantalones,* the Ergo Sum book-object with which we began this study. But I have, nonetheless, made this book by hand.

APPENDIX 1

Registry of Ergo Sum Book-Objects

Because most Ergo Sum book-objects do not carry a year of publication, it is difficult to determine with total certainty the year in which each book-object was published. The following list was complied with the help of Resha Cardone and Gabriela Aguilera, and represents our best possible attempt at accuracy.

1985 *Ergo Sum*
1986 *21 son los relatos*
Los incontables (single-authored book-object by Pedro Mardones)
1987 *Ensacados: 26 cuentos ilustrados*
1988 *25 cuentos a la bolsa*
1989 *Machismo se escribe con m de mamá (29 cuentos ilustrados)*
Cartas al azar
1990 *Microcuentos de 32 autores*
1991 *Por un zapato roto (Microcuentos)*
1992 *Cuentos reciclados*
1993 *Secretos y pecados*
1994 *Cuentos de guarda*
1995 *Problemáticos y febriles: microcuentos*
1996 *Secretos envasados*
1997 *Cuentos para iluminarse*
1998 *Con-presión*
1999 *En crisis*
2000 *Desaforados*
2001 *Tras la puerta*
2003 *41 ficciones súbitas*
2004 *Que sea la llave, ¿y por qué no?*

2005 *Diversos y estilados*
2006 *Tenemos pantalones*
2007 *Ni una más*
2008 *Perraje en crisis*
Homenaje a Juan Armando Epple
2009 *Bolsa de valores*
2010 *Aterramiento*
2011 *Letra chica*
2012 *No molestar*
2013 *Silencio roto*
2014 *Temblorosos y esenciales*
2015 *País Tanguero*

APPENDIX 2

Registry of Cartonera Presses Worldwide

This table includes only those Cartonera Publishers whose identities could be verified. It is not a comprehensive list. The publishers are presented according to country of origin, with countries listed in alphabetical order. Publishers with multiple countries of origin are presented last. The years listed represent the earliest identifiable date of existence for each press. This list was complied with the help of Alexandra Missirian and Jonathan Velásquez, and represents our best possible attempt at accuracy.

Name	*City*	*Country*	*Year*
Eloísa Cartonera	Buenos Aires	Argentina	2003
Cartonerita Solar	Neuquén	Argentina	2009
Editorial Retazos	Buenos Aires	Argentina	2009
Nasaindy Cartonera Editorial	Formosa	Argentina	2009
Textos de Cartón	Córdoba	Argentina	2009
Klóketen Tintea Cartonera	Río Grande	Argentina	2010
Cartoneros del Espacio	Buenos Aires	Argentina	2011
Cieneguita Cartonera	Mendoza	Argentina	2011
Me muero de muerta Cartonera	Ezeiza	Argentina	2011
Editora Cartonera Amarillo, Rojo y Azul	Buenos Aires	Argentina	2012
La Sofia Cartonera	Córdoba	Argentina	2012
Niñobúho Cartonera	Buenos Aires	Argentina	2012
Poderosa Lectura	San Juan	Argentina	2012
Casimiro Bigua Cartonera	Puerto Madryn	Argentina	2013
El Cid Cartonero	Córdoba	Argentina	2014
Hilo de Agua	Paraná	Argentina	unknown

Name	City	Country	Year
Mandrágora Cartonera	Cochabamba	Bolivia	2004
Yerba Mala Cartonera	La Paz	Bolivia	2006
Nicotina Cartonera	Santa Cruz	Bolivia	2009
La Aparecida Cartonera	Santa Cruz	Bolivia	2010
Rostro Asado Cartonero	Oruro	Bolivia	2010
Dulcinéia Catadora	São Paulo	Brazil	2007
Katarina Kartonera	Santa Catarina	Brazil	2008
Sereia Cantadora	São Paulo	Brazil	2010
Dengo-Dengo Cartoneiro	Santa Catarina	Brazil	2011
Ediçoes Serpentinas	Belo Horizonte	Brazil	2011
Estação Catadora	São Paulo	Brazil	2011
Querubim Cartonera	Recife	Brazil	2012
Rubra Cartoneira	Paraná	Brazil	2012
Severina Catadora	Garanhuns	Brazil	2012
CArtonerA CArAAtApA	Rio de Janeiro	Brazil	2013
Estrela Cartonera	Santa Maria	Brazil	2013
La Gurisa Cartonera	Alto Paraná	Brazil	2013
Maria Papelão Editora	Santa Maria	Brazil	2013
Mariposa Cartonera	Recife	Brazil	2013
Therezinha Cartonera	Foz do Iguaçu	Brazil	2013
Universo Cartoneiro	Igarassu	Brazil	2015
Animita Cartonera	Santiago	Chile	2005
Canita Cartonera	Alto Hospicio	Chile	2009
Cartonera Helecho	Puerto Montt	Chile	2009
Cizarra Cartonera	Santiago	Chile	2009
Nuestra Senora Cartonera	La Serena	Chile	2010
Isidora Cartonera	Santiago	Chile	2011
Benicia Cartonera Editorial	Santiago	Chile	2012
Calafate Cartonera	Santiago	Chile	2012
Editorial Letras de Cartón	Santiago	Chile	2012
Kiltra Cartonera	Valparaiso	Chile	2012
La Vieja Sapa Cartonera	Santiago	Chile	2012
Olga Cartonera	Santiago	Chile	2012
Warp Zone Cartonera	Arica	Chile	2012
Costalazo Ediciones	Santiago	Chile	2013
Infracción Ediciones	Concepción	Chile	2013
Juanita Cartonera	Santiago	Chile	2013

Name	*City*	*Country*	*Year*
La Fonola Cartonera	Santiago	Chile	2013
La Gata Viuda Cartonera	Santiago	Chile	2013
Loquita Cartonera	Santiago	Chile	2013
Varonas de Cartón Edición	Santiago	Chile	2013
Fugitiva Cartonera	Arica	Chile	2014
La Grullita Cartonera	Santiago	Chile	2014
La Joyita Cartonera	Santiago	Chile	2014
Mil Hojas	Beijing	China	2010
Patasola Cartonera	Bogotá	Colombia	2009
Cartonero Delahogado el sombrero	Cali	Colombia	2010
Amapola Cartonera	Bogotá	Colombia	2012
Cartón Grafías	Bogotá	Colombia	2014
Mamacha Cartonera	unknown	Colombia	unknown
Cartonera Tica	San José	Costa Rica	2010
La Cartonera Tuanis	Coronado	Costa Rica	2010
Ukecleta Cartonera	Guápiles	Costa Rica	2014
Luz Azul Cartonera	unknown	Dominican Republic	unknown
Dadaif Cartoenra	Guayaquil	Ecuador	2009
Matapalo Cartonera	Riobamba	Ecuador	2009
Murcielagario Kartonera	Quito	Ecuador	2009
Camareta Cartonera	Guayaquil	Ecuador	2010
Matrioska Cartonera	Guayaquil	Ecuador	2011
Ninacuro Cartonera	Cuenca	Ecuador	2013
Dadaif Cartonera	Guayaquil	Ecuador	2014
Luna Verde Cartonera	Macas	Ecuador	2014
Gato Negra Cartonera	Guayaquil	Ecuador	unknown
Cizarra Cartonera	unknown	El Salvador	2009
La Cabuda Cartonera Editorial	San Salvador	El Salvador	2009
Pirata Cartonera	San Salvador	El Salvador	2013
Karu Kartonera	unknown	Finland	2010
La Guêpe Cartonnière	Saint-Ouen	France	2010
Yvonne Cartonera	Paris	France	2010
Babel Cartonera	Bagnères de Luchon	France	2011
Cephisa Cartonera	Clermont-Ferrand	France	2011
Julieta Cartonera	Toulouse	France	2012
La Marge	Angers	France	2013
Kartocéros Editions	Clermont-Ferrand	France	2014

Name	*City*	*Country*	*Year*
PapperLaPapp	Berlin	Germany	2009
Papka Cartonera	Halle	Germany	2010
Alambique	Cobán	Guatemala	2009
Cartonera Maximon	Guatemala City	Guatemala	2011
Industria Cartonera	Guatemala City	Guatemala	unknown
ZonaFranca Casa Editrice Di Cartoni	Lucca	Italy	2009
FernAnda Pappetrice	Verona	Italy	2012
Storie di Cartone	Turin	Italy	2012
Cuxitali Cartonera	San Cristóbal de las Casas	Mexico	2005
La Cartonera	Cuernavaca	Mexico	2008
Santa Muerte Cartonera	Mexico City	Mexico	2008
Cohuiná Cartonera	Chiapas	Mexico	2009
La Ratona Cartonera	Cuernavaca	Mexico	2009
La Regia Cartonera	Monterrey	Mexico	2009
La Rueda Cartonera	Guadalajara	Mexico	2009
Cascada de Palabras Cartonera	Mexico City	Mexico	2010
Iguanazul Cartonera	Zongolica	Mexico	2010
Klitoris Kartonera	San Cristóbal de las Casas	Mexico	2010
Kodama Cartonera	Tijuana	Mexico	2010
La Marchanta Cartonera	Mexico City	Mexico	2010
La Verdura Cartonera	Mexico City	Mexico	2010
Nuestro Grito Cartonero	Pachuca de Soto	Mexico	2010
Tegus La Cartonera del Toro	Puebla	Mexico	2010
Bakcheia Cartonera	Chihuahua	Mexico	2011
Cartonera La Cecilia	Zacatecas	Mexico	2011
Cartonera Nieve de Limón	Zacatecas	Mexico	2011
La Cleta Cartonera	Cholula	Mexico	2011
Plástica Cartonera	Monterrey	Mexico	2011
Orquesta Eléctrica Cartonera	Mexico City	Mexico	2011
Siete Lenguas Cartonera	Aguascalientes	Mexico	2011
Cartonera LaAurora	unknown	Mexico	2012
Cosa Nostra Cartonera	Querétaro	Mexico	2012
Ediciones Cartonera Hortera	Cancún	Mexico	2012
Infinita Cartonera	Mexico City	Mexico	2012
Jauja Ediciones	Mexico City	Mexico	2012

Name	*City*	*Country*	*Year*
Mamá Dolores Cartonera	Querétaro	Mexico	2012
Maya Cartonera	Tuxtla Gutiérrez	Mexico	2012
Nauyaca Cartonera	Toluca	Mexico	2012
Pachuk' Cartonera	Pachuca de Soto	Mexico	2012
Fantasma Cartonera	Querétaro	Mexico	2013
La Milpa Cartonera	Guanajuato	Mexico	2013
Cartonera Nómada Editorial	Xalapa	Mexico	2014
El Chaneke Cartonero	Colima	Mexico	2014
Cartarsis Cartonera	Pachuca de Soto	Mexico	2015
La Tolvanera Cartonera	Coahuila	Mexico	unknown
Kutsemba Cartão	Maputo	Mozambique	2010
Livaningo Cartão d'Arte	Maputo	Mozambique	2012
Diablo Rojo Cartonera	Panama City	Panama	2011
Ediciones Pelo Malo	Panama City	Panama	2012
Yiyi Jambo	Asunción	Paraguay	2007
Felicita Cartonera	Asunción	Paraguay	2008
Mamacha Kartonera	Asunción	Paraguay	2008
Mburukujarami Kartonera	Luque	Paraguay	2008
La Cancha ava de Kumikova	Lambaré	Paraguay	2012
Sarita Cartonera	Lima	Peru	2004
Cartonazo Editores	Lima	Peru	2007
My Lourdes Cartonera	Cerro de Pasco	Peru	2009
Otra Cosa Cartonera	Huaraz	Peru	2009
Casa Katatay	Lima	Peru	2010
Eqquss Editorial Cartonera	Piura	Peru	2011
Qinti Qartunira	Lamas	Peru	2011
Amaru Cartonera	Lima	Peru	2013
Efraín y Enrique Editores	Lima	Peru	2013
Viringo Cartonero	Lima	Peru	2013
Charca Cartonera	Lima	Peru	2014
La Apacheta Cartonera	Lima	Peru	2014
Sullawayta Cartonera	Lima	Peru	2015
Bela Cartonera	Lisbon	Portugal	2012
Atarraya Cartonera	San Juan	Puerto Rico	2009
Mambru	unknown	Puerto Rico	2013
Coquí Cartonero	Añasco	Puerto Rico	2015
Paquita Cartonera	Barcelona	Spain	2007

Name	*City*	*Country*	*Year*
Editorial Ultramarina Cartonera	Seville	Spain	2009
Cartonerita Niñabonita	Zaragoza	Spain	2010
Cartopiés Cartonera	Madrid	Spain	2010
Boquita Cartonera	Blanes	Spain	2011
El Mamut Clonado Editorial Cartonera	Madrid	Spain	2011
Cartonera Island	Canary Islands	Spain	2012
Ediciones Cordeleria Ilustrada	La Puebla de Híjar	Spain	2012
Ediciones Karakartón	Mallorca	Spain	2012
Libertarios de Cartón	Tarragona	Spain	2012
Palmera Cartonera	Cáceres	Spain	2012
Zapaticos Rotos Cartonera	Zaragoza	Spain	2012
Aida Cartonera	Segovia	Spain	2013
Carmela Cartonera	Barcelona	Spain	2013
La Veronica Cartonera Editorial	Barcelona	Spain	2013
Pensaré Cartoneras	Valencia	Spain	2013
Poesia con C	Malmö	Sweden	2007
Rosalita Cartonera	Madison, WI	United States	2010
Cartonera Santanera	Santa Ana, CA	United States	2012
Cardboard House Press	Bloomington, IN	United States	2013
La Propia Cartonera	Montevideo	Uruguay	2009
Caracoles y Kurupies	unknown	Uruguay	unknown
HarKalya Kartonera	La Azulita	Venezuela	2011
Cartón en Mano Cartonera	Caracas	Venezuela	2014
Dirtsa Cartonera	Maracay	Venezuela	2014
Editorial Cartonera Intercultural	Guayaquil, Cuenca New York City, NY	Ecuador, United States	2008
Casamanita Cartonera	Mexico City and Saltillo San Salvador Galicia	Mexico El Salvador Spain	2009
Meninas Cartoneras	Santiago Mexico City Madrid	Chile Mexico Spain	2009
Anfibia Cartonera	Bogotá Madrid	Colombia Spain	2013

Notes

Introduction

Epigraph: [In Spanish] "Hay que retomar las cartes a la mano, combinar convicción, voluntarismo, un grado de testadurez [*sic*], con la tradición de una práctica y el aprendizaje de nuevas formas de comunicarse, producir y organizarse." When published English translations of original Spanish texts are available, I have cited them; otherwise, all translations are my own.

1. [In Spanish] "*Tenemos pantalones*® Talleres Ergo Sum, Dirigidos por Pía Barros, 2006."

2. [In Spanish] "Santiago de Chile, noviembre de 2006."

3. This book does not include an historical explanation of Chile's 1973 military coup, the seventeen-year dictatorship of General Augusto Pinochet that followed it, or the process through which that dictatorship ended. For this history, see Mary Helen Spooner, *Soldiers in a Narrow Land: The Pinochet Regime in Chile* (Berkeley: University of California Press, 1999), and *The General's Slow Retreat: Chile after Pinochet* (Berkeley: University of California Press, 2011); and Pamela Constable and Arturo Valenzuela, *A Nation of Enemies: Chile under Pinochet* (New York: Norton, 1991).

4. [In Spanish] "todos los medios de comunicación, así como al conjunto de las expresiones artísticas y culturales." Comisión Chilena de Derechos Humanos y Fundación Ideas, *Nunca más en Chile: Síntesis corregida y actualizada del Informe Rettig* (Santiago: LOM Ediciones, 1991), 6.

5. There have been other national and international meetings of Cartonera presses in Latin America, the United States, and Europe; however, to my knowledge none of them have been as large or diverse as the three held in Chile.

6. Robert Neustadt, *CADA día: La creación de un arte social* (Santiago: Editorial Cuarto Propio, 2012).

7. Francine Masiello's study of art and literature in postdictatorship Chile and Argentina demonstrates how the act of public performance changed as a result of the transition from dictatorship to democracy in both countries. She argues that under dictatorship, "when the state posited a need for fixed subjectivities and stable positions of meaning as a way to control citizen's movement," artistic performances of gender and sexual difference often relied on impersonation, copy, and disguise. On the other hand, the neoliberal nature of postdictatorship societies has produced public spheres dominated by visual materials and ways of seeing that commodify performance to such a degree that it becomes the very definition of citizenship. Francine Masiello, *The Art of Transition: Latin American Culture and Neoliberal Crisis* (Durham: Duke University Press, 2001), 59.

8. This is the central thesis of Alice A. Nelson's book, *Political Bodies: Gender, History, and the Struggle for Narrative Power in Recent Chilean Literature* (Lewisburg: Bucknell University Press; London: Associated University Presses, 2002).

9. Raquel Olea, *Lengua Víbora: Producciones de lo femenino en la escritura de mujeres Chilenas* (Santiago: Editorial Cuarto Propio; Corporación de Desarrollo de la Mujer la Morada, 1998). In *The Art of Transition,* Francine Masiello locates a similar emphasis on the materiality of language in queer literature of postdictatorship Argentina, which she argues unleashes a plurality of subjectivities from the body of the text (72). She finds the works of Néstor Perlongher and Arturo Carrera filled with mixed registers and textures of speech that make language, as she puts it, "almost physical" (70) and the sign on the page "material in form" (75).

10. Olea, *Lengua Víbora,* 13.

11. Nelly Richard, *Margins and Institutions: Art in Chile since 1973* (Melbourne, AU: Art and Text, 1986).

12. See Idelber Avelar, *The Untimely Present: Postdictatorial Latin American Literature and the Task of Mourning* (Durham, NC: Duke University Press, 1999); Kathrin Bergenthal, "El Mini-Boom de la Nueva Narrativa Chilena," in *Crisis, apocalipsis y utopías: Fines de siglo en la literatura latinoamericana; XXXII Congreso Internacional de la Literatura Iberoamericana,* ed. Rodrigo Cánovas and Roberto Hozven (Santiago: Instituto Internacional de la Literatura Iberoamericana; Instituto de Letras, Pontificia Universidad Católica de Chile, 2000); Luis E. Cárcamo-Huechante, *Tramas del mercado: Imaginación económica, cultura pública y literatura en el Chile de fines del siglo veinte* (Santiago: Editorial Cuarto Propio, 2007); Guillermo García-Corales, *Dieciseis entrevistas con autores chilenos contemporáneos: La emergencia de una nueva narrativa* (Lewiston, ME: The Edwin Mellen Press, 2005); and Bernardo Subercaseaux, *Historia del libro en Chile: Desde la Colonia hasta el Bicentenario* (Santiago: LOM Ediciones, 2000).

13. Cárcamo-Huechante, *Tramas del mercado,* 51–52. Cárcamo-Huechante singles out Isabel Allende, Luis Sepúlveda, Marcela Serrano, Gonzalo Contreras, Alberto Fuguet, and Hernán Rivera Letelier as authors who released titles in the late 1980s and early 1990s that quickly experienced large commercial success (51).

14. Ibid., 50.; and Ángel Rama, "El 'boom' en perspectiva," in *Más allá del boom: Literatura y Mercado,* ed. David Viñas (Mexico City: Marcha Editores, 1981), 91–110.

15. Bergenthal, "El Mini-Boom de la Nueva Narrativa Chilena," 224–29; Ksenija Bilbija, "¡Cartoneros de todos los países, uníos!: Un recorrido no tan fantasmal de las editoriales cartoneras latinoamericanas en el tercer milenio," in *Akademia Cartonera: A Primer of Latin American Cartonera Publishers, Academic Articles, Cartonera Publications Catalog and Bibliography,* ed. Ksenija Bilbija and Paloma Celis Carbajal (Madison: University of Wisconsin–Madison Libraries / Parallel Press, 2010), 7.

16. Bergenthal, "El Mini-Boom," 224–29.

17. Cárcamo-Huechante, *Tramas del mercado,* 57.

18. Masiello, *The Art of Transition,* 17.

19. [In Spanish] "la industria cultural convierte a los individuos en consumidores." Jorge Larraín, *Identidad Chilena* (Santiago: LOM Ediciones, 2001), 246.

20. Ibid., 248.

21. [In Spanish] "escritores-consumidores." Cárcamo-Huechante, *Tramas del mercado,* 52.

22. See Sergio Villalobos-Ruminott, *Soberanías en suspenso: Imaginación y violencia en América Latina* (Buenos Aires: Ediciones La Cebra, 2013), 75; and Néstor García Canclini, *Consumer Citizens: Globalization and Multicultural Conflicts,* trans. George Yúdice (Minneapolis: University of Minnesota Press, 2001). The latter takes this argument as its central theme.

23. The most egregious of those contradictions stem from the fact that the Chilean govern-

ment is still functioning under the 1980 constitution written by the Pinochet regime. While the 1980 constitution has been amended numerous times since the end of the dictatorship in 1990, many aspects of it are still severely problematic and anti-democratic. One example is that this constitution granted legal immunity to military and state officials who violated human rights during some of the dictatorship's most brutal years (Comisión Chilena de Derechos Humanos y Fundación Ideas, *Nunca más en Chile,* 7). Thus while the newly democratic state has named two commissions to investigate violations of human rights committed by the regime, the findings of those commissions do more to suture the psychic trauma of Chile's body politic than they do to actually effect social justice. The first state commission assigned to investigate the military's abuse of human rights was the Comisión Nacional de Verdad y Reconciliación (National Truth and Reconiliation Commision), which reported in 1991 that just under three thousand people had either been killed or disappeared by the military regime between 1973 and 1990. The second state commission, La Comisión Nacional sobre Prisión Política y Tortura (the National Commission on Political Imprisonment and Torture), formed by President Ricardo Lagos in 2003, shows a more complete picture of state violence: thirty thousand people voluntarily came forward to provide verbal testimonies to this commission about their experiences as victims of state torture. See Comisión Chilena de Derechos Humanos y Fundación Ideas, *Nunca más en Chile,* and Comisión Nacional sobre Prisión Política y Tortura, "Informe," *DerechosHumanos.net,* www.derechoshumanos.net. Some people see the failures of the newly democratic governments to dismantle the political and economic infrastructure erected by Pinochet's regime as reason to question the very use of the term "transition" to describe the early postdictatorship period. One of these critics is Sergio Villalobos-Ruminott, who sees the dictatorship and the postdictatorship periods as two moments in a continuous trajectory of the Chilean Republic's violent march toward modernization. Villalobos-Ruminott understands the very idea of a "neoliberal democracy" as an oxymoron. See Sergio Villalobos-Ruminott, *Soberanías en suspenso: Imaginación y violencia en América Latina* (Buenos Aires: Ediciones La Cebra, 2013), 36–44.

24. Michelle Bachelet is a prime example of Chile's successful re-establishment of procedural democracy since she represents so much of what Pinochet fought to eradicate from Chile: she is the daughter of a general whose open opposition to Pinochet resulted in his murder and the detention and eventual exile of his family, including the future president. She is also a socialist, an agnostic, and an unwed mother who held the position of defense minister and was twice elected as president of the Republic. On April 18, 2015, President Bachelet vowed to rewrite the constitution—a goal that critics believe will be difficult to realize.

25. Philip J. Costopoulos and Zaki Laidi, "Democracy in Real Time," in *Democracy Journal* 13, no. 3 (July 2012): 76.

26. Doris Sommer, ed., *Cultural Agency in the Americas* (Durham: Duke University Press, 2006) 19.

27. Michel de Certeau is best known for his research into how average citizens make creative and symbolic meaning through everyday objects and everyday acts of living. See Michel de Certeau, *The Practice of Everyday Life,* trans. Steven F. Rendall (Berkeley: University of California Press, 1984). A good source for this kind of research within the context of Latin America is the book *El consumo cultural en América Latina,* ed. Guillermo Sunkel (Santafé de Bogotá: Convenio Andrés Bello, 1999).

28. [In Spanish] "[*La producción literaria*] *está directamente relacionad[a] con el desarrollo cultural y la creatividad de la sociedad.* No necesariamente para desarrollar nuevas [ideas] sino para inventar nuevas formas de producir, de comunicar y de vivir. Porque, en el fondo, [la producción literaria] es la capacidad social y personal de transformar la creatividad en fuerza

productiva que permita a su vez el desarrollo de esa creatividad, en un círculo virtuoso entre el arte de vivir y la eficiencia de producir." Manuel Castells, *Globalización, desarrollo y democracia: Chile en el contexto mundial* (Santiago: Fondo de Cultura Económica, 2005), 112 (emphasis in the original).

1. Chilean Literary Culture since 1970

Epigraph: [In Spanish]"¿Cómo hacer que la cultura, que el gesto cultural se haga a cada rato en este país y con todos los ciudadanos, todos?" Gregory Cohen, "La rotura de nexo," in *Escritores por el fomento del libro y la lectura: Tercer encuentro; Actas* (Santiago: Gobierno de Chile; Letras de Chile; Mosquito Comunicaciones, 2001), 121.

1. Chilean book historian Bernardo Subercaseaux associates Allende's vision to democratize Chilean culture with the developmental agenda of presidents Arturo Alessandri, Carlos Ibáñez del Campo, Pedro Aguirre Cerda, Juan Antonio Ríos, and Eduardo Frei Montalva. Bernardo Subercaseaux, *Historia del libro en Chile: Desde la Colonia hasta el Bicentenario* (Santiago: LOM Ediciones, 2000), 177–78.

2. Ibid., 184–85.

3. Ibid., 188.

4. [In Spanish] "asegura[r] el acceso de las mayorías a los bienes artísticos." Ibid., 180.

5. Ibid., 177.

6. Subercaseaux writes that Quimantú set forth "una valoración del producto libro como un medio superior a otros medios, una visión iluminista de la cultura que la enfatiza como alta cultura, como un legado al que se accede solo a través de ciertos soportes capaces de contenerla: los libros (a valorization of the book product as a media superior to other media, an enlightenment vision of culture that accentuates it as high culture, as a legacy that is only accessed through certain mediums capable of housing it: books). Ibid., 184.

7. Ibid., 165.

8. Communications scholar Kristin Sorensen has shown how this also happened in the television industry during the dictatorship period, when formerly public networks were privatized and sold to foreign owners. Kristin Sorensen, *Media, Memory, and Human Rights in Chile* (New York: Palgrave Macmillan, 2009), 39.

9. Belén Bascuñán identifies some of the most serious raids as including the 1985 raid of the factory where the book *Y quién va a caer,* by Matilde Ladrón de Guevara, had been printed; the 1986 raid of Ediciones Pehuén; and the 1986 raid of Editorial Terranova. Belén Bascuñán, "Editores y editoriales en dictadura" (Santiago: Museo de la Memoria, June 2012), 6, www.cedocmuseodelamemoria.cl.

10. [In Spanish] "la fundación, edición y circulación de nuevas publicaciones." Subercaseaux, *Historia del libro en Chile,* 159.

11. Ibid., 159–60.

12. Horacio Eloy credits historian Víctor Muñoz Tamayo as introducing this term in the 1977 "Las Jornadas del Libro y la Lectura" (Conference on the Book and Reading), organized by La Universidad Católica de Chile (The Catholic University of Chile). Horacio Eloy, *Revistas y publicaciones literarias en dictadura (1973–1990)* (Santiago: Piso Diez Ediciones / Mago Editores, 2014), 14.

13. Pamela Constable and Arturo Valenzuela, *A Nation of Enemies: Chile under Pinochet* (New York: Norton, 1991), 147.

14. This last percentage differs a bit depending on whether we use Eloy's figure for national book production for 1975 or that provided by Subercaseaux: Eloy cites 618 books produced

in Chile in 1975 (*Revistas y publicaciones literarias,* 14), and Subercaseaux cites 513 (*Historia del libro en Chile,* 211).

15. Subercaseaux, *Historia del libro en Chile,* 202–207.

16. Ibid., 201.

17. Pía Barros, in discussion with the author, Santiago, March 5, 2007.

18. Subercaseaux identifies Chilean publishing houses in Mexico, Canada, and Spain. (201).

19. Alejandra Basualto, in discussion with the author, Santiago, March 14, 2007.

20. [In Spanish] "Hubo que enterrarla y allá en Concepción está todavía, más que una vez he pensado que así como en la Segunda Guerra Mundial la gente enterraba joyas o dinero, nosotros en Chile tuvimos que esconder o quemar libros." Subercaseaux, *Historia del libro en Chile,* 200.

21. [In Spanish] "símbolos de una historia que esper[a] quede sepultada definitivamente en el pasado." Diego Muñoz, "Discurso de Digo Muñoz Valenzuela, vicepresidente de la Corporación Letras de Chile," in *Escritores por el Fomento del Libro y la Lectura: Tercer Encuentro; Actas* (Santiago: Gobierno de Chile; Letras de Chile; Mosquito Comunicaciones, 2001), 19.

22. [In Spanish] "los bienes simbólicos son valorados pero no valorizados." Pía Barros, "Movimientos culturales, industria cultural" (unpublished essay, 2005), copy in author's collection.

23. Horacio Eloy, *Revistas y publicaciones literarias,* 14.

24. Consejo Nacional de la Cultura y las Artes (CNCA), Ministerio de Educación, DIBAM, *Plan Nacional de Fomento de la Lectura: Lee Chile Lee* (Santiago: CNCA, 2011), 72, www.cultura.gob.cl.

25. Constable and Valenzuela, *A Nation of Enemies,* 155. No one embodies the capitalist purpose of Chilean television and consumer culture of the postdictatorship period better than the figure of Don Francisco, the host of Chile's now world-famous television spectacular *Sábado Gigante* (Gigantic Saturday). Don Francisco rose to power as one of the nation's leading cultural icons during the dictatorship years of the 1980s partly because his public persona embodied the excessive emphasis Chilean society placed on the materiality of culture during these years (audience participants were frequently awarded home appliances and other items of consumer culture). *Sábado Gigante* is representative of how Pinochet's authoritarian regime privileged the spectacle over substance within the cultural realm. For more on the history and importance of *Sábado Gigante* in Chilean culture, see Óscar Contardo and Macarena García, *La era ochentera: Tevé, pop y under en el Chile de los ochenta* (Santiago: Ediciones B, 2005).

26. Statistics show that throughout the postdictatorship period, the literary industry has grown more steadily (albeit slowly) and in a more diversified way than other national culture industries. Bárbara Negrón, "Industrias culturales: Preguntas y desafíos," in *Políticas Culturales: Contingencia y Desafíos, Número 1. Año 1* (Santiago: Observatorio de Políticas Culturales / LOM Ediciones, 2011), 135.

27. Of course it is difficult to quantify the opinions of all Chilean literary producers of the postdictatorship period; I derive my statement here from numerous conversations I have had over many years with literary producers in Chile, as well as statements published by many of these individuals. Representations of these opinions can be found in *Escritores por el fomento del libro y la lectura: Tercer Encuentro; Actas;* and CNCA, *Plan Nacional.*

28. To give just one example of this growth, in 1977 there were 51 libraries in all of Chile; in 2011 there were over 450 (CNCA, *Plan Nacional,* 31).

29. Consejo Nacional de la Culturla y las Artes, *Plan Nacional,* 19–22.

30. Enrique Ramos Curd, "Plan de fomento de la lectura en Chile: Un proceso de construcción participativa," *Serie Bibliotecología y Gestión de Información* no. 45 (July 2009): 15, http://eprints.rclis.org.

31. Fundación la Fuente, Adimark-GFK, *Chile y los libros: Índice de Lectura y Compra de Libros, 2006,* www.fundacionlafuente.cl.

32. Universidad de Chile, Departamento de Economía, CNCA, *Estudio de Comportamiento Lector* (Santiago: Universidad de Chile, Departamento de Economía; CNCA, 2011), 37, www.cultura.gob.cl.

33. [In Spanish] "La democracia está basada, supuestamente, en la libre circulación de las ideas y de las palabras. Cuestión bien difícil cuando la existencia de una prensa independiente se ve truncada a medio camino entre la zozobra económica y el control de los grandes consorcios." Jaime Pinos, "La calabaza del diablo," in *Escritores por el fomento del libro y la lectura. Tercer Encuentro; Actas,* 87.

34. [In Spanish] "La libertad de expresión parece ser más un eslogan que una realidad debido a la total concentración de los medios de comunicación y a la virtual censura que imponen las empresas avisadoras de publicidad." Paulo Slachevsky, "El camino que vamos haciendo," in *Escritores por el fomento del libro y la lectura. Tercer Encuentro: Actas,* 91.

35. Ibid., 94.

36. The examples she gives are *Lumpérica,* by Diamelta Eltit, which was published by Las Ediciones del Ornitorrinco and then bought by Casa de las Américas in 2008; *Silendra,* by Elizabeth Subercaseaux, also published by Las Ediciones del Ornitorrinco, and then bought by Alfaguara in 2000, *Fidel Castro y la religión, conversaciones con Frei Betto,* by Carlos Alberto Libanio Christo, which was published by Pehuén and then bought by Ocean Press in 2006; and *El viejo que leía novelas de amor,* by José Luis Sepúlveda, which was published by Emisión and then bought by Tusquets in 2009. Bascuñán, "Editores y editoriales en dictadura," 9–10.

37. [In Spanish] "ser independiente de la lógica del mercado, ser una editorial de tamaño medio pequeño, y tener una política editorial distinta a las de las multinacionales." Quoted in Meninas Cartoneras, "Editoriales Cartoneras en Casa Américas," *MeninasCartoneras.BlogSpot.com,* June 22, 2013, http://meninascartonerasEditorial.blogspot.com.

38. [In Spanish] "Difundir el libro es hacer democracia, es posibilitar que al otro se asuma como ciudadano y no como consumidor, es invitarlo a pensar, a estar alerta. En ese sentido, creo que el trabajo con el libro desde la perspectiva cultural, es en alguna medida un trabajo militante. Creo que los editores independientes nos asumimos como militantes en el ámbito cultural." Paulo Slachevsky, "El camino que vamos haciendo," 93.

39. Kathrin Bergenthal, "El Mini-Boom de la Nueva Narrativa Chilena," in *Crisis, apocalipsis y utopías: Fines de siglo en la literatura latinoamericana; XXXII Congreso Internacional de la Literatura Iberoamericana,* ed. Rodrigo Cánovas and Roberto Hozven (Santiago: Instituto Internacional de la Literatura Iberoamericana; Instituto de Letras, Pontificia Universidad Católica de Chile, 2000), 224–29; and Ksenija Bilbija, "¡Cartoneros de todos los países, uníos!: Un recorrido no tan fantasmal de las editoriales cartoneras latinoamericanas en el tercer milenio," in *Akademia Cartonera: A Primer of Latin American Cartonera Publishers,* ed. Ksenija Bilbija and Paloma Celis Carbajal (Madison: University of Wisconsin–Madison Libraries / Parallel Press, 2010), 7.

40. Pinos, "La calabaza del diablo," 83; and Curd, "Plan de fomento de la lectura en Chile," 8.

41. It has become common for scholars to put the "Boom" in quotes in order to question its authenticity as an organic literary movement and to suggest that it was instead a marketing construction of Spanish publishers.

42. Quoted in Alejandro Herrero-Olaizola, "Consuming Aesthetics: Seix Barral and José Donoso in the Field of Latin American Literary Production," Hispanic Issue, *MLN* 115, no. 2 (March 2000): 324.

43. Similar associations and organizations of cultural producers from various industries,

including radio, film, television, and music, have increased in impressive numbers throughout the postdictatorship period. The 2005 state publication on culture policy, *Chile quiere más cultura* (Chile wants more culture), cites 4,225 such organizations (23). La Unión Nacional de Artistas de Chile (The National Union of Chilean Artists) also provides a comprehensive list of such associations, as do Agustín Squella and José Weinstein. See CNCA, *Chile quiere más cultura: Definiciones de política cultural 2005–2010,* May 2005, 23, www.cultura.gob.cl; La Unión Nacional de Artistas de Chile, "Afiliados," www.unionnacionaldeartistas.cl; Agustín Squella, *El jinete en la lluvia: La cultura en el gobierno de Lagos,* ed. Eduardo Carrasco (Santiago: Aguilar, 2005), 122–23; and José Weinstein, "Discurso de inauguración," in *Derecho de autor: Un desafío para la creación y el desarrollo,* ed. Eduardo Carrasco (Santiago: LOM Ediciones / CNCA, 2004), 14.

44. A prime example of this is María Sol Vera, who explains that during the dictatorship years her press, Editorial Cuarto Propio (Room of One's Own Publishers), functioned as a publicity firm in order to hide its editorial output; now under a neoliberal democracy, her press still has to find other ways of making money in order to finance its book production. María Sol Vera, in discussion with the author, Santiago, January 9, 2014.

45. Raymond Williams, *Culture* (Glasgow: Fontana Paperbacks, 1981), 62.

46. [In Spanish] "la nueva institucionalidad cultural de Chile." Coincidentally, Allende and Pinochet also referred to the "cultural institutionalization" of their respective administrations. With regard to the cultural institutionalization of the newly democratic governments, Agustín Squella has written a book, *El jinete en la lluvia: la cultura en el gobierno de Lagos,* documenting the formation and emergence of Chile's new cultural institutionalization. Here he explains that while the CNCA is essentially a state ministry (as civil society requested), the government intentionally rejected naming it as such, or labeling it with other titles such as "directorate" or "subsecretary," since none of those names adequately expressed both the importance of *culture* in the state's overall administrative agenda nor the importance of *civil society* in the construction and administration of this dual public-private organism (99). On the other hand, the word "council" identifies the essential role civil society plays within this institution as counselor to the state. For more on the development of Chile's new cultural institutionalization within the postdictatorship period, see Cristián Antoine, "La nueva institucionalidad cultural en Chile" *Revista Ius Publicum,* no. 12 (2004): 89–103; Manuel Antonio Garretón, "Las políticas culturales en los gobiernos democráticos en Chile," in *Políticas Culturais na Ibero-América* (Salvador Bahia: Editora da Universidade Federal da Bahía, 2008); and Observatorio de Políticas Culturales, *Políticas Culturales: Contingencia y Desafíos, Número 1. Año 1 Mayo* (Santiago: Observatorio de Políticas Culturales / LOM Ediciones, 2011).

47. The councils of the CNCA are Architecture, Visual Arts, Artisan Culture, Circus Arts, Dance, Design, Audiovisual Arts, Music, Photography, New Media, Theater, and Books and Reading.

48. Editores de Chile y Fundación Chile Veintiuno, *Una política de Estado para el libro y la lectura: Estrategias para el fomento de la lectura y el desarrollo de la industria editorial en Chile* (Santiago: Fundación Chile Veintiuno / Editores de Chile, 2005), www.chile21.cl.

49. CNCA and Consejo Nacional del Libro y la Lectura, *Política Nacional del Libro y la Lectura* (Santiago: CNCA, 2006).

50. Squella, *El jinete en la lluvia,* 99; CNCA, *Plan Nacional de Fomento de la Lectura,* 24.

51. [In Spanish] "Hemos creado el Consejo Nacional de la Cultura y los Consejos del Libro, de la Música y ahora del Audiovisual. Estos Consejos son los instrumentos públicos a través de los cuales debemos canalizar las políticas estatales dirigidas a fortalecer las industrias culturales." José Weinstein, "Simposio internacional sobre industrias culturales, discurso inaugural,"

in *Industrias culturales: un aporte al desarrollo,* ed. Eduardo Carrasco and Bárbara Negrón (Santiago: LOM Ediciones / CNCA), 18.

52. [In Spanish] "En estos tiempos en que se busca a toda costa la ganancia rápida, vale la pena recordar que la lectura sirve para compartir, para reconocerse en la alegría y el sufrimientos de otros, para vivir emociones profundas, para autocuestionarse, para ganar capacidad crítica y no dejarse engañar, para poder conocer de manera más compleja y diversa este mundo y otros mundos." CNCA, *Plan Nacional de Fomento de la Lectura,* 7.

53. [In Spanish] "el Fondart se ha transformado en una especie de estipendio que el Estado asigna a artistas que de otra manera no podrían sobrevivir por sí mismos. Eso no puede ser. . . . **¿Quién legitima al artista sino su obra?**" Quoted in Ricardo Brodsky, "¿Reforma en los fondos de cultura?" in *Políticas Culturales: Contingencia y Desafíos, Número 1. Año 1. Mayo,* 103–104.

2. Ergo Sum

1. Resha Cardone, "Refashioning the Book in Pinochet's Chile: The Feminist Literary Project, Ergo Sum," *Confluencia* 29, no. 1 (Fall 2013): 137.

2. María Luisa Ortiz, "RE: investigación: autopublicaciones en dictadura," e-mail to the author, March 11, 2014.

3. [In Spanish] "De este modo, tanto en Santiago como en Temuco, Valparaíso, Concepción, Valdivia, Iquique, Antofagasta, Chiloé, Punta Arenas y otras localidades la publicación de revistas se va convirtiendo en una real propuesta contestataria, en una postura cultural alternativa que, paso a paso y contra todas las dificultades, se revela como una fuerza y movimiento de mucho ingenio e imaginación para lograr cambios." Horacio Eloy, *Revistas y publicaciones literarias en dictadura (1973–1990)* (Santiago: Piso Diez Ediciones / Mago Editores, 2014), 15. Horacio Eloy and Jorge Montealegre curated a collection of self-published literary magazines of the dictatorship period that was on display at Chile's National Library for a limited time. Examples from the collection have been digitally archived as part of the library's "Memoria Chilena" (Chilean Memory) project and can be viewed on the library's website (www.memoriachilena.cl); this site is one of the best resources available for studying this underground publishing movement. El Museo de la Memoria y los Derechos Humanos (Museum of Memory and Human Rights) also has a substantial (but certainly not exhaustive) collection of underground self-publications of all kinds, not only literary. The seventh volume of the journal *Simpson 7,* published by the Sociedad de Escritores de Chile in 2000, is dedicated to the topic of Chilean literary journals and magazines from before, during, and after the dictatorship. It also contains an article written by Eloy that he eventually published in book form and that is one of the most authoritative pieces of scholarship published on this topic: *Revistas y publicaciones literarias en dictadura (1973–1990).*

4. Eloy lists some, but not all, literary workshops that were operating in Chile in the late 1970s and early 1980s: "Se generó de esta manera el discurso de la resistencia desde talleres, colectivos, asociaciones y grupos literarios como: Tralca, Tragaluz, Taller Urbano, Tranvía, Agrupación Cultural Santa María, Talleres del Mar, Taller Sol, Aumen, Índice, Grupo Salar, Ergo Sum, Mestizo, Literabierta, Talleres Andamio, Unión de Escritores Jóvenes, Agrupación Cultural Universitaria (ACU), y el Colectivo de Escritores Jóvenes, entre otros" (Such it was that a conversation about resistance coming from workshops, collectives, associations, and literary groups such as: Tralca, Tragaluz, Taller Urbano, Tranvía, Agrupación Cultural Santa María, Talleres del Mar, Taller Sol, Aumen, Índice, Grupo Salar, Ergo Sum, Mestizo, Literabierta, Talleres Andamio, Unión de Escritores Jóvenes, Agrupación Cultural Universi-

taria [ACU], and the Colectivo de Escritores Jóvenes, among others); *Revistas y publicaciones literarias,* 13. Chileans living in exile abroad during the dictatorship also participated actively in the autoedición movement. See Pía Barros, "Mujeres, creatividad y contracultura," symposium address, "Chilean Women and the Global Politics of Writing," University of California, Irvine, CA, February 4, 2008; and Lorène d'Etudes, "Revistas culturales del exilio Chileno (1973–1989)," *MuseodelaMemoria.cl,* June 2012, www.cedocmuseodelamemoria.cl.

5. [In Spanish] "trípticos, hojas de poesía, periódicos y revistas que difundidas [*sic*] con grandes dificultades y riesgos circularon a través de su venta en lecturas poéticas, recintos universitarios, peñas, bares, manifestaciones políticas, teatros, ferias de artesanía y, por supuesto, mano a mano." Eloy, *Revistas y publicaciones literarias,* 13. Chileans living abroad also self-published literary works as a form of solidarity with compatriots still in Chile and as a means of educating foreign communities about what was happening in their homeland. They sometimes contributed to Chilean autoediciones as well. Some self-published magazines produced in Chile in the 1980s also labeled themselves as international publications, including *Extramuros, Revista Internacional de Poesía,* and *Palabra de Mujer.* Many other independent literary publications list contributors from foreign countries, including *Nos=Otras,* the literary journal published by Barros that served as a precursor to Ergo Sum.

6. [In Spanish] "'De algún modo como no habían muchas posibilidades ni de prensa o editoriales para dar a conocer lo que uno escribía, de alguna manera esta[s] revista[s] era[n] el carril que tenía esta generación de escritores para dar a conocer lo que estaban haciendo.'" Susana Freire, "La hidalga existencia de los caballeros de la poesía," *La Nación,* August 25, 2001.

7. Underground literary publications also included cultural criticism by José Joaquin Brunner, Lotty Rosenfield, Soledad Bianchi, and Jorge Edwards, although it is difficult to know for sure if these were reprinted (with or without permission) or if they were original publications. For example, the self-published literary journal *La Obsidiana* published a story by Ray Bradbury, which it most likely did not have permission to do and which was certainly not an original publication.

8. Museo de la Memoria y los Derechos Humanos, "Humor Gráfico Bajo Estado de Sitio: Seis dibujantes en revistas de prensa alternativa en dictadura," 2012, www.museodelamemoria.cl.

9. Andrea L. Bell, "Creating Space in the Margins: Power and Identity in the *cuentos breves* of Pía Barros and Cristina Peri Rossi," *Studies in Short Fiction* 33, no. 3 (Summer 1996): 346.

10. [In Spanish] "se planteó por algunos investigadores como una metáfora que designa el período más duro y violento de la dictadura (1973–1981), en el cual se hace evidente la falta de protagonismo de los creadores en esta etapa depresiva para el desarrollo del Arte y la Cultura." Eloy, *Revistas y publicaciones literarias,* 13.

11. [In Spanish] "una arma de batalla por la democracia." Belén Bascuñán, "Editores y editoriales en dictadura," *MuseodelaMemoria.cl,* 2012, 4, www.cedocmuseodelamemoria.cl.

12. In 1983 the government lifted the decree that required prior permission from the state to produce and circulate printed works; however, the 1980 constitution gave Pinochet as head of state the authorization to restrict all cultural communications and freedom of information as he saw fit. Bernardo Subercaseaux, *Historia del libro en Chile: Desde la Colonia hasta el Bicentenario* (Santiago: LOM Ediciones, 2000), 202. In the early 1980s, the military state also granted permission to a small number of pro-democratic journals and magazines to circulate materials, even though those journals worked under constant harassment from government officials. Pamela Constable and Arturo Valenzuela, *A Nation of Enemies: Chile under Pinochet* (New York: Norton, 1991), 157.

13. Communications scholar Kristin Sorensen also includes within this category the Jesuit journal *Mensaje,* first published in 1951, and *Solidaridad,* which was also connected with the

Catholic Church. Kristin Sorensen, *Media, Memory, and Human Rights in Chile* (New York: Palgrave Macmillan, 2009), 156.

14. Carol Díaz Allendes and Hugo Neira Gasc, "La lucha de CAUCE: Análisis de la batalla contra la dictadura desde la prensa y desde tribunales en 1984," *MuseodelaMemoria.cl,* July 2013, 6, www.cedocmuseodelamemoria.cl. Sorensen documents that "many of these journals were funded with international support—a combination of solidarity groups and commercial advertisers, especially from Europe." Sorensen, *Media, Memory, and Human Rights,* 111.

15. [In Spanish] "reivindicaban un discurso veladamente opositor." Eloy, *Revistas y publicaciones literarias,* 15.

16. Bascuñán, "Editores y editoriales en dictadura," 9.

17. Bascuñán cites the current editor of CESOC, Julio Silva Montes, who explains that CESOC opened in 1983 as a book press precisely because at that time there was a ban on opening new journalistic publications, so rather than starting a journal, he and his colleagues opened a publishing house instead (ibid., 10). With regard to the journal *Cauce,* Carol Díaz Allendes and Hugo Neira Gasc point out that it was published by Editorial Antártica, but they do not mention its relation to Pensamiento Ediciones ("La lucha de CAUCE").

18. Unlike all of the oppositional periodicals and many of the oppositional publishing houses that functioned during this same time, Cuarto Propio, Pehuén, and CESOC not only survived the country's transition to democracy but have also established themselves as some of Chile's most important book publishers of the postdictatorship period. See Bascuñán, "Editores y editoriales en dictadura," 11.

19. Subercaseaux, *Historia del libro en Chile,* 231–38.

20. Patricia Verdugo's *Los Zarpazos del puma* was an almost instant hit and sold sixteen thousand copies in its first month of circulation. Paula Espinoza O., *Editado en Chile (1889–2004)* (Valparaíso: Quilombo Ediciones, 2012), 187. Despite the fact that the state banned it almost immediately, the book still circulated illegally in Chile throughout the remaining years of the dictatorship. In an interview with Belén Bascuñán, Julio Silva Montes, current editor of CESOC, says that it is still the press's all-time bestseller. Bascuñán, "Editores y editoriales en dictadura," 21.

21. Bascuñán, "Editores y editoriales en dictadura," 7–9; Díaz Allendes and Neira Gasc, "La lucha de CAUCE"; Espinoza O., *Editado en Chile,* 11–15; and Subercaseaux, *Historia del libro en Chile,* 231–38.

22. Bascuñán, "Editores y editoriales en dictadura," 8–9.

23. Ibid.," 8.

24. [In Spanish] "aunque los diarios (vigilados por el régimen militar), hablaban de 'apagón cultural' el país vivió un masivo movimiento de contra cultura que no tenía registro en los medios de comunicación de masa, pero sí a pequeña escala puesto que se inundó de micro medios, tales como revistas, trípticos, dípticos y un sinfín de precarias publicaciones." Barros, "Mujeres, creatividad y contracultura." Sorensen argues that documentary films were also an important part of underground cultural production during the dictatorship years. Sorensen, *Media, Memory, and Human Rights,* 59.

25. The self-published literary works to which I had access promoted Editorial Sinfronteras, Cultrún Editores, and Editorial Universitaria.

26. This chapter does not cover the entire range of editorial diversity that existed in Chile during the dictatorial regime. For a more comprehensive view, see chaps. 6 and 7 of Subercaseaux, *Historia del libro en Chile,* as well as Espinoza, *Editado en Chile.* While incredibly exhaustive, Subercaseaux limits his research to Chile's professional book industry, leaving

much room open for further investigations into the history of non-industrial book production in Chile.

27. Subercaseaux, *Historia del libro en Chile,* 255.

28. Eloy, *Revistas y publicaciones literarias,* 13; Jorge Montealegre, cited in Eloy, *Revistas y publicaciones literarias,* 121; Barros "Mujeres, creatividad y contracultura"; and Bascuñán, "Editores y editoriales en dictadura," 10.

29. [In Spanish] "una forma muy artesanal de imprimir." Bascuñán, "Editores y editoriales en dictadura,"10.

30. [In Spanish] "la época en que más trípticos y dípticos se publicaron en este país: una hoja carta doblada en dos partes que informaban actividades, hacían denuncias." Ibid.

31. [In Spanish] "No es raro encontrarse en los lugares menos esperados con aquella hojita doblada graciosamente en tres partes y que casi todo el mundo llama 'Tríptico.'" *Botella al mar: Hoja Literaria,* no. 1 (Spring 1985): 2.

32. Barros, "Mujeres, creatividad y contracultura."

33. [In Spanish] "convertir la miseria en dignidad." Jorge Montealegre, "Algunas notas (autocomplacientes y hasta nostálgicas) sobre La Castaña," *Revista de Crítica Cultural* no. 31 (June 2005): 17.

34. Unlike in opposition periodicals, colored ink was only occasionally used in the sample of autoediciones to which I had access. One outstanding example is the women's self-published literary journal *Palabra de Mujer.*

35. [In Spanish] "Así como el afiche asume en manos de incontaminados dibujantes una categoría muy superior a la manipulación comercial, así también los trípticos no sólo revelan ser la hojita de ensayo para cubrir primarias y modestas inquietudes literarias. Y esto por una razón muy simple: ahí tiene que fundirse la gracia de un buen diseño gráfico y la calidad del mensaje escrito." *Botella al mar: Hoja Literaria,* no. 1 (Spring 1985).

36. [In Spanish] "todo significaba." Montealegre, "Algunas notas," 17.

37. In 1985, Chilean writer Juan Cameron compiled a bibliography of literary texts published by Chilean authors that year. Of the 141 publications that appear in this bibliography, Cameron lists 38 as published by "Author." Cameron's list also includes publications by some of the self-publishing workshops and collectives cited by Eloy and some of the oppositional publishing houses discussed by Bascuñan. See Juan Cameron, "Bibliografía 1985," *El espíritu del valle* (Fundación Cooperación Chile-Canadá / Ediciones Cordillera Ottowa, Candadá), no. 1 (December 1985): 92–97.

38. Subercaseaux, *Historia del libro en Chile,* 167.

39. [In Spanish] "editoriales privadas que publican casi exclusivamente las obras de sus propietarios." Ibid., 216.

40. [In Spanish] "criterios de marketing." Examples include Enrique Lafourcade, who opened Ediciones de La Fourcade; Pablo Huneeus, who opened Editorial Nueva Generación; and Jorge Sasía, who opened Ediciones Cerra Santa Lucía. Subercaseaux, *Historia del libro en Chile,* 216. For more on Zurita and Editores Asociados, see Espinoza O., *Editado en Chile,* 179.

41. [In Spanish] "Los autores y autoras pasaron por todo el proceso del texto: desde el taller donde se aprendía y creaba el texto, hasta el proceso de ver el texto en el diálogo privado con el artista gráfico . . . , la impresión, doblado, alzado e insertado en el objeto de turno, hasta el proceso directo de la venta. Nada les fue ajeno, ni siquiera la negativa a la compra." Barros, "Mujeres, creatividad y contracultura." There is no doubt that members of underground literary collectives handmade their own publications, but it is not certain that all underground groups followed the same technique that Barros explains here, in which *every* member of the

workshop engaged in the material production of each publication. Evidence that they did not all adhere to this model is the fact that many of these journals (including Barros's own *Nos=Otras*) published authors living abroad who obviously would not have been present to participate in the material production of these texts.

42. Raymond Williams, *Culture* (Glasgow: Fontana Paperbacks, 1981).

43. [In Spanish] "reivindicaba sobre todo el derecho a expresión de los que se quedaron y sufrieron, de los que adquirieron una conciencia colectiva frente a la dictadura y la represión." Barros, "Mujeres, creatividad y contracultura." When Barros says "those who stayed behind and suffered," she is referring to those Chileans who did not go into exile, but rather remained in Chile during the duration of the military regime.

44. It must be noted that while it was far easier for members of the general public to join underground literary workshops than it was for them to join the writing staff of an oppositional periodical, and even though these collectives did exist all over the country rather than just in Santiago, their membership was not massive in scale. When we compare them to similar cultural projects of the postdictatorship period, for instance, we note that these earlier collectives were rather limited in size compared to the much larger and truly "massive" participation in alternative forms of literary production that we see taking place after 1990.

45. [In Spanish] "Quisimos ser legales, pedimos autorización para circular, pero no la obtuvimos. (Es que había Dictadura amigos). Valga la explicación [marginal] porque para nosotros la marginalidad no fue una opción ni una vocación. Simplemente estábamos al margen." Eloy, *Revistas y publicaciones literarias*, 124.

46. [In Spanish] "Circulación Restringida"; "publicación de circulación interna"; "permiso en trámite." From the self-published literary journals I was able to access directly, I found the words "Circulación Restringida" printed on *Tira Lineas, Botella al Mar, Barbaria,* and *Cuadernos de la Maga. Lapizlázuli* carried the label "permiso en trámite" on its inside cover; *Carmina, SECH '85,* and *El boletín del coordinador cultural* also printed "publicación de circulación interna" on their publications.

47. [In Spanish] "sin permiso de nadie." Eloy, *Revistas y publicaciones literarias*, 11.

48. As Juan Carlos Vega explains, "Las primeras publicaciones no tienen autoría, no tienen imprenta, no tienen derecho de autor, porque se trabaja en esas condiciones" (The first publications do not include the name of the author, do not give the name of the publisher, and are not copyrighted because of the conditions in which they were produced). Quoted in Bascuñán, "Editores y editoriales en dictadura," 10.

49. [In Spanish] "Lo que no se podía hacer era fundar medios sin autorización." Bascuñán, "Editores y editoriales en dictadura," 8.

50. The two authorized workshops were conducted by the writers Enrique Lafourcade and Miguel Arteche respectively, and both were held in Chile's National Library. Cardone, "Refashioning the Book," 139.

51. Freire, "La hidalga existencia de los caballeros de la poesía."

52. [In Spanish] "los tiempos que aquí se viven son no sólo urgentes e inseguros, sino que dolorosos y hasta inhumanos. De ahí que, cualquier vía de comunicación, cualquier dato o instancia que la fuerza de jóvenes escritores puedan asumir, adquiere en sí un valor testimonial." *Botella al mar: Hoja Literaria,* no. 1 (Spring 1985), 2.

53. Nelly Richard, *Margins and Institutions: Art in Chile since 1973* (Melbourne, AU: Art and Text, 1986), 23.

54. [In Spanish] "la vuelta a la democracia era posible creando conciencia en sus lectores." Allendes and Gasc, "La lucha de CAUCE," 9.

55. I have only had access to *Somos trece: Soffia,* which was printed by Editorial Arcilla. It has

no ISBN or copyright, but it does have an inscription number and the notation of "Derechos Reservados" (Rights Reserved) to "Pía Barros y otros" (Pía Barros and others).

56. Cardone, "Refashioning the book in Pinochet's Chile,"142.

57. [In Spanish] "se inició en forma completamente autónoma, sin ningún apoyo institucional, lo que marca, pues, fuertemente, la gesta de su formación, su independencia creativa." Carmen Berenguer, Eugenia Brito, Diamela Eltit, Raquel Olea, Eliana Ortega, and Nelly Richard, eds., *Escribir en los bordes: congreso internacional de literatura femenina latinoamericana, 1987* (Santiago: Editorial Cuarto Propio, 1987), 9–10.

58. For more on the CEMAS and Chilean women's recent political action on the Right and the Left, see Lisa Baldez, *Why Women Protest: Women's Movements in Chile* (Cambridge: Cambridge University Press, 2002). For readings on feminism and Chilean political history, see Alicia Frohmann and Teresa Valdés, *"Democracy in the Country and in the Home": The Women's Movement in Chile* (Santiago: FLASCO, 1993); and Julieta Kirkwood, *Ser política en Chile: Las feministas y los partidos* (Santiago: FLASCO, 1986). For readings on women and feminist literature of the dictatorship period, see Berenguer et al., *Escribir en los bordes: Congreso internacional de literatura femenina latinoamericana, 1987;* Raquel Olea, *Lengua Víbora: Producciones de lo femenino en la escritura de mujeres chilenas* (Santiago: Editorial Cuarto Propio; Corporación de Desarrollo de la Mujer la Morada, 1998); and Alice A. Nelson, *Political Bodies: Gender, History, and the Struggle for Narrative Power in Recent Chilean Literature* (Lewisburg: Bucknell University Press; London: Associated University Press, 2002).

59. Richard identifies exactly to whom she is referring with the term "avanzada" in a footnote: "Surgida desde las artes visuales (Carlos Leppe, Eugenio Dittborn, Catalina Parra, Carlos Altamirano, el grupo CADA, Lotty Rosenfield, Juan Castillo, Juan Dávila, Víctor Hugo Codocedo, Elías Adasme, etc. . . .) y en interacción con las textualidades poéticas y literarias de Raúl Zurita y Diamela Eltit, la escena de 'avanzada' armó una constelación de voces de críticas de la que participaron filosófos y escritores como Ronald Kay, Adriana Valdés, Gonzalo Muñoz, Patricio Marchant, Rodrigo Cánovas, Pablo Oyarzun y otros" (Emerging from the visual arts [Carlos Leppe, Eugenio Dittborn, Catalina Parra, Carlos Altamirano, the CADA group, Lotty Rosenfield, Juan Castillo, Juan Dávila, Víctor Hugo, Codocedo, Elías Adasme, etc. . . .] and in interaction with the poetic and literary textualities of Raúl Zurita and Diamela Eltit, the "advanced" scene assembled a constellation of voices of critics in which philosophers and writers such as Ronald Kay, Adriana Valdés, Gonzalo Muñoz, Patricio Marchant, Rodrigo Cánovas, Pablo Oyarzun, and others participated). Richard, *Margins and Institutions,* 15.

60. [In Spanish] "El gesto de la 'avanzada' de desobedecer las asignaciones de formato convencionales que fija la tradición artística y literaria (el cuadro para la pintura; el libro para la poesía o la narrativa), denunciaba figuradamente los abusos de autoridad con los que el régimen militar custodia las fronteras del Orden." Ibid., 17.

61. Alejandro Herrero-Olaizola, "Consuming Aesthetics: Seix Barral and José Donoso in the Field of Latin American Literary Production," Hispanic Issue, *MLN* 115, no. 2 (March 2000): 325.

62. Cardone, "Refashioning the book in Pinochet's Chile," 136.

63. Teresa Calderon led a poetry workshop through the Sociedad de Escritores de Chile (The Chilean Society of Writers, SECH); Catalina Ruiz directed a short story workshop also with SECH; and Ana María del Río and Carmen Berenguer each led their own individual writing workshops in the 1980s. See Pía Barros "Las senoras de los tecitos," *Nos=Otras,* ed. Pía Barros, vol. 2 (n.d.). *Safo* was produced out of Rancagua. The only edition of this work I am aware of was published in 1989, and I do not know if it was associated with any literary workshop. See Memoria Chilena, "Revistas y Publicaciones Literarias (1960–1990)," Biblioteca Nacional de

Chile, *MemoriaChilena.cl,* 2013, accessed March 11, 2013, www.memoriachilena.cl. I was able to access approximately eight issues of *Palabra de mujer* that were published between 1989 and 1992, but I do not know if other issues exist. The magazine was produced by a literary workshop of the same name, although it published works by women who did not participate in the workshop, including known authors from all over Latin America and elsewhere.

64. [In Spanish] "escrita en ella." Adriana Valdés, *Composición de lugar: escritos sobre cultura* (Santiago: Editorial Universitaria, 1995), 71–72.

65. Cardone, "Refashioning the book in Pinochet's Chile," 147–48.

66. Cardone has carefully researched the way in which Ergo Sum shaped its editorial project in relation to the first presidency of Michelle Bachelet, explaining how the physical form of multiple book-objects published in the mid-2000s represents goals and accomplishments of Chile's first female president. Cardone, "The Hands That Make the Books," paper presented at the Women's Studies Conference, Southern Connecticut State University, New Haven, CT, 2011.

67. *Sudaca* is a pejorative term used to refer to people from South America. *Sud* refers to "south," as in *Sud América* ("South America"), whereas *-aca* connotes *caca,* meaning "shit." We might, therefore, literally translate this word as "South American shit." For more on this term and its use in Eltit's work, see Olea, *Lengua Víbora,* chap. 2.

68. Diamela Eltit, *The Fourth World,* trans. Dick Gerdes (Lincoln: University of Nebraska Press, 1995), 114.

69. See Eustasio A. García, "Historia de la empresa editorial en Argentina: Siglo XX," *Historia de las empresas editoriales de América Latina, siglo XX,* ed. Juan Gustavo Cobo Borda (Bogotá: CERLALC, 2000), 15–104; Alejandro Herrero-Olaizola, "Consuming Aesthetics: Seix Barral and José Donoso in the Field of Latin American Literary Production," Hispanic Issue, *MLN* 115, no. 2 (March 2000): 323–39; and Donald L. Shaw, "The Post-Boom in Spanish American Fiction," Special Issue, *Studies in 20th Century Literature* 19, no. 1 (1995): 11–27.

70. Grupo Planeta, for example, owns 29 publishing companies, 9 communications companies, 3 audiovisual media companies, 8 special collectibles companies, 10 professional training companies, 8 sales and distribution companies, and 2 distance learning companies.

71. Richard, *Margins and Institutions,* 24.

72. Cuarto Propio is one of the best examples of the way in which Chilean women attempted to use literary publishing as a form of political protest and pro-democratic mobilization during the 1980s. Its name, "a room of one's own," is of course a reference to the famous line by English writer and feminist Virginia Woolf. Since the return to democracy, Cuarto Propio has expanded its catalog to include more than just women's and feminist publications. It has become one of the most important producers of literature and intellectual scholarship in the postdictatorship period.

73. It is true that Ergo Sum book-objects were never sold for profit under dictatorship. However, individual writers often sold their text to friends and acquaintances in order to recuperate the resources required for production. Barros, "Mujeres, creatividad y contracultura." Their sales never produced any tax revenue for the state nor did they produce any kind of surplus income for the group or its authors.

74. Kathrin Bergenthal, "El Mini-Boom de la Nueva Narrativa Chilena," in *Crisis, apocalipsis y utopías: Fines de siglo en la literatura latinoamericana; XXXII Congreso Internacional de la Literatura Iberoamericana,* ed. Rodrigo Cánovas and Roberto Hozven (Santiago: Instituto Internacional de la Literatura Iberoamericana; Instituto de Letras, Pontificia Universidad Católica de Chile, 2000), 226.

75. Luce Irigaray, *This Sex Which Is Not One* (Ithaca: Cornell University Press, 1985), 176.

76. Cardone, "Refashioning the Book," 140.

77. Ibid.

78. Ibid., 146.

79. [In Spanish] "¿Qué se espera de una caja con 'cosas de mujeres'? Seguramente botones, con aguja e hilo; aros, 'pinches' para el pelo; cachureo. Cualquier cosa, en definitiva, propia de las 'labores del sexo' y no del seso; un lapis labial; nunca uno de los otros." Barros, "Mujeres, creatividad y contracultura."

80. Cardone argues that Ergo Sum book-objects take the shape of "inoffensive containers." Cardone, "Refashioning the Book," 147.

81. Judith Butler, *Bodies that Matter: On the Discursive Limits of Sex* (New York: Routledge, 1993), 15.

82. Cardone, "Refashioning the Book," 147.

83. Resha Cardone, "Acting Up and Carrying On: Women Writers of Chile, 1945–2006" (PhD diss., University of Kansas, 2006), 91. In her essay "Refashioning the Book in Pinochet's Chile," Cardone uses this objective of female self-empowerment to explain the collective's name and signature logo. In reference to the name, she argues that the words "Ergo Sum" necessarily bring "to mind René Descartes' philosophical rumination: 'Cogito ergo sum' (I think; therefore I am). The chosen phrase highlights classical Western thought, and implicitly, a tradition that reserved thinking and writing for a select male elite." According to Cardone, Ergo Sum reverses this masculine model of the subject by combining these words with the visual image of Ergo Sum's logo: an ink pen with the universal sign of "women" (♀) embedded in it. This resymbolizes Descartes' "I think; therefore I am" to read, as Cardone claims, " 'I am woman who writes; therefore, I am.' " Cardone, "Refashioning the Book," 143–44.

84. Butler, *Bodies that Matter,* 15.

85. See Bascuñán, "Editores y editoriales en dictadura," 9. Although it formed in the 1990s, after the end of the dictatorship in Chile, the sardonic newspaper *The Clinic* epitomized the power of parody in its critique of the military regime and its legacies in postdictatorship Chile. According to one of its first directors, Patricio Fernández, when the paper started it "was more like a pamphlet" than an actual newspaper—evidencing yet another linkage to forms of an alternative press that originated under dictatorship. Sorensen, *Media, Memory, and Human Rights,* 123.

86. Constable and Valenzuela, *Nation of Enemies,* 157.

87. Irigaray, *This Sex Which Is Not One,* 196 and 173.

88. Pierre Bourdieu, *The Field of Cultural Production* (New York: Columbia University Press, 1993), 35.

3. Cartonera Publishers

1. [In Spanish] "o el libro se integra a los mecanismos de la industria cultural o corre el riesgo de ser un producto marginal e incluso de tener que reciclarse en materia prima." Bernardo Subercaseaux, *Historia del libro en Chile: Desde la Colonia hasta el Bicentenario* (Santiago: LOM Ediciones, 2000), 166.

2. [In Spanish] "están destinados a ser picados, molidos y convertidos en materia prima. . . . Se trata de una especie de resurrección al revés, en que fenece el alma del libro para resucitar su cuerpo, un cuerpo que se transforma en papel para envolver, en servilletas y sobres." Ibid., 209.

3. [In Spanish] "la lucha vital de las especies por los espacios y por sus funciones dentro de ellos." Luis E. Cárcamo-Huechante, *Tramas del mercado: Imaginación económica, cultura pública y literatura en el Chile de fines del siglo veinte* (Santiago: Editorial Cuarto Propio, 2007), 58.

4. [In Spanish] "Esto hace más patente aún el efecto petrificante que tiene el concepto de nicho de mercado, en tanto modalidad de *encajonamiento* del autor-obra-producto, como entidad sin vida, sin movimiento." Ibid., 59.

5. This state of mourning could be induced by the death of democracy in Chile or by the individual deaths of all those citizens who lost their lives to state terrorism. Resha Cardone, "Refashioning the Book in Pinochet's Chile: The Feminist Literary Project, Ergo Sum," *Confluencia* 29, no. 1 (Fall 2013): 145.

6. Ibid., 148.

7. [In Spanish] "adquiridos por papeleros, para ser revendidos por kilo a las industrias manufactureras de papeles y cartones." Subercaseaux, *Historia del libro en Chile,* 209.

8. Luís Díaz Calderón and Nélida Códova (editors of La Fonola Cartonera) in discussion with the author, Santiago, August 21, 2013.

9. Kika Valdés, "Introducción" Taller de Memoria y libros de Cartón (Workshop in Memory and Cardboard Books), Museo de la Memoria y los Derechos Humanos (Memory and Human Rights Museum) and Meninas Cartoneras, Santiago, August 24, 2013; [In Spanish] "medio y mensaje de protesta. Exquisitamente diverso, reivindicativamente diverso." Meninas Cartoneras, "Editoriales Cartoneras en Casa de América," *MeninasCartonerasEditorialBlogSpot.com,* June 22, 2013, http://meninascartoneraseditorial.blogspot.com.

10. Amanda Espejo and Karen Peñaloza (editors of Calafate Cartonera) in discussion with the author, Santiago, January 2, 2013.

11. Cartonera Publishers Conference 2009, University of Wisconsin, Madison, www.library.wisc.edu. This conference was organized by University of Wisconsin professor Ksenija Bilbija and University of Wisconsin librarian Paloma Celis Carbajal. The following Cartonera Publishers were in attendance: Eloísa Cartonera, Sarita Cartonera, Animita Cartonera, Mandrágora Cartonera, Herba Mala Cartonera, Dulcinéa Catadora, Yiyi Jambo, and La Cartonera.

12. [In Spanish] "la solidaridad, el trabajo comunitario y, por cierto, la búsqueda de la relativa independencia de los libros." Felipe Almazán, "Libros de Cartón (y las editoriales cartoneras)," Felipealmazan.bligoo.com, accessed May 11, 2009 (no longer available).

13. [In Spanish] "revalorización"; "reivindicativamente."

14. In Spanish, the "ito/a" suffix is added to nouns in order to denote smallness, but it also connotes affection and caring rather than just physical size.

15. Walter Benjamin, "The Work of Art in the Age of Mechanical Reproduction," in *Illuminations,* ed. Hannah Arendt, trans. Harry Zohn (New York: Schocken Books, 1969), 222.

16. [In Spanish] "nueva institucionalización cultural."

17. [In Spanish] "explosión cartonera." Canita Cartonera, "Inicio," *CanitaCartoneraWordPress.com,* July 2010, http://canitacartonera.wordpress.com.

18. The ephemeral nature of Cartonera presses makes it difficult to know with exact certainty how many of these presses exist at any given time, or how many of those that have come into being are presently functioning. This ephemeral nature is an important characteristic of Cartonera publishing. See appendix 2 for a list of all Cartonera presses that I was able to locate at the time of publication.

19. The family of Chilean Cartoneras includes (in order of appearance): Animita Cartonera (Santiago, 2005), Canita Cartonera (Alto Hospicio-Iquique, 2009), Cizarra Cartonera (2009), El Helecho Cartonera (Puerto Montt, 2009), Meninas Cartonera (Santiago, Madrid, Mexico City, 2009), Nuestra Señora Cartonera (La Serena, 2010), Benicia Cartonera (Santiago, 2011), Olga Cartonera (Santiago, 2011), Calafate Cartonera (Santiago, 2012), Editorial Letras de Cartón (Santiago, 2012), Kiltra Cartonera (Valparaíso, 2012), La Vieja Sapa Cartonera (Santiago, 2012), Warp Zone Cartonera (Arica, 2012), La Cartonera (Santiago, 2013),

Costalazo Ediciones (Santiago, 2013), Juanita Cartonera (Santiago, 2013), Varonas de Cartón Edición (Santiago, 2013), La Gata Viuda Cartonera (Santiago, 2013), Infracción Ediciones (Concepción, 2013), Isidora Cartonera (Santiago, 2013), Fugitiva Cartonera (Arica, 2014), La Grullita Cartonera (Santiago, 2014), and Opalina Cartonera (Santiago 2014).

20. Valdés, "Introducción," Taller de Memoria y libros de Cartón.

21. Ibid. The first Chilean Cartonera press, Animita Cartonera, came into being after its founding editors, Ana Moraga, Ximena Ramos, Fernanda Arrau, Tanya Núñez, became aware of Eloisa Cartonera in Argentina; the four young women wrote to the editors of Eloisa, who advised them on how to set up the first Chilean cardboard press (Santi). Canita Cartonera was formed because of a cross-cultural exchange between its founding editors and the Bolivian press Yerba Mala Cartonera (Canita Cartonera). Meninas Cartoneras originated in Spain after its founding editors, Carolina Escalona, Carolina Espinoza, Kika Valdés, and Beatriz Martínez, heard about the growing number of Cartoneras in Latin America and decided to bring the trend to Spain, making Meninas the first Cartonera in Europe (Meninas Cartoneras). Meninas later spread its editorial project to Mexico and Chile, becoming a truly transnational publishing house. The press began offering workshops in Santiago, teaching Chileans the art of cardboard bookmaking. Santiago residents Olga Sotomayor and Karen Peñaloza attended these workshops and consequently opened Olga Cartonera and Calafate Cartonera (Olga Sotomayor, in discussion with the author, Santiago, December 26, 2012; Espejo and Peñaloza in discussion with the author). Olga Cartonera has in turn been highly influential in spreading the Cartonera trend throughout Chile, leading its own workshops on cardboard bookmaking, organizing various Cartonera cultural events, giving lectures about the trend, and advising new Chilean Cartonera editors who are in the process of establishing their own presses. Olga Cartonera supported Luís Díaz and Nélida Muñoz in their formation of La Fonola Cartonera, and an event that Olga initiated, El Primer Encuentro de las Editoriales Cartoneras de Chile (The First Meeting of Chilean Cartonera publishers), in May 2013, inspired one of its attendees, Roberto Toledo, to create La Gata Viuda Cartonera. At the time of writing, Chile's newest Cartonera, Opalina Cartonera, was formed as a result of its connection with Isidora Cartonera.

22. Some Cartonera editors choose to alter the spelling of the name, often replacing the "C" with a "K," and still others translate the word into the native language in which they live and work.

23. Resha Cardone's research on the Ergo Sum collective shows that it was heavily influenced by the arpillera tradition and that Pía Barros used the arpillera practice as a model for how to structure her underground literary workshop and press. "Both groups shared the objective to establish the worth of female forms of *artisanal* expression traditionally considered artistically insignificant." Cardone, "Refashioning the Book," 147 (emphasis added). For more on the Chilean arpillera tradition, see Marjorie Agosín, *Tapestries of Hope, Threads of Life: The Arpillera Movement in Chile* (Lanham, MD: Rowman and Littlefield, 2008).

24. [In Spanish] "coser y cantar." Valdés, "Introducción."

25. The name "Eloisa" was chosen for purely sentimental rather than political or symbolic reasons. When Barilaro, Cucurto, and Laguna founded the press, Barilaro had romantic feelings for a Bolivian woman named Eloisa and affectionately named his new artistic project after her. Ironically, we could argue that this positioning of the real woman Eloisa as an artistic muse stands in contradiction to the feminist politics I am here reading into the matriarchal Cartonera family and its material methods of cardboard book production. For a fuller history of the formation of Eloisa Cartonera, see *Akademia Cartonera: A Primer of Latin American Cartonera Publishers,* ed. Ksenija Bilbija and Paloma Celis Carbajal (Madison: University of Wisconsin–Madison Libraries / Parallel Press, 2009), http://digicoll.library.wisc.edu.

26. When the editors of Animita Cartonera contacted Washington Cucurto in 2005 to ask for permission to start the first Chilean cardboard press, he asked them only to respect the founding principle of the project, which was to buy the cardboard from cartoneros at a higher price than they typically sold it on the street and, thus,"trabajar con personas que realmente necesitan la plata, dejándoles libertad para expresarse artísticamente" (to work with people who really needed the money, giving them the freedom to express themselves artistically). Marietta Santi, "Animita Cartonera: Mosqueteras de la literatura." *La Tercera,* January 21, 2007. In addition to being the only Chilean Cartonera that I know of to buy its cardboard from cartonero street vendors, Animita Cartonera is the only Chilean press I know of that ever asked Eloisa for permission to start a Cartonera press. The fact that the twenty-two other Chilean Cartonera presses did not ask permission provides yet another example of the general disregard for authorized forms of copying characteristic of Chilean Cartonera publishers.

27. Tanya Núñez and Ximena Ramos (editors of Animita Cartonera) in discussion with the author, Santiago, January 3, 2013.

28. Roberto Toledo (editor of La Gata Viuda Cartonera) in discussion with the author, Chile, August 16, 2013.

29. La Gata Viuda Cartonera and Editorial Letras de Cartón both employ the latter method. La Gata Viuda editor Roberto Toledo creates an original design that he prints onto small sheets of paper and then manually adheres to the cover of each individual cardboard book he makes. In order to ensure the individuality of each book despite the repeated cover design, he manually stamps each copy with a number to mark its position within a given print run. Ibid.

30. Isidora Cartonera, La Fonola Cartonera, and La Vieja Sapa Cartonera have all solicited works from the general public in this way.

31. Olga Cartonera, La Gata Viuda Cartonera, and Isidora Cartonera all opened for the purpose of publishing works written by their founding editors although they are all now publishing titles by third parties, including international authors and re-editions of other Cartonera original publications. The very fact that Olga Sotomayor named her press after herself underscores the importance of self-publishing. The founding editors of Isidora Cartonera, Ignacio Cuevas and Francisco Escobar, were only able to start the project after they received funding from their university, Universidad Alberto Hurtado, to teach a public workshop in self-publication. Isidora Cartonera considers its titles self-publications because all authors participate in the material production of their own books. La Vieja Sapa Cartonera and Calafate Cartonera also have aspirations of publishing works by their own editors. Mario Aravena and César Rey (editors of La Vieja Sapa Cartonera) in discussion with the author, Santiago, August 20, 2013; Amanda Espejo and Karen Peñaloza (editors of Calafate Cartonera) in discussion with the author, Santiago, January 2, 2013; Ignacio Cuevas (editor of Isidora Cartonera) in discussion with the author, Santiago, August 14, 2013; Olga Sotomayor (editor of Olga Cartonera) in discussion with the author, Santiago, December 26, 2012; Toledo in discussion with the author.

32. The only exception to this is of course the example I cited above in which Animita Cartonera pays two young women to make books for them. These women do not make enough money from this work to fully support themselves, however, and rely on other jobs for their subsistence. Núñez and Ramos in discussion with the author.

33. See appendix 2.

34. Aravena and Rey in discussion with the author; Cuevas in discussion with the author; Toledo in discussion with the author; Díaz Calderón and Muñoz Códova in discussion with the author. It is because little-to-no financial resources are needed to open and run a Cartonera press that there is an ever-growing number of them around the world. The lack of financial

capital needed to start a Cartonera press is also why the existence of such presses is often so fleeting, or to repeat a word I used before, ephemeral. Because founders are not preoccupied with recuperating their financial investment in their presses and because they have no intention of making a living from the endeavors, these projects die very easily. This of course limits the impact that they can have on the public, and it is also one reason why arriving at a definitive number of how many Cartonera presses currently exist in the world is so challenging.

35. Canita Cartonera, "Fanzines," *CanitaCartonera.WordPress.com,* 2010, https://canitacartonera.wordpress.com.

36. [In Spanish] "hacer de un projecto algo que es parte de la base de uno." Isidora editors are also musicians and will sometimes play shows in bars as a means of raising the money needed to finance their editorial production. Cuevas in discussion with the author.

37. Aravena and Rey in discussion with the author.

38. [In Spanish] "la plata que ganemos es para hacer más libros." Rodrigo Alvarado, "Historias de cartón," *La Nación,* November 5, 2006, accessed August 18, 2015, www.lanacion.cl.

39. Sotomayor in discussion with the author.

40. [In Spanish] "preservar una idea de acercar la cultura a la gente, porque Animita es un proyecto social." Alvarado, "Historias de cartón."

41. [In Spanish] "generar la humanidad." Toledo in discussion with the author.

42. [In Spanish] "llevar la creación literaria a todos los rincones posibles." Aravena and Rey in discussion with the author.

43. [In Spanish] "en la democracia, queda gente afuera." Toledo in discussion with the author.

44. [In Spanish] "basada en la solidaridad, y donde el valor de intercambio predominante es la lógica de transformar la basura en arte." Heidi Schmidlin Moore, "Cuando la pobreza genera riqueza," *La Panera,* May 2012, 33–34, http://issuu.com. Ecological conservation and respect for the natural environment are of course also a political consequence of this editorial method, although the environmental impact is only of principal concern to a small minority of Chilean Cartoneras (La Fonola Cartonera especially, but also Animita Cartonera, Meninas Cartonera, and Isidora Cartonera). Meninas's self-description fits that of most Chilean (and other) Cartoneras; the editors describe their press as follows: "El proyecto en el que nos hemos embarcado es en esencia literario. Pero también artístico. Y ecológico. Y social. Y solidario. Sin pudor le colgamos la etiqueta de 'PROYECTO ÍNTEGRO'" (The project we have embarked upon is in essence literary. But it is also artistic. And ecological. And social. And conscientiously committed. We unabashedly label it an "INTEGRAL PROJECT"). Meninas Cartoneras, *Meninas CartonerasEditorial.Blogspot.com,* accessed September 2, 2015, http://meninascartoneraseditorial.blogspot.com).

45. Raymond Williams, *Culture* (Glasgow: Fontana Paperbacks, 1981), 50.

46. See Néstor García Canclini, *Transforming Modernity: Popular Culture in Mexico,* trans. Lidia Lozano (Austin: University of Texas Press, 1993), chaps. 4, 5, and 6.

47. Toledo in discussion with the author.

48. María Sol Vera (editor of Editorial Cuarto Propio) in discussion with the author, Santiago, January 9, 2014.

49. For a history on the Chicago Boys and their implementation of neoliberalism in Chile, see Cárcamo-Huechante, *Tramas del mercado;* Pamela Constable and Arturo Valenzuela, *A Nation of Enemies: Chile under Pinochet* (New York: Norton, 1991); Naomi Klein, *The Shock Doctrine: The Rise of Disaster Capitalism* (New York: Picador, 2007); and Juan Gabriel Valdés, *Pinochet's Economists: The Chicago School of Economics in Chile* (Cambridge: Cambridge University Press, 2008).

50. Aravena and Rey in discussion with the author; Espejo and Peñaloza in discussion with the author; Sotomayor in discussion with the author.

51. [In Spanish] "los proyectos cartoneros nacen como una forma de resistencia al mercado maximizador de las casas editoriales." Nuestra Señora Cartonera, "Bienvid@ a Nuestra Señora Cartonera," 2010, http://nuestrasenoracartonera.blogspot.com.

52. We have already discussed how La Fonola Cartonera's name cites Chile's history of military dictatorship. For its part, La Vieja Sapa Cartonera is named after the popular national character of the neighborhood busybody: *la sapa. Sapa* literally means female frog, but in Chilean vernacular it carries this connotation.

53. *Calafate* is "caulk" in English and thus the name creates a coincidental vibration with La Fonola Cartonera's choice of the word *fonola;* whereas "caulk" denotes a waterproofing material, *fonola,* which literally means "earpiece" or "megaphone," also carries the cultural connotation in Chile of a weatherproofing material. Espejo and Peñaloza in discussion with the author.

54. [In Spanish] "recuperando con autogestión la identidad de barrio, el encuentro e intercambio." Benicia Cartonera, "A participar en la Feria del Trueke!!!!!!! Casona Protectora-MPL," *BeniciaCartonera.BlogSpot.com,* April 2011, www.beniciacartonera.blogspot.com.

55. García Canclini, *Transforming Modernity,* chaps. 4 and 5.

56. Aravena and Rey in discussion with the author; Espejo and Peñaloza in discussion with the author; Díaz Calderón and Muñoz Códova in discussion with the author; Sotomayor in discussion with the author; Toledo in discussion with the author.

57. Espejo and Peñaloza in discussion with the author.

58. Ksenija Bilbija, "¡Cartoneros de todos los países, uníos!: Un recorrido no tan fantasmal de las editoriales cartoneras latinoamericanas en el tercer milenio," in *Akademia Cartonera: A Primer of Latin American Cartonera,* ed. Ksenija Bilbija and Paloma Celis Carbajal (Madison: University of Wisconsin–Madison Libraries / Parallel Press, 2010), 8 (emphasis added), http://digicoll-dev.library.wisc.edu.

59. Craig Epplin, "Theory of the Workshop: César Aira and Eloísa Cartonera," in ibid. 56. While the workshop is a defining element of the Chilean tradition of cardboard publishing, it functions differently than it has in Eloísa Cartonera's editorial project. Few Chilean Cartoneras center their production out of a single physical space as Eloísa Cartonera originally did with its workshop in the Boca neighborhood of Buenos Aires. Instead, they "stage"—to use Epplin's term—workshops in various locations depending on the purpose of the workshop and its target participants. Many of these workshops are offered through a cooperative relationship between a Cartonera press and a school, community group, or state organization. For example, Meninas Cartoneras has given writing and bookmaking workshops in Chile's Museo de la Memoria y los Derechos Humanos (Museum of Memory and Human Rights); Isidora Cartonera has offered self-publishing workshops in la Biblioteca de Santiago (Santiago Library); Animita Cartonera has run workshops out of Balmaceda 1215, a state-owned cultural center for underprivileged urban youth; Benicia Cartonera works intimately with a community organization called Movimiento de Pobladores en Lucha (Workers in Struggle Movement) that fights for the economic and cultural uplift of the working classes; and Canita Cartonera and Fugitiva Cartonera ground all their editorial production in workshops they give for prison inmates in the Alto Hospicio state penitentiary. Other Cartoneras give workshops to schoolchildren (Benicia Cartonera, Helecho Cartonera, Meninas Cartonera), victims of domestic violence (Meninas Cartoneras), and socio-economically impoverished communities (Calafate Cartonera, Olga Cartonera). Marcelo Ibarra, former prisoner of Alto Hospicio prison in the north of Chile, has participated in Cartonera literary production in that prison. For more on his story, see the YouTube video *Marcelo Ibarra,* by Antonio Belfegor, May 24, 2010, www.youtube.com.

60. [In Spanish] "crear un sentido comunitario que atienda los intereses de las distintas personas ya que creemos que el arte es una herramienta generadora de espacios de diálogo e intercambio de experiencias e ideas." Animita Cartonera, www.animita-cartonera.cl.

61. Esther Leslie, "Walter Benjamin: Traces of Craft," *Journal of Design History* 11, no. 1 (1998): 6, www.jstor.org.

62. Ibid.

63. The connection between sewing the language of the text and sewing the material form of the book is even more emphatic in the previously discussed Ergo Sum book-object *Tenemos pantalones.*

64. Cuevas in discussion with the author; Espejo and Peñaloza in discussion with the author; Toledo in discussion with the author.

65. [In Spanish] "Este libro es único, original e irrepetible y está hecho a mano por OlgaCartonera."

66. [In Spanish] "Objeto de arte realizado y pintado a mano con la ayuda de recolectores y jóvenes."

67. Chilean Cartoneras that employ this method include Olga Cartonera, La Gata Viuda Cartonera, Calafate Cartonera, La Vieja Sapa Cartonera, and La Fonola Cartonera.

68. Aravena and Rey in discussion with the author.

69. [In Spanish] "inscriben sus identidades en los libros." Bilbija, "¡Cartoneros de todos los países, uníos!: Un recorrido no tan fantasmal de las editoriales cartoneras latinoamericanas en el tercer milenio," 11.

70. Benjamin, "The Work of Art in the Age of Mechanical Reproduction," 221 (emphasis added).

71. The well-cited example of this, as we saw in chapter 1, is the emergence of what has come to be known as La Nueva Narrativa Chilena (The New Chilean Narrative) that some claim represents the Chilean literary experience of the postdictatorship and that others, in contrast, see as a marketing ploy invented by foreign publishers. See Cárcamo-Huechante, *Tramas del mercado,* 47–49; and Kathrin Bergenthal, "El Mini-Boom de la Nueva Narrativa Chilena," in *Crisis, apocalipsis y utopías: Fines de siglo en la literatura latinoamericana; XXXII Congreso Internacional de la Literatura Iberoamericana,* ed. Rodrigo Cánovas and Roberto Hozven (Santiago: Instituto Internacional de la Literatura Iberoamericana; Instituto de Letras, Pontificia Universidad Católica de Chile, 2000), 224–29.

72. [In Spanish] "La importancia mayor de las [industrias culturales] no puede medirse tanto por su dimensión económica . . . sino *por lo que los valores simbólicos producidos aportan, o pueden aportar, al mejoramiento del espacio público nacional y regional.* Es decir, a la información, la educación, la cultura y el conocimiento, atendiendo a sus necesidades de su desarrollo equitativo y democrático." Octavio Getino, "Las IC en el MERCOSUR: Apuntes para un proyecto de política de Estado," in *Industrias culturales: un aporte al desarrollo* (Santiago: LOM Ediciones / CNCA, 2005), 37.

73. Ksenija Bilbija writes, "Las fronteras nacionales todavía [son] irónicamente mantenidas por las grandes editoriales multinacionales, que tienden a distribuir sus escritores sólo dentro de los ámbitos locales, creando así una ilusión del mercado nacional. Lo problemático del tal mercado literario nacional es que no está producido por la industria nacional, financiado por la capital nacional, desde adentro, sino por las multinacionales regidas por las inversiones del mercado globalizado que basan sus listas en lo vendible y competetivo que es un libro, trantándolo así como cualquier objeto de consumo y perdiendo de vista su valor cultural y artístico" (National borders are still ironically maintained by large multinational publishers who tend to distribute their writers only within local circuits, and as such create the illusion of

a national market. What is problematic about this national market is that it is not produced by the national industry or financed by national capital, from within, but rather by multinationals who are governed by investments from the globalized market and who base their lists on how sellable and competitive a book is, and in so doing treat it like any other consumer object and lose sight of its cultural and artistic value). Bilbija, "¡Cartoneros de todos los países, uníos!" 7.

74. Jaime Pinos, "La calabaza del diablo," in *Escritores por el fomento del libro y la lectura: Tercer Encuentro; Actas* (Santiago: Mosquito Comunicaciones; Letras de Chile; Gobierno de Chile, 2001), 83.

75. [In Spanish] "nace de la necesidad de llevar a la calle y masificar un mensaje que está atrapado en la fauces de la mala voluntad de las editoriales del mercado." Toledo in discussion with the author.

76. Aravena and Rey in discussion with the author.

77. Leslie, "Walter Benjamin," 11. The question of how artisanal book production compares to both the national and global publishing industries is further complicated by the fact that Chile's new cultural institutionalization of the postdictatorship years has made structural advancements in the industrialization of Chilean artisanal culture. Like culture at large, artisanal culture has received growing attention by the state and culture industries alike throughout Chile's postdictatorship period. In 2003, the Chilean Ministry of Culture created the Área de Artesanía (Area of Artisanry) under its Division of Culture with the objective of "trabajar por [el] reconocimiento, valoración y fomento" (working toward the recognition, valuation, and promotion) of artisanal culture. CNCA, "Información," Cultura.gob.cl. In addition to the projects and programs administered by this agency, the state has also passed cultural policy on artisanal culture and invested resources to support academic investigations into Chilean artisanry in order to better understand its position within Chile's newly democratic cultural landscape and how that position can be improved. CNCA, *Política de fomento para la Artesanía, 2010–2015* (Valparaíso: CNCA, 2010), www.cultura.gob.cl.

78. Williams, *Culture,* 44.

79. Ibid.

80. García Canclini, *Transforming Modernity,* 59.

81. [In Spanish] "Ley sobre Propiedad Literaria y Artística"; "Ley sobre Propiedad Intelectual."

82. CNCA, *Guía de propiedad intelectual y derecho de autor, Cultura.gob.cl,* October 2013, 53, www.cultura.gob.cl.

83. José Weinstein, "Discurso de inauguración," in *Derecho de autor: Un desafío para la creación y el desarrollo,* ed. Eduardo Carrasco (Santiago: LOM Ediciones / CNCA, 2004), 15; Asociación de Editores de Chile y Fundación Chile Veintiuno, *Una política de Estado para el libro y la lectura: Estrategias para el fomento de la lectura y el desarrollo de la industria editorial en Chile* (Santiago: Fundación Chile Veintiuno / Asociación de Editores de Chile, 2005), 52.

84. Agustín Squella, *El jinete en la lluvia. La cultura en el gobierno de Lagos* (Santiago: Aguilar, 2005), 128.

85. In its 2005 document *Una política de Estado para el libro y la lectura,* the Asociación de Editores de Chile (Association of Chilean Publishers) claims that what they call the "copyright industry" has become of one of the principle factors of wealth in the era of globalization (37). In other venues, local independent editors have argued that anti-piracy policies protect the integrity of creative production and help local businesses compete against multinational corporations. See Santiago Schuster, "Sociedad del conocimiento, industrias culturales y propiedad intelectual," in *Industrias Culturales: Un aporte al desarrollo,* 85; and Ricardo de Zavalía,

"Necesidad de una protección efectiva contra la piratería de obras intelectuales," in *Industrias Culturales: Un aporte al desarrollo,* 101.

86. Williams, *Culture,* 47, 62.

87. Ibid.

88. [In Spanish] "Ley del Fomento del Libro y la Lectura."

89. [In Spanish] "en todo libro impreso en el país se dejará constancia del Número Internacional de Identificación (ISBN) que figurará en un registro público a cargo de la entidad pública o privada que represente el International Standard Book Number." Cámara Chilena del Libro, "Agencia ISBN," http://camaradellibro.cl.

90. On its website, the organization describes itself as an "asociación gremial" (professional association). See Cámara Chilena del Libro, "Quienes Somos," http://camaradellibro.cl.

92. [In Spanish] "Es importante destacar que el ISBN es aplicable independiente del destino que el editor le asigne al libro ya sea para venta, obsequio o circulación interna." Cámara Chilena del Libro, "Agencia ISBN," http://camaradellibro.cl.

93. Examples of Cartonera publishers who license their publications with Creative Commons and/or Copyleft include but are not limited to La Gata Viuda Cartonera, Isidora Cartonera, and Olga Cartonera. Examples of those who acknowledge names of individuals who participated in the production process include but are not limited to Olga Cartonera, La Gata Viuda Cartonera, Calafate Cartonera, and Isidora Cartonera. Examples of Cartonera presses who publically thank the author for giving over her rights to the work include but are not limited to Kiltra Cartonera and La Vieja Sapa Cartonera.

94. Espejo and Peñaloza in discussion with the author; Sotomayor in discussion with the author.

95. [In Spanish] "Cualquier copia, reproducción o falsificación está plenamente permitida, incluso, promovida por esta editorial. Es más, luego de ser leído, es recomendable doblar muy cuidadosamente este libro y hacer de él un avión de papel. Quizá dándole alas pueda volar hasta donde no hemos llegado aún. La propiedad es un robo."

96. Toledo in discussion with the author.

97. [In Spanish] "liberar voces que nunca nadie hubiese escuchado." Canita Cartonera, "Fanzines: N°2 enero 2010," *CanitaCartoneraWordPress.com,* January 2010, https://canitacartonera.wordpress.com.

98. [In Spanish] "derecho patrimonial." CNCA, *Guía de propiedad intelectual y derecho de autor,* 14, 48.

99. Aravena and Rey in discussion with the author.

100. Espejo and Peñaloza in discussion with the author.

101. [In Spanish] "piratas." Ibid.

102. Paul Steidlmeier, "The Moral Legitimacy of Intellectual Property Claims: American Business and Developing Country Perspectives," *Journal of Business Ethics* 12, no. 2 (February 1993): 157.

103. [In Spanish] "la necesidad de establecer el derecho de autor se consolida con el inicio del proceso de afirmación de los derechos individuales que desde esa ya lejana época [del siglo diesiocho] se expande progresivamente hasta nuestros días." Weinstein, "Discurso de inauguración," 11.

104. Carole Pateman, *The Sexual Contract* (Stanford: Stanford University Press, 1988).

105. Laikwan Pang, *Cultural Control and Globalization in Asia: Copyright, Piracy, and Cinema* (London: Routledge, 2006), 38.

106. Williams, *Culture,* 44–47.

107. Ibid., 47.

108. Steidlmeier, "Moral Legitimacy of Intellectual Property Claims," 158.

109. Lawrence Lessig, "The People Own Ideas! Do We Want Music, Software, and Books to Be Free—or Not?" *Technology Review,* Massachusetts Institute of Technology, June 1, 2005, 8 (emphasis in the original), www.technologyreview.com.

110. [In Spanish] "sin permiso de nadie." Horacio Eloy, *Revistas y publicaciones literarias durante la dictadura (1973–1990)* (Santiago: Piso Diez Ediciones / Mago Editores, 2014), 11.

111. Squella, *El jinete en la lluvia,* 126.

112. Pang, *Cultural Control and Globalization in Asia,* 45.

113. See Hans-Otto Dill, "The Riders Get Off the Horse: David Viñas and the Demise of the Authoritarian Argentine Military," in *Post-Authoritarian Cultures: Spain and Latin America's Southern Cone,* ed. Roberto Ampuero and Luis Martín-Estudillo (Nashville: Vanderbilt University Press, 2008).

114. Ampuero and Martín-Estudillo, eds., *Post-Authoritarian Cultures,* xvi.

115. [In Spanish] "Las políticas culturales democráticas son—en un sentido más general—políticas formales. Persiguen arreglos institucionales más que aplicar contenidos cognitivos a la sociedad. Persiguen crear estructuras de oportunidades (mercados, sistemas de elección, pluralidad de ofertas, vareidad) y, al mismo tiempo, impedir (mediante contrabalances, procedimientos, formas de control, medidas de competencia apertura de cierres, etc) que esas estructuras de oportunidades sean objeto de social closure, de cierre ideológico o de cualquier otra forma de manipulación monopólica." José Joaquín Brunner, "Políticas Culturales y Democracia: Hacia una Teoría de las Oportunidades," in *Políticas culturales en América Latina,* ed. Néstor García Canclini (México, D.F.: Grijalbo, 1987), 198.

116. Ronald V. Bettig, *Copyrighting Culture: The Political Economy of Intellectual Property* (Boulder: Westview Press, 1996), 20.

117. See Steidlmeier, "The Moral Legitimacy of Intellectual Property Claims: American Business and Developing Country Perspectives," 157; and Lessig, "The People Own Ideas!" 6.

118. Pang, *Cultural Control and Globalization in Asia,* 10.

119. Here the authors are referring to the worldwide standards for Trade-Related Aspects of Intellectual Property (TRIPS), which were put in place during the 1992 Uruguay Round of the General Agreement on Tariffs and Trade. James D. Gaisford and R. Stephen Richardson, "North-South Disputes over the Protection of Intellectual Property," *The Canadian Journal of Economics / Revue Canadienne d'Economique* 29 (April 1996): 380.

120. Bettig, *Copyrighting Culture,* 226.

121. Ibid., 7.

122. Ibid., 23.

123. Lessig, "The People Own Ideas!" 6–9.

124. Bettig, *Copyrighting Culture,* 103.

125. Kelly Gates, "Will Work for Copyrights: The Cultural Policy of Anti-Piracy Campaigns," *Social Semiotics* 16, no. 1 (April 2006): 57.

4. Libros de Mentira

1. CNCA, "Anuario de Cultura y Tiempo Libre, Recopilación de Ocho Años, 2003–2010. Sectores destacados" (Santiago: CNCA, Departamento de Estudios, Sección de Estadísticas, 2011), www.cultura.gob.cl; La Tercera, "Informe de la ONU asegura que Chile lidera la penetración de usuarios de internet en América Latina," *La Tercera,* September 26, 2012, www.latercera.comtml.

2. World Economic Forum, *The Global Information Technology Report, 2014: Rewards and Risks of Big Data,* ed. Beñat Bilbao-Osorio, Soumitra Dutta, and Bruno Lavin (World Economic Forum; Insead, 2014), xxi–13, www.weforum.org.

3. Ibid., 26.

4. CNCA, Ministerio de Educación, and DIBAM, *Plan Nacional de Fomento de la Lectura: Lee Chile Lee* (Santiago: CNCA, 2011), 20, www.leechilelee.cl (hereafter cited as *PNFL*).

5. Fundación la Fuente and Adimark-GFK, *Chile y los libros, 2010,* November 2010, www.fundacionlafuente.

6. CNCA, Ministerio de Educación, and DIBAM, *PNFL,* 51.

7. Escritores y Poetas en Español, "Página Chilena al servicio de la Cultura," ed. Luis Martínez Solorza, www.letras.s5.com.

8. The press's website does have a "Tienda" (Store) page where users would expect to find merchandise for sale; however, this page has been nonfunctional for the entire period that I have been researching this website (www.tienda.librosdementira.org).

9. Luis Cruz Sánchez and Mauricio Sanhueza Arce (founders of Libros de Mentira), in discussion with the author, Santiago, August 16, 2011.

10. [In Spanish] "destacados escritores"; "prestigiosos autores." Libros de Mentira, "Presentación," www.librosdementira.com.

11. Cruz Sánchez and Sanhueza Arce, in discussion with the author, 2011.

12. [In Spanish] "Esta es una iniciativa de carácter colaborativo e independiente, por lo que no responde a intereses de mercado." Libros de Mentira, "Cosas que deben saber," LibrosdeMentiraBlog.com, www.librosdementira.com.

13. [In Spanish] "Esta iniciativa es gratuita y de libre acceso, pluralista e integradora, se fundamenta en el concepto de la democratización de la publicación y utiliza Internet como soporte para contenidos literarios y creativos." Libros de Mentira, "Presentación," www.librosdementira.com.

14. Raffaele Simone, "The Body of the Text," in *The Future of the Book,* ed. Geoffrey Nunberg (Berkeley: University of California Press, 1996), 250.

15. Sven Birkerts, *The Gutenberg Elegies: The Fate of Reading in an Electronic Age* (London: Faber and Faber, 2006), 154–55 (emphasis added).

16. Simone, "Body of the Text," 239.

17. Ted Striphas, *The Late Age of Print: Everyday Book Culture from Consumerism to Control* (New York: Columbia University Press, 2009), 24.

18. David Gauntlett, *Making is Connecting: The Social Meaning of Creativity from DIY and Knitting to YouTube and Web 2.0* (Cambridge, UK: Polity Press, 2011), 80.

19. Electronic literature genres include kinetic poetry, code work, generative art, locative narratives, hypertext fiction, network fiction, and interactive fiction. See Electronic Literature Organization, "What is E-Lit?" https://eliterature.org; N. Katherine Hayles, *Electronic Literature: New Horizons for the Literary* (Notre Dame, IN: University of Notre Dame Press, 2008), 5–30.

20. Hayles, *Electronic Literature,* 4.

21. Ibid., 35.

22. Ibid.

23. Ibid., 20 (emphasis added).

24. Chilean poet Vincente Huidobro, writing in the first half of the twentieth century, was known for writing poems whose words were typed on the page in such a way as to create unique shapes and images that of course directly interacted with the words of the poems to create an overall poetic aesthetic. See Naín Nómez, *Poesía Chilena Contemporánea: Breve Antología*

Crítica (Santiago: Fondo de Cultura Económica / Editorial Andrés Bello, 1992), chap. 2. But even in cases when the author does not make typographical decisions affecting the aesthetics of the literary text, it is nevertheless true that individuals other than the author—specifically editors and designers—also make typographic choices in the editorial process that contribute to the text's overall aesthetic quality. Both of these examples—the author's own manipulation of typography and the typographical maneuvers of individuals who are not the text's author—complicate if not contradict the notions that printed works are the sole product of the author herself and that the material support through which texts reach readers does not participate in the work's symbolic meaning.

25. Hayles, *Electronic Literature,* 159–86.

26. Electronic Literature Organization, "What Is E-Lit?" (emphasis added).

27. Paul Duguid, "Material Matters: The Past and Futurology of the Book," in *The Future of the Book,* ed. Geoffrey Nunberg, 78.

28. Ibid., 75, 79.

29. Ibid., 81.

30. Ibid., 82.

31. Kristin Sorensen, *Media, Memory, and Human Rights in Chile* (New York: Palgrave Macmillan, 2009), 73.

32. Robert W. McChesney, *Digital Disconnect: How Capitalism is Turning the Internet against Democracy* (New York: The New Press, 2013), 72; Ithiel de Sola Pool, *Technologies of Freedom* (Cambridge: Harvard University Press, 1983), 5.

33. Sola Pool, *Technologies of Freedom,* chap. 2; McChesney *Digital Disconnect,* 72–82; Lawrence Lessig, "The People Own Ideas! Do We Want Music, Software, and Books to be Free—or Not?" *Technology Review* (February 15, 2006), 3–5, www.technologyreview.com.

34. Gauntlett, *Making Is Connecting,* 6.

35. Ibid., 6–7.

36. For an overview of the Internet's "celebrants" and "skeptics," see McChesney, *Digital Disconnect,* 5–12; Henry Jenkins and David Thorburn, "Introduction: The Digital Revolution, the Informed Citizen, and the Culture of Democracy," in *Democracy and New Media,* ed. Henry Jenkins and David Thorburn (Cambridge, MA: MIT Press, 2004), 1–17; and Gauntlett, *Making Is Connecting,* chaps. 4 and 8.

37. Gauntlett, chaps. 1, 4, and 8.

38. Lloyd Morrisett, "Technologies of Freedom?" in *Democracy and New Media,* 22–23.

39. Benjamin Barber, "Which Technology and Which Democracy?" in *Democracy and New Media,* 42; Gauntlett, *Making Is Connecting,* chaps. 1 and 4; Morrisett, "Technologies of Freedom?" 28–29; Dolores Romero López, "From Analogue to Hypermedia Texts in Hispanic Literatures," *Neohelicon* 36, no. 2 (December 2009): 463–75.

40. Jenkins and Thorburn, "Introduction," 2.

41. Digital books are in no way penalized for not receiving votes. All books are equally accessible on the site; the only difference that votes make is in determining which books will be highlighted on the site's homepage.

42. [In Spanish] "Desde el siglo XIX, . . . se habla de la alienación en la producción capitalista. Y no deja de ser cómico que en un ámbito en que podríamos hacer experiencia diferentes, reproduzcamos un quehacer marcado por la segmentación: el autor escribe, el editor selecciona y edita, el impresor imprime, el distribuidor distribuye, el librero vende y el comprador lee. Cada uno se limita a hacer solo que le toca en su parte de la cadena y eso mata al libro, en su posibilidad y en su realidad." Paulo Slachevsky, "El camino que vamos haciendo," in

Escritores por el fomento del libro y la lectura: Tercer Encuentro; Actas (Santiago: Letras de Chile; Gobierno de Chile; Mosquito Comunicaciones, 2001), 91–92.

43. [In Spanish] "Sobre el autor"; "Libros publicados por el autor."

44. Resha Cardone, "Refashioning the Book in Pinochet's Chile: The Feminist Literary Project, Ergo Sum," *Confluencia* 29, no. 1 (Fall 2013): 137–53.

45. Morrisett, "Technologies of Freedom?" 22.

46. Lessig, "The People Own Ideas!" 51.

47. Bernardo Subercaseaux, *Historia del libro en Chile: Desde la Colonia hasta el Bicentenario* (Santiago: LOM Ediciones, 2000), 214 and 270–72.

48. Hayles, *Electronic Literature,* 22–30.

49. Print publishers of course also offer electronic versions of their titles at an ever-increasing rate, but they are charging money for these e-books. Libros de Mentira is not.

50. La Tercera, "Informe de la ONU asegura que Chile lidera la penetración de usuarios de internet en América Latina."

51. [In Spanish] "Quienes somos"; "Nunca había tenido la posibilidad de leer algo de [Alberto] Fuguet, [pero] hoy gracias a su ayuda pude leer un libro suyo, así que gracias." Jenny Maturana, comment to "Quienes somos," LibrosdeMentiraBlog.com, August 4, 2008, www.librosdementira.com.

52. Gauntlett, *Making Is Connecting,* 191–93.

53. Cruz Sánchez and Sanhueza Arce, in discussion with the author, 2011.

54. [In Spanish] "La editorial realizará selecciones periódicas del material que los usuarios suban al sitio. Las obras elegidas pasarán a formar parte de los libros DESTACADOS EN PORTADA. Librosdementira se reserva el derecho de editar y/o modificar las obras que pasen a esta sección con el fin de que cumplan con los requerimientos de calidad exigidos por la editorial." Libros de Mentira, "Términos de uso," www.librosdementira.com (emphasis in the original).

55. [In Spanish] "publicar y promocionar obras con fines comerciales, siempre y cuando suscriban al acuerdo específico para este tipo de entidades. Queda explícitamente prohibida la venta de libros (en formato físico o digital) fuera de los canales que Librosdementira establece para esta labor." Ibid.

56. Jeff Jarvis, *Public Parts: How Sharing in the Digital Age Improves the Way We Work and Live* (New York: Simon and Schuster, 2011), 13.

57. Libros de Mentira member Estéban Espinoza openly admits on his member profile page that he was tortured and exiled by Pinochet's regime. He has lived in New Zealand since going into exile during the dictatorship and publishes with Libros de Mentira. There are likely many other Chileans from the diaspora using the site who do not identify themselves as such, and more likely still other members using the site who live in Chile and are also victims of the regime's violence but who do not make this information public on the site.

58. [In Spanish] "mayor interés." Libros de Mentira, "Cumplimos un año," e-mail to Libros de Mentira members, April 26, 2012, www.librosdementira.com.

59. Of course once a title makes it into the "Most Read" and "Most Votes" categories it is more likely to be read again and receive even more votes since it is highlighted on the site's homepage. Still, in order to make it into this category in the first place, a title needs to receive a requisite number of votes and reads, which still proves the point that members prefer to read and vote on works uploaded by other members like themselves.

60. Jorge Larraín, *Identidad Chilena* (Santiago: LOM Ediciones, 2001), 231.

61. [In Spanish] "Cristian, me ha encantado tu libro. No sé por qué pero hay partes que

me recuerdan los Macanudos de Liniers. Tienes gracia y profundidad, te agradezco que hayas compartido tus poemas con nosotros (hablo en plural, pues compartir un libro en este sitio mentiroso es un acto de generosidad con los lectores). Te doy 5 estrellas y un gran abrazo. Y que la administración lo pase a Destacados!" Carlos Toledo, comment to *Pandemonium*, September 5, 2011, www.librosdementira.com.

62. Benedict Anderson, *Imagined Communities: Reflections on the Origin and Spread of Nationalism* (London: Verso, 1983).

63. Gauntlett, *Making Is Connecting*, 88–107.

64. [In Spanish] "caus[ó] un placer casi culpable de tener este libro de mentira en papel, para compartirlo con mis estudiantes. Feliz recibo una copia." María Francisca Sasso Lorca, comment to *Martín Warp*, May 26, 2012, www.librosdementira.com.

65. [In Spanish] "Quiero tenerlo en mis manos, para poder ver los estupendos dibujos una y otra vez, sin prender el computador!" Mariel Sanhueza, comment to *Martín Warp*, May 28, 2012, www.librosdementira.com.

66. [In Spanish] "Me encantó este libro! Lindísimo, sin lugar a dudas, un libro que quisiera tener en mi pequeña biblioteca para hojearlo todos los días. Saludos, CG." Carmen Gloria Salas Jara, comment to *Baila*, February 11, 2012, www.librosdementira.com.

67. In the age of Web 2.0 it has become somewhat commonplace for the general public to have direct access to celebrities, government officials, and other authority figures through social media web applications such as Facebook and Twitter, creating the effect that the line dividing elite and commoner has been, if not totally erased, at least significantly shortened.

68. In speaking directly about this with Pía Barros and Jorge Montealegre, both of whom have works published on the Libros de Mentira website, neither author remembered having any participation in the design of their respective digital books or member pages.

69. Cruz Sánchez and Sanhueza Arce, in discussion with the author, 2011.

70. An excellent example is Editorial Viceral, which chose to use Libros de Mentira's online press to promote its book *Martin Warp*. The digital version of the text contains a video interview with the author in which he explains that the Internet is an appropriate venue for the dissemination of his book because, as he claims, it as a more participatory public space than bookstores, which he equates to museums. He also gives instructions for how readers can order a hard copy of the book or download it for free at www.viceral.cl.

71. Members such as Marco Kasaneva (www.marcokasaneva.com), Daniela Viviana Guerrero González (www.dielago.blogspot.com), Mariel Sanhueza (www.vimeo.com), Javier Aguirre (www.tallersayenco.blogspot.com), and Simón Soto all use the Libros de Mentira online platform to self-promote their burgeoning artistic careers. They use the site to find and direct new audiences to their larger artistic oeuvre and also to offer their services (such as writing and drawing classes) for hire.

72. In his description of the text on the Libros de Mentira site, Uribe states that some of this material was first published by Editorial Santillana, one of the largest publishers of Spanish-language educational materials in the world; however, there is no mention of Santillana in the actual digital book, where Uribe describes the book as the result of "active research" performed at various Chilean schools. The book reads like a textbook and seems to be written for use in the high school classroom. This editorial inconsistency point to the alternative nature of Libros de Mentira's digital publishing since such seeming contradictions and lack of previous editorial information (if there is any) would not happen in the commercial publishing industry (www.librosdementira.com).

73. [In Spanish] "sea más agradable"

74. [In Spanish] "labores como la tuya dan sentido a nuestro trabajo diario." Libros de

Mentira, comment to *Educación Tecnológica Primero Medio Guías y Experiencias en borrador,* September 22, 2011, www.librosdementira.com.

75. [In Spanish] "una escritora aficionada." Jessica Fuentes Sáez, "Sobre el autor," www.librosdementira.com. [In Spanish] "lector común y escritor de vez en cuando." Francisco García Mendoza, "Sobre el autor," www.librosdementira.com. [In Spanish] "la escritura como medio de expersión de mi visión del mundo." Sebastián Olivares Maureira, "Sobre el autor," www.librosdementira.com.

76. [In Spanish] "Inicié la escritura de este texto a mediados del año 2008 . . . en el 2009 lo dí por terminado y olvidado, hasta hora, en que me decidí a editarlo y publicarlo. Espero disfruten la lectura." Jeanette González, Comment to *Al arrogante pájaro,* January 26, 2012, www.librosdementira.com.

77. [In Spanish] "Simplemente por placer." Roberto Rabi, "Sobre el autor," www.librosdementira.com.

78. The press gets around legal issues surrounding republications by making it clear that "queda prohibido el uso de material que vulnere los derechos de autor de terceros" (the use of material that violates the intellectual property of others is prohibited). Libros de Mentira, "Términos de Uso," May 20, 2014, www.librosdementira.com. It also puts the responsibility on individual authors to obtain the rights for their own original work. But ultimately the strongest way in which Libros de Mentira protects itself from copyright problems is by not charging money for any of its services. The press neither profits from its distribution of digital books nor does it hold the rights to any of them. All responsibility belongs to the members who make these books. Some register their books with Creative Commons, some list the press that originally published the text in print, and some (such as Felix Albert Ventura) register their works with an ISBN number on their own.

79. Villegas notes in his description of this digital book that it was to be used in a psychology class at the University of Santiago. The first page of the text lists the citation of the original text from which this excerpt was taken: "*Obras escogidas de Carlos Marx y Federico Engels en Tres Tomos.* Editorial Progreso, Moscú. 1981. Tomo 3, pp 66–79." No translator is mentioned in the citation.

80. [In Spanish] "Pero falta que gente con talento como tú sea difundida, que se conozca su trabajo." Roberto Rabi, comment to *Los Pituflaites,* March 15, 2012, www.librosdementira.com. The title (and Torres's entire book) *Los Pituflaites* is a Chilean spoof on The Smurfs, whose name in Spanish is Los Pitufos. *Flaite* is a derogatory Chilean slang word used to refer to urban youth of low socio-economic standing. We could think of its U.S. English equivalent as "ghetto" when used in reference to how urban working-class people dress, speak, and behave. *Los Pituflaites* rewrites The Smurfs from a uniquely urban and working-class Chilean perspective.

81. [In Spanish] "Ojalá le den cabida a autores inéditos. Porque las influencias, el compadrazgo, el pituto, y otras pestes, siguen saturando hasta a las editoriales más pequeñas e independientes. Falta una válvula de escape al respecto, espero que ustedes lleguen a ser esa válvula." Gato, comment to "Quienes Somos," LibrosdeMentiraBlog.com, June 8, 2008, www.librosdementira.com.

82. [In Spanish] "Les agradezco que con sus letras vayan en son de la élite cultural se rebaje al ciudadano medio a un solo click. Gracias. Gracias. Gracias." Charol, comment to "Quienes Somos," LibrosdeMentiraBlog.com, January 29, 2008, www.librosdementira.com.

83. Sola Pool, *Technologies of Freedom,* 5.

84. Lessig, "The People Own Ideas!" 49.

85. Ibid., 50.

86. Jenkins and Thorburn, eds., *Democracy and New Media,* 10.

5. Santiago en 100 Palabras

Epigraph: [In Spanish] "Creemos en una sociedad plural y heterogénea, donde los espacios que permiten la expresión creativa de sus ciudadanos resultan indispensables para democratizar la cultura y visibilizar su diversidad" (http://plagio.cl).

1. World Book and Copyright Day was founded by the United Nations Educational, Scientific and Cultural Organization (UNESCO) in 1996 to "promote reading, publishing, and the protection of intellectual property through copyright." The organization chose April 23 as World Book and Copyright Day because on this same day in 1616 three literary giants, Cervantes, Shakespeare, and el Inca Garcilaso de la Vega, all died. UNESCO, "World Book and Copyright Day-April 23," *Unesco.org,* 2015, www.unesco.org.

2. For more on the artistic projects Plagio organizes, see the group's website: http://plagio.cl.

3. Ignacio Arnold and Sylvia Dümmer (founders of Plagio) in discussion with the author, Santiago, March 3, 2007.

4. [In Spanish] "profesionales destacados del ámbito literario nacional." Santiago en 100 Palabras, "Preguntas Frecuentes: ¿Quienes son los encargados?" www.santiagoen100palabras.cl.

5. In recent years, national literary professionals who have served as judges on the preselection committee have included Luis López-Aliaga, Cristián Barros, Roberto Fuentes, Kurt Folch, Daniel Villalobos, Francisco Ortega, Rodrigo Olavarría, and Alan Meller. Finalist judges have included José Miguel Varas, Diamela Eltit, Alberto Fuguet, Alejando Zambra, Roberto Fuentes, Rafael Gumucio, Nona Fernández, Carmen García, Alejandra Costamagna, Roberto Merino, Sergio Gómez, Alejandro Cabrera, Andrea Jeftanovic, and Manuel Peña Muñoz. It should be noted that of the judges listed here, Nona Fernández, Alejandra Costamagna, and Andrea Jeftanovic all participated in the Ergo Sum writing workshop and press at early stages in their literary careers.

6. Metro de Santiago, "Gobierno Corporativo: Nuestra Organización," *Metro.cl,* accessed August 19, 2015, www.metro.cl.

7. [In Spanish] "objeto de uso cotidiano." Santiago en 100 Palabras, "Preguntas Frecuentes: ¿Dónde se publican y difunden los cuentos?" *Santiagoen100palabras.cl,* www.santiagoen100 palabras.cl.

8. *Santiago en 100 Palabras,* www.santiagoen100palabras.cl.

9. Throughout this chapter I refer to the way in which this contest affects Chile on a national level, which is not completely accurate since not all Chileans live in a city where the contest functions. However, the majority of them do. The popularity of the contest has caused it to expand to four other Chilean cities—Valparaíso, Antofagasta, Iquique, and Concepción—four of the six most highly populated cities in Chile behind Santiago. The contest has also expanded into other media, including short films. See www.plagio.cl.

10. Minera Escondida writes that its philanthropic organization, Fundación Minera Escondida (Minera Escondida Foundation), donates 1 percent of the company's annual profits before taxes to philanthropic programs related to education, health, social development, and culture. Minera Escondida, *Santiago en 100 Palabras: Los mejores 100 cuentos* (Santiago: Plagio, 2003), www.santiagoen100palabras.cl.

11. For more on representations of nationalism in Chilean literature, see Juan Poblete, *Literatura chilena del siglo XIX: Entre públicos lectores y figuras autoriales* (Santiago: Cuarto Propio, 2003).

12. See Pierre Bourdieu, *The Field of Cultural Production* (New York: Columbia University Press, 1993).

13. Esperança Bielsa, *The Latin American Urban Crónica: Between Literature and Mass Culture* (New York: Lexington Books, 2006), chap. 1; Manuel Castells, *Globalización, desarrollo y*

democracia: Chile en el contexto mundial (Santiago: Fondo de Cultura Económica, 2005), 32–34; Gregory Sholette, *Dark Matter: Art and Politics in the Age of Enterprise Culture* (New York and London: Pluto Press, 2011), 1–22. Sholette does not limit his argument to Latin America but rather describes how the global neoliberal economy posits the masses as marginalized cultural producers in all regions of the world.

14. Marcy Schwartz, "The Writing on the Wall: Urban Cultural Studies and the Power of Aesthetics," in *City/Art: The Urban Scene in Latin America,* ed. Rebecca E. Biron (Durham, NC: Duke University Press, 2009), 127–31.

15. [In Spanish] "lecturas colectivas." Jesús Martín-Barbero, "Recepción de medios y consumo cultural: Travesías," in *El consumo cultural en América Latina,* ed. Guillermo Sunkel, 2–25.

16. Michel De Certeau, *The Practice of Everyday Life,* trans. Steven F. Rendall (Berkeley: University of California Press, 1984), xiii.

17. [In Spanish] "Pues si el producto o la pauta de consumo son el punto de llegada del proceso de producción, son también el punto de partida, y la materia prima, de otro proceso de producción silencioso y disperso, oculto en los usos." Martín-Barbero, "Recepción de medios y consumo cultural," 3–4.

18. [In Spanish] "el proceso educativo . . . discurre entre un polo activo que detenta el saber—la élite, el intelectual, el maestro—y otro pasivo por ignorante: el pueblo, la masa, el niño. Con la consiguiente legitimación de la división entre la esfera de la producción y creatividad de un lado, y la del consumo, la pasividad y el conformismo del otro. Está aún por hacerse la *historia social de la lectura* que nos permita romper ese dualismo, desplazarnos del lugar teórico-político en que se origina, y poder así desentrañar los rasgos diferenciales de la lectura popular." Ibid., 4 (emphasis in the original).

19. Schwartz, "Writing on the Wall," 129.

20. Asociación de Editores de Chile y Fundación Chile Veintiuno, *Una política de Estado para el libro y la lectura. Estrategias para el fomento de la lectura y el desarrollo de la industria editorial en Chile* (Santiago: Asociación de Editores de Chile / Fundación Chile Veintiuno, 2005), 40.

21. Julio García Espinosa, "For an Imperfect Cinema," in *New Latin American Cinema,* ed. Michael Martin, trans. Julianne Burton (Detroit: Wayne State University Press, 1997), 76.

22. [In Spanish] "La industria cultural convierte a los individuos en consumidores." Jorge Larraín, *Identidad Chilena* (Santiago: LOM Ediciones, 2001), 246.

23. Ibid., 248.

24. Tomás Moulian, *Chile actual: Anatomía de un mito* (Santiago: LOM Ediciones / Arcis, 1997), 102.

25. Larraín, *Identidad Chilena,* 221 and 270.

26. Bielsa, *The Latin American Urban Crónica,* 2.

27. Ibid.

28. García Espinosa, "For an Imperfect Cinema," 76.

29. [In Spanish] "La 'mediatización de lo popular'—esto es, la incorporación y difusión masiva de géneros a veces considerados como expresión de lo 'auténtico' latinoamericano. . . . [M]anifestaciones culturales populares [son] readaptadas para un consumo masivo y, en ciertos casos, para un consumo de élite." Guillermo Sunkel, "Introducción: El consumo cultural en la investigación en comunicación-cultura en América Latina," in *El consumo cultural en América Latina,* xxiii.

30. [In Spanish] "la mediatización de lo popular también implica una readaptación y por tanto una transformación que . . . provoca cambios de forma y de contenido." Ibid.

31. Néstor García Canclini, *Transforming Modernity: Popular Culture in Mexico,* trans. Lidia Lozano (Austin: University of Texas Press, 1993), 76.

32. [In Spanish] "Todas las mañanas amanece a los pies del caballo de Valdivia, sintiéndose un ciudadano, un chileno. No puede ir al baño que está en la plaza porque cien pesos al amanecer son una fortuna para el Negrito, como sus conocidos le dicen. Su rostro está cubierto por una capa de mugre y sus manos también. Todos comentan que hace cinco años que no se baña. Un día un pintor de la plaza lo retrató. En dos días terminó el óleo. De inmediato lo vendió a un turista por cien dólares." María Isabel Toro, "El Negrito," in *Santiago en 100 Palabras: Los 100 mejores cuentos III (incluye cuentos de los concursos 2005–2006)* (Santiago: Plagio; Metro Santiago; Minera Escondida, 2007), 58, www.santiagoen100palabras.cl.

33. Ricardo Greene, " 'Monstruos urbanos': Figuras cardinales de la experiencia cotidiana santiaguina," *Revista electrónica de arquitectura e urbanismo* (Universidade São Judas Tadeu), no. 2 (second semester 2009): 160, www.usjt.br.

34. García Espinosa, "For an Imperfect Cinema," 75.

35. Ibid., 76.

36. It is important to note that both the state's new cultural institutionalization and Metro Santiago have individually initiated creative means of bringing libraries to citizens rather than expecting citizens to go to libraries. Such programs include library trucks that move throughout the city space and libraries stationed throughout the subway system.

37. [In Spanish] "gente común y corriente." Plagio, *Santiago en 100 Palabras.*

38. Ángel Rama, *La ciudad letrada* (Hanover: Ediciones del Norte, 1984).

39. Fundación La Fuente and Adimark GFK, *Chile y los libros: Índice de Lectura y Compra de Libros, 2008, FundaciónlaFuente.cl,* 2008, 12, www.fundacionlafuente.cl. Books in Chile are consistently more expensive than in other countries. Matías Cociña compared the sales price in U.S. dollars of J. K. Rowling's book *Harry Potter: The Order of the Phoenix* in fifteen different countries from all over the world. The same book cost $9.99 in the USA, $12.25 in Germany, $14.99 in the UK, $16.48 in New Zealand, $18.74 in Mexico, $18.87 in Spain, $20.38 in Switzerland, and $23.73 in Chile. See Matías Cociña, "Determinantes de la lectura en Chile," master's thesis, Universidad de Chile, 2007, cited in Enrique Ramos Curd, "Plan de fomento de la lectura en Chile: Un proceso de construcción participativa," *Serie Bibliotecología y Gestión de Información,* no. 45 (July 2009): 19, http://eprints.rclis.org.

40. The contest rules state: "Podrán participar todas las personas con domicilio estable en Chile y Chilenos viviendo en el exterior, a excepción de los empleados de Plagio, Metro de Santiago y Minera Escondida" (Contest participation is open to all persons holding established residency in Chile and Chileans living abroad, with the exception of anyone employed by Plagio, Metro Santiago and Minera Escondida). Santiago en 100 Palabras, "Preguntas frequentes."

41. María Constanza Mujica, "Santiago en 100 palabras: Escenas y fragmentos de la memoria," *Revista Eure* 31, no. 92 (May 2005): 3; [In Spanish] "escribir un cuento en 100 palabras suena como algo fácil, pero no lo es." Equipo Bifurcaciones, "Santiago en más de 100 palabras: Entrevista a Carmen García y Sylvia Dümmer, de Revista Plagio," *Bifurcaciones.cl,* no. 1 (Summer 2004): 5, www.bifurcaciones.cl.

42. I actually found this to be the case while researching this contest in Santiago in 2007. I frequently shared conversations with people outside the space of the subway in which we discussed stories we had, at separate times, read while traveling across the city. In particular I remember a conversation I had with a friend about a story that addressed the topic of child molestation ("Pena remitida" [Deferred Shame], First Place, 2005 by Patricia Middleton). The brevity of the narrative (only forty-five words) in no way prevented it from addressing such a complicated and controversial topic, nor did it prevent the story from serving as a catalyst for

my friend and me to discuss this topic in more depth after having separately read it while on the subway.

43. In his book *Identidad chilena,* Jorge Larraín explains that the Pinochet regime constructed Chilean identity according to the ideologies of patriarchy, militarism, Christianity, and free market capitalism (8).

44. [In Spanish] "un nuevo espacio para el imaginario urbano de nuestra capital." Plagio, *Santiago en 100 Palabras: Los 100 mejores cuentos III (incluye cuentos de los concursos 2005 y 2006).*

45. [In Spanish] "Quizás la pregunta por la identidad esté lejos de la academia y de los grandes discursos, y se encuentre en nosotros mismos, en el día a día, en nuestras experiencias cotidianas. 'Santiago en 100 Palabras' logra rescatar y entrelazar esas pequeñas historias que componen nuestra cotidianeidad. . . . El tercer volumen de los mejores cien cuentos de 'Santiago en 100 Palabras' es la recopilación de las respuestas de miles de chilenos a la pregunta sobre quiénes somos. . . . Los escritores que escriben estos cuentos] escriben la historia de este país a diario." Ibid.

46. [In Spanish] "Santiago de Nueva Extremadura." Jorge Aguilera, "Santiago de Nueva Extremadura," in Plagio, *Santiago en 100 Palabras: Los mejores 100 Cuentos,* 21.

47. [In Spanish] "Éste es el lugar. Aquel río nos brindará agua y desde esta cima veremos si el enemigo se aproxima."

48. Larraín, *Identidad chilena,* 10.

49. [In Spanish] "Desapareceremos uno o dos cerros para ventilar la cuenca y evitar el smog."

50. Larraín, *Identidad chilena,* 253.

51. [In Spanish] "¿Qué opina Gamboa, que estaré exagerando? ¿Sí? Entonces olvide lo que he dicho y que sea a su voluntad."

52. Mujica, "Santiago en 100 palabras," 3–4.

53. For related discussions of urban space as art, see Robert Neustadt, *CADA día: La creación de un arte social* (Santiago: Editorial Cuarto Propio, 2001); and Schwartz, "The Writing on the Wall".

54. [In Spanish] "como dicta la etiqueta no escrita de este mundo subterráneo—no miran a nadie, no conversan con el vecino y fijan la vista fuera, en la oscuridad de los túneles o en los anuncios publicitarios de brillantes colores y grandes letras." Mujica, "Santiago en 100 palabras," 1.

55. [In Spanish] " 'Santiago en 100 Palabras' permite que a través de la literatura se produzca un encuentro entre las personas." Bifurcaciones, "Santiago en más de 100 palabras," 4.

56. Ibid.

57. Ibid., 2.

58. [In Spanish] "La avidez irreflexiva de las masas, exacerbada por la publicidad, las llevaría a abalanzarse obsesivamente sobre objetos innecesarios." Néstor García Canclini, "El consumo cultural: una propuesta teórica," in *El consumo cultural en América Latina,* ed. Guillermo Sunkel, 28.

59. [In Spanish] "Si me llamas hoy, no te contestaré yo, sino otro. No tengo cómo avisarte, pues todos los datos estaban ahí y sólo ahí. Si lees esto te enterarás y quizá nos encontremos frente al afiche, yo deseando que lo leas y tú riéndote de la despistada que perdió el celular." María Inés Peranchiguay, "Lo perdí," in *Santiago en 100 Palabras: Los mejores 100 cuentos III (incluye cuentos de los concursos 2005–2006),* 33.

60. Larraín, *Identidad chilena,* 227.

61. Pamela Constable and Arturo Valenzuela, *A Nation of Enemies: Chile under Pinochet* (New York: Norton, 1991).

62. [In Spanish] "No se me ocurrió otra forma de ubicarlos para que lo supieran. Mamá,

papá: estoy bien y los perdono." Jorge Gutiérrez, "Escrito hallado en un respaldo de asiento de micro," in *Santiago en 100 Palabras: Los mejores 100 cuentos III (incluye cuentos de los concursos 2005–2006),* 14.

63. See Bifurcaciones "Santiago en más de 100 palabras," 2; and Greene, " 'Monstruos urbanos,' " 153.

64. [In Spanish] "Aquí llega el metro, atestado de gente como todas las mañanas. Escojo con la mirada desde el andén a mi víctima, mientras repaso mentalmente el plan. Se abren las puertas. El último en bajar es un hombre todavía somnoliento. 'Mi víctima,' digo para mis adentros." Pablo Figueroa, "Metro los Héroes," in *Santiago en 100 Palabras: Los mejores cuentos,* 43.

65. [In Spanish] "Él me mira de reojo y entonces ataco: "Hola, ¿cómo está?", le digo, mientras subo y avanzo por el carro. Él gira. Las puertas se cierran y veo con satisfacción su cara de incertidumbre. Pobre hombre, pensará todo el día quién lo saludó, y yo, no puedo esperar hasta mañana a mi siguiente víctima." Ibid.

66. Mujica, "Santiago en 100 palabras," 3.

67. Larraín, *Identidad chilena,* 46.

68. Ibid., 244.

69. Ibid., 270.

70. Ibid., 269.

71. [In Spanish] "Habría observado con detención a las personas salir humeantes de la boca del Metro. Habría atravesado estupefacto la Moneda bajo la lluvia. Pensativo, le habría comprado una sopaipilla a un perro hambriento cerca del Santa Lucía." Ernesto Guzmán, "Dostoievski," in *Santiago en 100 Palabras: Los mejores 100 cuentos III (incluyen los cuentos de los concursos 2005–2006),* 3.

72. [In Spanish] "A Fedor Dostoievski le habría gustado Santiago en invierno."

73. Like the success of this individual story, the success of the contest as a whole reverses the flow of cultural influence and imitation between Chile and its international counterparts. Whereas Santiago as a city, like all Latin American capitals, was constructed and designed in the image of European, specifically Spanish metropoles, the success of Santiago en 100 Palabras has reversed this trajectory by inspiring the European cities of Berlin and Barcelona to follow in its footsteps and create their own copies (*plagios*) of the contest.

74. "Concertación" stands for "Concertación de Partidos por la Democracia" (Coalition of Political Parties for Democracy), a center-left coalition of political parties that banned together in the latter half of the 1980s in opposition to the military regime. Four of the five presidents to govern Chile since the return to democracy in 1990 have belonged to the Concertación.

75. According to Manuel Castells, throughout the 1990s Chilean natural resources and extracted materials became the largest export out of all Latin American countries except for exports from Brazil. Chile maintained mining as its top industry of exported goods throughout the 1990s. Manuel Castells, *Globalización, desarrollo y democracia: Chile en el contexto mundial* (Santiago: Fondo de Cultura Económica, 2005), 33–34.

76. Fundación Minera Escondida, "Minera Escondida," www.fme.cl.

77. Ibid.

78. Minera Escondida, *Santiago en 100 Palabras: Los mejores 100 cuentos II* (Santiago: Plagio; Metro de Santiago, 2005), www.santiagoen100palabras.cl.

79. [In Spanish] "Y el patrocinio de empresas o personas tiene dos características: busca reconocimiento y aprovecha estímulos tributarios. ¿Por qué negarlo?" Arturo Navarro, *Cultura: ¿Quién paga?; Gestión, infraestructura y audiencias en el modelo chileno de desarrollo cultural* (Santiago: RIL Ediciones, 2006), 209.

80. Chin-tao Wu, *Privatising Culture: Corporate Art Intervention since the 1980s* (New York and London: Verso, 2002), 23.

81. [In Spanish] "Distribución Gratuita / Prohibida Su Venta."

82. For more information about Cultural Donations Law, see *Donaciones Culturales*, www.donacionesculturales.gob.cl; and Navarro, *Cultura*, chaps. 1 and 6–10. It is important to note that Minera Escondida also sponsors many cultural projects that are not distributed for free, namely feature films. In fact, Minera Escondida's cultural sponsorship of Chilean arts projects is vast and diverse, and deserves greater scholarly investigation.

83. In the introduction to the first book of best one hundred stories submitted to the contest, Minera Escondida writes that between 1990 and 2001, it paid the Chilean government an average of U.S. $148 million a year in taxes (Minera Escondida, *Santiago en 100 Palabras: Los mejores 100 cuentos*).

84. See Mark W. Rectanus, *Culture Incorporated: Museums, Artists, and Corporate Sponsorships* (Minneapolis: University of Minnesota Press, 2002), chaps. 1 and 3.

85. Ibid., 30.

86. Wu, *Privatising Culture*, 129–31.

87. [In Spanish] "Uno de nuestros objetivos estratégicos es ser un ciudadano responsable y ser reconocido como tal." Minera Escondida, *Mineraescondida.cl*, accessed March 29, 2009 (no longer available).

88. [In Spanish] "Hace más de diez años nadie se imaginaba crear una fundación minera para trabajar con la gente. Porque siendo realistas, la experiencia y el negocio de la compañía era producir cobre. . . . [T]ambién era fundamental aumentar los **vínculos con la comunidad**, la que en ese entonces veía a la actividad minera como lejana y distante a sus intereses y necesidades. Y no la relacionaba con una posibilidad para mejorar su **calidad de vida**." Fundación Minera Escondida, "Nuestros Inicios," Fml.cl, accessed May 23, 2009 (emphasis in the original; site no longer available).

89. See Wu, *Privatising Culture*, chap. 8.

90. Roland Kushner, *Strategy, Structure and Organizational Effectiveness: A Study of Nonprofit Arts Organizations* (Bethlehem, PA: Lehigh University Press, 1994).

91. Rectanus, *Culture Incorporated*, 10.

92. Wu, *Privatising Culture* 158.

93. Ibid., 14–15.

94. Ibid., 17.

95. [In Spanish] "Las empresas privadas que a través de sus actos de mecenazgo exhiben su generosidad, orientan el arte para debilitar su espíritu crítico o cubren los rasgos negativos que pueden afectar sus marcas." Jorge Orlando Melo, "Economía, cultura y mecenazgo," in *Economía y Cultura: la tercera cara de la moneda* (Convenio Andrés Bello, Bogotá, 2001), 209.

96. This is evidenced by the 2010 Copiapó accident in which 33 miners were trapped 700 meters below the earth's surface for 69 days.

Conclusion

1. [In English] "Chilean Letters."

2. [In Spanish] "Es necesario fomentar . . . la ambición de hacer un trabajo que intervenga en la sociedad en que vivimos. Decía que la idea era no quedarse en el lamento, pues si bien frente a la adversidad y las transformaciones en nuestro alrededor solemos muchas [*sic*] responder con el quejido, ello limita nuestro actuar, nuestra posibilidad de intervención." Paulo Slachevsky, "El camino que vamos haciendo," in *Escritores por el fomento del libro y la lectura: Tercer Encuen-*

tro; Actas (Santiago: Letras de Chile; Gobierno de Chile; Mosquito Comunicaciones, 2001), 90–91.

3. [In Spanish] "Hay que retomar las cartes a la mano, combinar convición, voluntarismo, un grado de testadurez [*sic*], con la tradición de una práctica y el aprendizaje de nuevas formas de comunicarse, producir y organizarse." Ibid., 91.

4. This is not unlike the view held by some that neoliberalism is incongruent to all forms of democracy, both political and also cultural. See Sergio Villalobos-Ruminott, *Soberanías en suspenso: Imaginación y violencia en América Latina* (Buenos Aires: Ediciones La Cebra, 2013), 75; and Néstor García Canclini, *Consumer Citizens: Globalization and Multicultural Conflicts,* trans. George Yúdice (Minneapolis: University of Minnesota Press, 2001).

5. "Ojalá le den cabida a autores inéditos. Porque las influencias, el compadrazgo, el pituto, y otras pestes, siguen saturando hasta a las editoriales más pequeñas e independientes. Falta una válvula de escape al respecto, espero que ustedes lleguen a ser esa válvula." Gato, comment to "Quienes Somos," LibrosdeMentiraBlog.com, June 8, 2008, www.librosdementira.com.

6. Benjamin Barber, "Which Technologies and Which Democracy," in *Democracy and New Media,* ed. Henry Jenkins and David Thorburn (Cambridge, MA: MIT Press, 2004), 43–44.

7. Julio García Espinosa, "For an Imperfect Cinema," trans. Julianne Burton, in *New Latin American Cinema,* ed. Michael Martin (Detroit: Wayne State University Press, 1997), 76.

8. Benedict Anderson, *Imagined Communities: Reflections on the Origin and Spread of Nationalism* (London: Verso, 1983).

9. Ángel Rama, *La ciudad letrada* (Hanover: Ediciones del Norte, 1984).

10. [In Spanish] "Quizás la pregunta por la identidad esté lejos de la academia y de los grandes discursos, y se encuentre en nosotros mismos, en el día a día, en nuestras experiencias cotidianas. . . . Los escritores que escriben estos cuentos] escriben la historia de este país a diario." Plagio, "Introducción," in *Los 100 mejores cuentos III (incluye cuentos de los concursos 2005 y 2006)* (Santiago: Plagio, 2007).

11. Kathrin Bergenthal, "El Mini-Boom de la Nueva Narrativa Chilena," in *Crisis, apocalipsis y utopías: Fines de siglo en la literatura latinoamericana; XXXII Congreso Internacional de la Literatura Iberoamericana,* ed. Rodrigo Cánovas and Roberto Hozven (Santiago: Instituto Internacional de la Literatura Iberoamericana; Instituto de Letras, Pontificia Universidad Católica de Chile, 2000), 224–29.

12. David Gauntlett, *Making Is Connecting: The Social Meaning of Creativity from DIY and Knitting to YouTube and Web 2.0* (Cambridge, UK: Polity Press, 2011).

13. Néstor García Canclini's early work, specifically *Las culturas populares en el capitalismo* (Mexico City: Nueva Imagen, 1982), and *Transforming Modernity: Popular Culture in Mexico* (Austin: University of Texas Press, 1993), did focus on material modes of cultural production. In more recent years, his research has followed the trend in cultural studies scholarship of focusing on processes of cultural consumption; see his books *Consumidores y ciudadanos: conflictos multiculturales de la globalización* (Mexico City: Grijalbo, 1995), and *Consumer Citizens: Globalization and Multicultural Conflicts,* trans. George Yúdice (Minneapolis: University of Minnesota Press, 2001.) There is general consensus that the primary role played by citizens living in Latin America within the global cultural economy is that of consumer, not producer, of material culture. See Guillermo Sunkel, ed., *El consumo cultural en América Latina: Construcción teórica y líneas de investigación* (Santafé de Bogotá: Convenio Andrés Bello, 1999); and García Canclini, *Consumer Citizens.*

14. Susan Hekman, *The Material of Knowledge: Feminist Disclosures* (Bloomington: Indiana University Press, 2010).

15. Ibid., 3.

16. [In Spanish] "o el libro se integra a los mecanismos de la industria cultural o corre el riesgo de ser un producto marginal e incluso de tener que reciclarse en materia prima." Bernardo Subercaseaux, *Historia del libro en Chile: Desde la Colonia hasta el Bicentenario* (Chile: LOM Ediciones, 2000), 166 (emphasis added).

17. Gilles Deleuze and Félix Guattari, *Kafka: Toward a Minor Literature,* trans. Dana Polan (Minneapolis: University of Minnesota Press, 1986).

18. Luce Irigaray, *This Sex Which Is Not One* (Ithaca: Cornell University Press, 1985), 196.

Afterword

1. Gesa E. Kirsch and Liz Rohan, "Introduction: The Role of Serendipity, Family Connections, and Cultural Memory in Historical Research," in *Beyond the Archives: Research as a Lived Process,* ed. Gesa E. Kirsch and Liz Rohan (Carbondale: Southern Illinois University Press, 2008), 8.

2. Pía Barros, *Los que sobran / Those not spared,* bilingual edition, trans. Resha Cardone and Jane D. Griffin (Santiago: Asterión Ediciones, 2010); Pía Barros, *El lugar del otro / The place of the other,* bilingual edition, trans. Resha Cardone and Jane D. Griffin (Santiago: Asterión Ediciones, 2012).

3. Resha Cardone, "Translating Chilean Women Writers: Same-Sex Collaboration and Feminist Activism in the Era of Multinational Publishing," paper presented at the New England Council of Latin American Studies Conference, Wheaton College, Norton, MA, November 9, 2013.

4. Elizabeth (Betsy) Birmingham, "I See Dead People: Archive, Crypt, and an Argument for the Researcher's Sixth Sense," in *Beyond the Archives,* 139–40.

5. Ibid., 139.

6. Pierre Bourdieu, *The Field of Cultural Production* (New York: Columbia University Press, 1993), 35.

7. Esther Leslie, "Walter Benjamin: Traces of Craft," *Journal of Design History* 11, no. 1 (1998): 6, www.jstor.org.

8. Christine Mason Sutherland, "Getting to Know Them: Concerning Research into Four Early Women Writers," in *Beyond the Archives,* 28.

Index

Page numbers in *italics* refer to illustrations.

JANE D. GRIFFIN is associate professor of Spanish in the Department of Modern Languages at Bentley University. She holds a PhD in comparative literature from the University of California, Irvine and a bachelor's degree from the University of Wisconsin–Madison. A native of Southern California, she currently lives in Watertown, Massachusetts.